TREES OF PARADISE

Richard Edmunds and Nigel Hughes

To the people of the Hunstein Range

Green
Press

First published 1991 by
GREEN PRESS
20734 Big Rock Drive, Malibu, CA 90265, USA

ISBN 0-9630312-0-1

Printed on recycled paper

Front Cover illustration: Kowane Bague
Back Cover illustration (Bird of Paradise) : Felix Endoi

Acknowledgements
We would like to thank all the following people for their valuable assistance in bringing this book to life.

Diana Ambache and Jeremy Polmear for their constant support and fax depot. Glenys Baylis for her proof-reading. Elizabeth and Grenville Clarke who held us together with plenty TLC and the best pizzas in Lawshall Green. Sandy Clough (Australia) for his idyllic house. Sue Copping for her incredible patience and generosity in loaning us her Mac and house. Joan Diamond for her brilliant suggestion that we use a dictaphone. Vanessa Doyle (Australia) for her typing of an initial draft. Barry Hart (New Zealand) for his perfect farm. Lesley Hetherington for her practical and moral support. Wendy Knight for her generous typing time. Sue Meyer for her sensational organizational skills. James Moran for his perspective on the first draft. The National Art School, Papua New Guinea, for encouraging our cover artists. Simon Pentanu and William Takaku (PNG) for their advice and inspiration. David Simpson for his design. John and Sue Stebbing for their generous donation of fax, typewriter and cucumbers. Diane West, our whizz editor (who 'it our 'eads very gently!). Jacqui Wilmot who did an incredible job deciphering our scrawls, interpreting our hieroglyphics and knocking it all together onto the computer.

And, of course, to our Fairy Godparents, Celia and Brian Wright.

In order to protect their identity we have found it necessary to change some people's names.

Contents

Richard Edmunds took an Honours degree in Biological Sciences at Kings College, London, before surprising his professors by becoming a playwright. His plays have been produced at the National Theatre, the New End Theatre, Hampstead, Theatr Clwyd and on BBC Radio Four.

He has also travelled widely and stayed with indigenous communities in such diverse places as Lapland, the Sahara and the Himalayas.

Nigel Hughes studied Fine Art at Exeter College of Art before training at the Bristol Old Vic Theatre School. An actor for fifteen years, he has worked widely in television, West End and provincial theatres, enjoying seasons with the National Theatre, the Bristol Old Vic and the Alan Ayckbourn Company.

Recently he turned to directing and his productions have ranged from Restoration Comedy to Brecht.

Together, in 1988, they founded Green Light Productions, an internationally operating theatre production company that links art and nature. Under GLP's banner they lead a programme of courses in artistic expression, creative writing and environmental awareness world-wide.

PART ONE

THE SEVERED HEAD
OF A TOUCAN

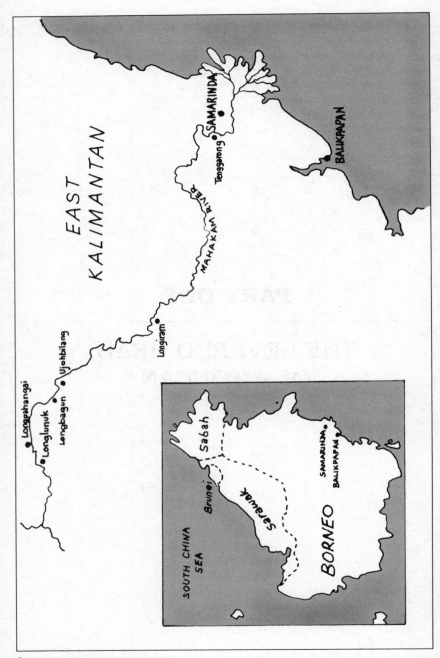

*Longpahangai, East Kalimantan, INDONESIA, BORNEO 21
January 1988*

Dear Friend Ray,

*What a pretty pickle Rick and I have found ourselves in! Find a map
of Indonesia. Find the largest island – Kalimantan (the major part
of Borneo). Look at the south east and find a town called Samarinda.
We are not there. Though that is indeed where we would like to be.
But circumstances extraordinary prevent us!*

*We are marooned – alas, not on a white-sanded, palm-fringed
desert island, sipping chilled coconut milk (oh, if only!), but six days
up the muddy, menacing Mahakam river, home of the Dyak tribes.
Marooned in a creaky-floor-boarded, hard-bedded Catholic Mission at Longpahangai, a remote outpost close to the Sarawak
border. . . . .*

*If you ever get this letter, save it, I may need it to remind me,
someday, of this predicament. I'll write again – hopefully from
Samarinda.*

*Your friend,
Nigel*

I

What ever were we doing in the heart of Borneo? I am a playwright and Nigel, my partner, was at that time an actor. Not much hope of getting a script accepted there and not many local auditions. And yet for me at least, it wasn't such a surprise. I have always had a great love of the wild, in all its extremes. This love was christened at the age of five when I climbed my first mountain. It was in Southern Ireland: one of the MacGiddycuddy's Reeks. I stood on the very top and peed into the precipice below. Then I perched on the cairn with my mother and father and two older sisters watching the mist, like a great rushing dragon, swallow up the emerald valley, leaving us stranded on a magic carpet above the clouds.

But maybe this love for the wild was also in my genes. As a young man, my father had been a traveller and had always inspired me with his tales. And my grandfather on my mother's side had been an ardent naturalist. One day, when he was still a little boy, he was playing on the South Downs in Sussex; in those days they were covered with butterfly and bee orchids. Suddenly, he spotted a brilliantly coloured bird and dashed all the way home to tell his mother. After he had described it to her in detail, she put down what she was doing and said with deep excitement and admiration, 'Cuthbert – you have seen a bee-eater!'

It took me much longer to see my bee-eater; I had to travel by horseback along the red foothills of the Sahara to glimpse it. But my great grandmother's excitement had been instilled in me long before. My childhood playground was the Ashdown Forest, not so far from the South Downs, and also in Sussex. There I had my first adventures and there the taste for nature got into my blood. As I grew up, I always longed to go to the remotest places: there, nature was at its most powerful; there, the taste was fresh. For, unlike my grandfather on his untrespassed orchid slopes, I was a child of the sprawling fifties and my favourite kingfisher lake had been ruined by an ugly housing estate. Later I wandered across the Shetland Islands and spent a summer on a tiny island beyond the Outer Hebrides. I chased the Midnight Sun across Lapland and revisited the windswept coasts of Southern Ireland. On these travels I was at my happiest. I felt carefree. I felt hopeful. It was a relief to be far away from the confusing conundrums of the twentieth century everyday. It was also a relief to be away from our family problems, which had clawed a gash across my youth.

At university in London I studied biological sciences. But I was not a success in the laboratory and, having struggled for and got my degree, I turned my back on science. But my college years did precipitate a romance with the city. I was swept away with the razzamatazz and became an actor. I was fascinated with the sordidness and became a writer. However, beneath the tinsel merry-go-round, my love for the natural world stayed with me and increasing news coverage of environmental destruction filled me with a horrible aching feeling of despair. Especially stories of the rainforest. So many thousand acres devastated, so many plant and insect species obliterated for ever. Plants and butterflies that no one would ever see, that no one would ever thrill to. I joined the Friends of the Earth. But I found their articles too painful to read. I felt it was my duty to know the terrible truth and yet I longed to bury my head in the sand.

Then something unexpected happened. I spent the New Year of 1987 on my annual Vipassana meditation retreat. I had first come across Vipassana on a trip to India in 1980 to fulfil my dream of walking in the Himalayas. It's a form of Bhuddist meditation from Burma; a practical technique for helping to concentrate and balance the mind. Throughout the silent ten-day course, the rainforest kept looming up before me; both its awe-inspiring splendour and the tragedy of its destruction. It was almost as if it were beckoning me, pulling me, urging me to hurry, before it was too late. And I realized with remorse that I had lost the tangy taste of the wild. Since India eight years before I had not travelled at all. I had got bogged down with trying to make it as a writer. I had got bogged down with those twentieth century conundrums. And my spirit was crying out for another adventure.

Back in our rented Notting Hill flat, I discussed the idea of a rainforest journey with Nod (my name for Nigel). To my delight, he was immediately enthusiastic. Professionally, we were both in a bit of a rut. We had been hitting our heads against too many brick walls. We were both ready for a change: a new kind of challenge.

When Rick came back from his meditation retreat he talked about his overwhelming desire to walk in primary rainforest. I didn't really know what it was. When he explained that it was forest that had stood for thousands of years, never cut or spoilt by man, images of huge wide trees set in steaming, leech-filled Amazon jungles flashed before me, giving me goose-pimples at the thought. His descriptions of his travels in the Sahara, Lapland and the

Himalayas had always tantalized me. His experiences of travelling were in stark contrast to my safer 'tourist' or 'holidaymaker' forays into Europe and America. When, for instance, the summer we met, he strode off with a knapsack on his back to a remote farm in Norway, I caught the ferry from Brindisi to bake on the beach in Mikonos. When he went trekking in the Himalayas, my adventure was to roller-skate along Venice Beach, Los Angeles, and enjoy the thrills and spills of Space Mountain, Disneyland. Now there was an opportunity to join him on a real adventure which would raise, in my mind, my status to one of 'explorer'.

During the previous two years I had embarked upon a journey of self-development, wanting to free myself from the trap of my rather rigid military upbringing. My father had been in the Army and I was the only one of four children who chose neither the Army nor the Air Force as a career. Despite a degree of ridicule and teasing from my elder brothers and sister, I had chosen a more artistic angle and had become an actor. I was born and lived in Glasgow, then moved to the beautiful red-cliffed Devonshire coast at five years old. There I developed a love for the sea, beaches, cliffs and wild life. As Rick talked in his wide-eyed, enthusiastic way, something stirred in me. I felt challenged, excited and somewhat daunted, to say the least, at the prospect of tramping in the deep, dark, dangerous jungle. I had become frustrated with my moderate success as an actor, and was ready for a change. I felt the compulsion to jump out of my life, the way I had recently jumped out of a plane – with a parachute on my back – in order to conquer my fear of heights. I reckoned that if I could risk my life at 2,000 feet it was time to do it on ground level. I wanted to shake myself up, widen my horizons, enrich my artistic work and get my hands dirty in the process. This felt like the perfect opportunity.

With Nod on my side, our first step was to start a Travel Fund. Ten per cent of our earnings would go to this fund and be deposited monthly. I was working with a project that rehoused young homeless people and Nod's time was divided between acting and leading workshops at The Actors Institute. Each month we faithfully made our deposits, not commenting on how small they were. We avoided making concrete plans and evaded our friends' probing questions. I wrote: 'Year of Preparation', across the cover of my 1987 diary. But preparation for what exactly? We still had no clear idea. To my chagrin I had discovered an unwanted truth:

I was afraid. The Unknown, which had always lured me on, now filled me with fear. So it was safer to stay vague. In compensation I wrote to an old friend in Brazil for advice and started reading Catherine Caufield's *In the Rainforest*.

The next real step didn't come until the summer and it just sort of happened to us. I do my writing in a tumbledown cottage in Suffolk where our farmer landlord charges a nominal rent in return for us looking after repairs. On a wet Sunday afternoon in late August we went to visit friends in a nearby village. They were out. So we took a walk round the neighbouring fields in the rain, and found ourselves talking in depth about the trip: our doubts, our fears, our hopes, our aspirations. As it poured, we pushed through brambles into a wood. Rain-wood. Rain-forest. A premonition of things to come? Soaked to the skin, we drove back to the cottage, lit a fire and wrote out our individual bids for the contours of the journey.

For me it was simply to walk in a primary rainforest, either in South America or Asia, the location didn't matter. Nod had three additional bids: Australia, to explore work possibilities; New Zealand, because his family had almost emigrated there; and India, because I had already whetted his appetite. Okay, so we'd build a journey to serve us both. There had been no letter from Brazil. Meanwhile an ex-university mate had recommended Borneo as the best alternative. This fitted in better with the other countries and we jotted down the following itinerary – India, Indonesia, Australia, New Zealand – and agreed we would give ourselves six months for the trip. We shook hands on it and wrote a departure date in our diaries – *Sunday 22 November 1987*. Excitement was beginning to shift the grip of fear.

A few days later, the then director of The Actors Institute, Lynne Lesley, visited. We proudly outlined our plan. 'Oh, you ought to go to Papua New Guinea as well,' she said; 'there's rainforest there too and it's always fascinated me.' 'Yes, of course', I answered, feeling foolish that I hadn't thought of it first. Nod nodded hard and, not even knowing where it was on the map, we added Papua New Guinea to the itinerary, there and then. There was only one problem: money. The Travel Fund had raised, so far, less than half of one of our estimated fares. Still, the commitment had been made. There was no turning back. So, as the good old English rain continued to batter the summer flowers, we underlined the fateful date of departure. One week later, Nod landed three commercials: one for France, one for Spain and one – a major coup – for an international credit card company. If successful, it had the

potential of earning him several thousand pounds. It was successful. The Travel Fund rose dramatically.

Now I tried to catch up on the research I should have been doing
all year. I wrote to Catherine Caufield, author of the rainforest
book, and to the Rainforest Department of Friends of the Earth
(FOE). I searched for books on Borneo and, via the publishers,
tried to contact the author of the only relevant one I could find. We
also visited a couple who had worked for several years in Papua
New Guinea. Meanwhile Nod investigated flights. To fulfil our
itinerary at a cheap rate proved a nightmare; the negotiations and
complications were endless. Several travel agents gave up on us
altogether, threatening nervous breakdowns. By October the pull
for us to give up too got stronger and stronger. We were far more
entrenched than we had realized. I have always prided myself on
my simple life-style – but the petty entanglements of twentieth
century living still seemed to go on for ever. To wrench ourselves
free was going to take supreme effort. Then to top it, Nigel's Agent
accused him of being totally irresponsible and stupid. This shook
his confidence severely. Was it irresponsible? Was it stupid?
Should he stay behind after all?

A few days before our departure, a colleague from the homeless
project told me that Mark, an ex-member of the management
committee, was now the Field Director in Indonesia for Voluntary
Service Overseas (VSO). I could only remember him vaguely, but
wrote to him straightaway. Though it seemed much too late and
I held little hope of hearing from him, I enclosed the address of our
first port of call in India, just in case.

We now had funds to last us (if we were stringent) for our six-
week stay in India and a following six weeks in Indonesia. After
that? Who knew? Now we had a more pressing problem. Our
tickets still hadn't been issued. Our flight was on a Sunday
morning and I only picked them up the day before, speeding down
Oxford Street on my bicycle and yelling at the meandering
Christmas shoppers in my haste to reach the travel office before
it closed at midday for the weekend. The tickets were as fat as little
books and when the assistant handed them over, I handed back
a bottle of wine to thank him for his untiring efforts. We were to
fly on Turkish Airways, Garuda, Quantas and Air New Zealand;
the outbound stops were Istanbul, Bombay, Singapore, Jakarta,
Sydney and Auckland. Papua New Guinea had proved too difficult
to include. We would have to sort that out later. The provisional
date of return was 22 May 1988.

Nod was up to his ears co-leading an intensive workshop that very weekend, and he came home to help me pack in between sessions. We were keen to travel as light as possible and limited ourselves to a sports bag each and the following items: one change of clothes (we would buy new things when they wore out); our rainforest boots (Vietnam combat specials from a US Army surplus store in Soho); groundsheet; sleeping sheet; medical kit; water bottle; camera; notebook; maps; small rucksack for trekking and one luxury – a walkman with a few cassettes.

Nod's best friend, Ray – to whom he wrote the 'marooned' letter – came to say goodbye to us at midnight. He got quite a shock when he saw the extensive range of our medicines. 'So you really do mean business, don't you?' 'Yes', we affirmed tremulously, trying to squeeze them into the oblong tupperware containers we had bought for the purpose. 'Wow. You really are going off the beaten track!'

II

The International Academy of Vipassana Meditation is situated on a hill outside the sprawling town of Igatpuri, four hours by train from Bombay. We had agreed to start the journey with a meditation course. After it, there was a letter waiting for me with Indonesian stamps on it. Mark's memory of me was as vague as mine of him; nonetheless, he would be happy to put us up in Jakarta. He also had contacts in Kalimantan who could help us plan our trek. And most surprising, he was also a Vipassana meditator.

But first, our sojourn in the ravaged land of pellucid eyes, coloured dust and holy hump-backed cows. We visited the Gir Forest, last home of the Asiatic lion; a terrain in polar opposite to a rainforest. There had been no rain at all for three years and many of the trees looked dead, having shed their leaves for moisture retention against the severe drought. Wild peacocks. Families of monkeys. And one early morning we stood 20 feet from a full-grown lioness and her yawning cub. Both gazed at us with disdain, then turned and padded off, easefully, crunching the carpet of dry dead leaves.

Then it was Christmas at Dwarka, birthplace of Lord Krishna, on the cobalt blue Arabian Sea, where the cheapest place to stay was a hostel teeming with noisy pilgrims; and New Year at Murud, a bustling fishing town on the Maharashtra coast, where we shared a room with a large extended family. From Murud, a clanking bus called 'The Night Queen' trundled us back to a sleeping Bombay and the airport. The rainforest journey began before we even touched down in Jakarta.

From Rick's journal. Monday 4 January 1988.
On the Garuda flight from Singapore, I meet Mr Uno, a short fat Jakarta business man. He asks about our trip; I tell him of my interest in the rainforest and my connections with FOE, etc. It develops into quite a big discussion. Mr Uno is from Kalimantan himself. He spent his childhood on the edge of the jungle. Whenever it was cut, he saw it growing back immediately – so what's the problem? I explain the problem is a question of scale. Multi-national logging companies. Thousands of acres being destroyed.

Mr Uno is suspicious of 'environment groups'. He has heard of Greenpeace and suspects that they are just after intellectual power. That is the image we have created to the Indonesian people. I explain that we are fighting powerful and intellectual governments. We have to fight them on their terms – otherwise we will be laughed off as 'eccentrics' and old 'hippies'.

Mr Uno propounds his theory of human nature. We all have spiritual qualities in our hearts. But we are also greedy and after power. That is the human condition. I argue that, yes, we *can* all fall prey to greed, but just because we have that negative potential, we don't *have* to follow it, do we? FOE workers, for example, earn peanuts. If they were really only after power, surely they would look elsewhere for gratification? We are not against all development. We are only against exploitation and irreversible destruction. Mr Uno listens with interest and suggests we meet again to talk further. He is keen and so we exchange addresses in Jakarta and shake hands.

I feel tested and shaken. Jumped in the deep end. Caught the Indonesian attitude full blast. A developing third world country – why should they refuse the help of the big companies? The forest will grow again. The forest grows fast. So leave us alone. Don't try to meddle in our affairs. It's not your business anyway! We had talked leaning against the emergency exit at the back of the plane. 'What on earth's the matter?' Nod asks when I return to my seat. I am tensed up, sweating profusely. For some reason I had felt the need to impress Mr Uno and had set myself up as an environmentalist. Why? What was wrong with just being a nature lover? I had even pretended that Nod was a photographer and he had asked who was funding us. Feeling transparent and embarrassed, I had got myself into a muddle. What a relief when the 'fasten your seat belt' sign came on and the crew prepared for landing.

At Jakarta's beautifully designed modern airport, Mark was waiting to meet us. To their surprise, it was he and Nod who recognized each other; they had met on two Vipassana courses several years before. After the dry heat of India, the wet humidity was a shock as we waded through it to the car. Mark's house was in a quiet side-street off the long, congested Jubba Watta Road. It was open plan, with large windows looking onto a central courtyard; a little bridge over an oblong fishpond; coloured shrubs and exotic moisture-loving ferns. Our room had a high-speed fan and springy beds. Next to it was the *mandi*, an Indonesian-style shower which comprises a large wooden tub and a plastic scoop. The procedure is to strip off and sluice oneself down with scoopfuls of water from the tub. Greedy for comfort, we sluiced and sluiced. After the hard conditions of India, this felt like the Sultan's palace.

In the elegant dining room, Pauline, Mark's wife, served us a delicious supper. Gorging myself, I boasted about my first Indonesian friend, Mr Uno. Mark became grave. I had not been wise to speak to Mr Uno so openly. An international business man was bound to have government connections. And the government would be less than tolerant of our environmental interests. Mark advised us not to contact Mr Uno and to be more careful in the future. 'Don't worry though,' he reassured, 'as long as you didn't give him this address, you should be OK.' 'No, of course I didn't', I lie. 'There you go then; if you always remember to keep things simple in Indonesia, you'll be fine.'

The mango ice-cream lost its flavour. How could I have been so stupid? Blunderer! Not only had I made a fool of myself, I had put us both at risk. The winking tropical luxury leaned in on me with a treacherous sneer. Indonesia was ruled by a ruthless military regime. Spontaneity was dangerous. It looked as if we ought to get out of Jakarta fast. Luckily Mark had plenty of contacts and was keen to help. There was Jaspar, a Dutch VSO worker, who was stationed up the great Mahakam river in East Kalimantan; we could visit him and explore the forest from there. Then there was Keith, a VSO teacher in Samarinda, the town at the mouth of the same river. There was also another Keith, who had been the previous VSO representative in Samarinda and now worked for a private concern in Jakarta. He would be able to fill us in on all the background information that we needed. Mark would arrange a meeting and also book our flight for us. 'Great; yes please'. I wasn't keen to hang around.

The next day was a kaleidoscope of contrasts. First, the city centre: angular sky-scrapers cutting harshly into the hot blue sky; formality bordering onto hostility; haze of yellow pollution over the jam-packed congestion. Next, a restaurant for lunch with Mark: spacious and tasteful; unfaultable service; avocado shakes and sumptuous seafood. Then a stroll in the afternoon: dappled alleyways; everything higgledy-piggledy; odd little houses, odd little corners; and from flower-trailing verandahs – 'Hello mister, hello mister' – round dumpy smiles from the lolling locals. In the evening we travelled by taxi to another part of the city to meet the Jakarta Keith. Here, bicycle rickshaws seemed to be fighting a losing battle with the relentless traffic, though Keith's airy house was well-protected down another leafy alley.

When we broached the topic of Kalimantan and the forest, he painted a depressing picture. Most of the primary forest had gone and what was left was inaccessible; there was no way we could reach it. Although there was an official logging quota per annum, the president's wife had been handing out extra concessions all over the place. There had also been a vast fire five years ago that had destroyed an area the size of Belgium. It was believed that this had been caused by over-logging and the over-heating of the humus layers beneath the forest floor. Further upriver from the village where Jaspar, the Dutch VSO worker, was based, there was a Catholic mission. Here we might find some primary forest. But we would have to charter our own boat and this would cost around £700! There was a forest reserve for the protection of the orang-utan, but the chances of reaching this were also dubious. Keith suggested we changed our plan to Sumatra. Though the destruction story was even worse there, at least the little that was left was more accessible.

I felt winded, punched in the stomach. I hadn't landed in Jakarta to be discouraged. I hadn't spent a year in preparation to hear this. Keith's young Indonesian friends were shrieking with laughter over the pudding. Apparently, his maid was obsessed with gelatin, and her puddings were getting more garish and more tasteless by the day. Tonight it was shocking purple with cream-crackers set in it like sails on a wobbly sea. Declared inedible by our host, it was removed. But for me the hilarity was a struggle.

I would sooner have gone up on the roof and bellowed.

In the night I more or less did. I am not a good sleeper at the best of times and when I travel I carry my bulging anti-insomnia kit with me. Meditation, yoga, a relaxation tape, a physical limber and, finally, if all else fails, a jotting down of all the rubbish in my mind. But that night, nothing worked. My head was raging. My glorious vision of Borneo had slipped off its stage and my wonderful dream of the perfect forest had been dashed to smithereens. Why had I failed to get better information before we left? The Rainforest Campaign at the Friends of the Earth had just been changing personnel. The publishers of the Borneo book had not been helpful in my efforts to track down the author. And I wasn't to receive Catherine Caufield's letter until after I had returned to Britain. But why hadn't I tried harder? In my absurd romanticism, I had imagined that a miraculous guiding hand would somehow lead us to our goal. That somehow a magical twist of fate would show me the signpost that I needed. Mr Uno might have been that guiding hand, that twist of fate; but look what I had done when I had met him. Urghh! And yet, somewhere in that confusing, conflicting city, there lay the key to the forest. But how to find it? How?

Suddenly, there was an almighty crash on the roof and a horrible screech. Nod sat up with a jolt. 'A feral cat', he whispered. Mark had mentioned them earlier. In my demented state, it felt like a sinister omen. At the very least, Mr Uno and an army of special police were surely on their way to arrest me. This merry self-flagellation continued until dawn, when the neighbouring family all got up; they seemed to have at least five mandies each. I tried to meditate, to balance my mind. Well, that was a joke. My head was still exploding. Would it never abate? Still, I did decide one thing. It would be foolhardy to ignore Keith's advice. After all, he had been over here for several years. We would just change our plan and go to Sumatra – it didn't matter where we went, as long as we found the primary forest.

But at breakfast Mark presented us with the tickets to Samarinda. He hadn't only booked them, he had bought them too. My brain ricocheted away again and my emotions catapulted into new extremes. I felt I had no option but to share them with Nod. The bewildering force of my anger, frustration and confusion had become too much to hold alone. Nod listened in his own attentive and patient way until my rantings were through. Then he helped me see that we could take it as a positive eruption; for it showed us just how much this journey to the forest mattered to me and it was time to acknowledge it. Perhaps that was why I had got into such a muddle with Mr Uno. Nod was right. Now I could turn my crazy night into strength and determination. We agreed not to be put off by Keith. If there was primary forest up the Mahakam river, we would find it somehow.

To assist us, we took out Nod's pack of Angel Cards. Each card has a positive attribute written on it, like Clarity, Flexibility, Harmony. The method is to think of a question and ask which attribute would best help solve it. I had always felt pretty cynical about these cards, but Nod had found them beneficial. Two 'angels' – Trust and Patience – that he had turned up previously had helped him a great deal. And anyway, what the hell, I was game for anything that morning. Our question was: what would help us reach our goal? Nod picked up Inspiration and I turned over Release. Well, I had to admit, they sounded like good ideas. We could undoubtedly do with some inspiration, and I certainly needed to get rid of the nonsensical violence in my head. Phew, time for a double mandi and a cold drink. Time to scribble down a poem in order to crystalize my feelings and to help us on our way. And then, time to get on with the business of our last Jakarta day.

Pick yourself up off the ground
And shake the chains off your feet
We are not impressed by a whimpering Knave

Light up your torch of courage
And sharpen your spear of hope
We want to see a Warrior

And wrapping yourself in the shield of your father's love
With the child of trust tucked safely in your heart
Go seek the mighty Forest of your dreams
And pay homage to the primordial forces of life.

From Nigel's journal. Samarinda. Saturday 9 January.
Rick and I left Mark's house at 4.30 a.m. yesterday. The journey to Samarinda was in four stages, each one in Merpati planes. Merpati is renowned as one of the world's unsafest airlines – we had just heard that they lost two planes last month. This information did nothing to alleviate my fear of flying or, rather, of crashing, or help my determination to trust more. The first hop was to

Surabaya on the Eastern tip of Java, followed by a half-hour ice-cream stop. Second hop: to Banjarmasin across the sea on the south coast of Kalimantan, Borneo. Another half-hour wait and then back on the same plane for the third hop to Balikpapan, the provincial capital of East Kalimantan. There we waited for one and a half hours in the sweltering departure lounge, with no cafeteria, while the pilot had lunch; then, finally, we got on a fifteen-seater plane that shuddered and lurched with every twist of its twin-propped engines. The experience of flying became more primitive and scary with each hop. Snacks of a hard boiled egg and a banana were served on two legs of the journey. My first view of tropical forest was disappointing. We saw a huge area that had been burned down leaving ugly charred stalks and black mess every-where.

To my surprise, Samarinda from the air was a big sprawling town; but the airport was only a hut. Alas, no Keith to meet us. Three Canadian project workers were on the same flight from Balikpapan. We asked the person meeting them if he knew how much a taxi would be to the University where Keith worked. He knew Keith and gave us a lift. The University comprised odd groups of prefab and cement buildings set in scraggy unkempt grounds. We found the right department and a boy who knew Keith and where he lived. We drove through the campus to a series of low-roofed flimsy bungalows. Keith's was locked. In dismay we asked a group of students who lived opposite if they knew where he was. They told us he may be back about 5 p.m. It was 3.15 p.m. We decided to wait. Merv, our willing Kiwi chauffeur, left his address with us in case we needed it.

The students invited us into their bare, lino-floored house. No one spoke English. A doughnut seller with his cart arrived; we bought doughnuts and the students gave us boiled water. A girl arrived with a big bunch of rambutan, a lychee-like fruit with prickly red skins, which they shared with us. We waited, wilting in the heat, trying to make ourselves understood with the few words of Indonesian we'd learned so far and much sign language. Around 5.30 p.m., unable to sit up on the hard floor anymore, and with concentration waning, we asked if we could lie down to sleep for an hour, explaining that we had been up since 4 a.m. Rick went to collect our bags from outside Keith's house and met Gabriel, a small, wide-faced young man, his heavily-marked face showing scars of smallpox, who rode up on his motorbike. He had come to invite Keith to a dancing party on Sunday. We looked through Keith's windows and discovered his motorbike locked inside. Now what to do? No Keith, no contact. My security began to waver.

We decided to search for Merv. Gabriel pushed his bike and we walked, lugging our bags, for three-quarters of an hour. Sweat poured over us in the intense humidity as we trudged back along the path and through tropical flora, to the edge of the campus. We found number B.10, surrounded by a well-kept garden, perched on the edge of a hill overlooking a valley of myriad greens. Merv and his wife Denise were not at all surprised to see us. They invited us in and gave us much-needed cold drinks. We were invited to stay for dinner. Their Indonesian cook, Maria, smiled happily, delighted at the prospect of three extra guests. When Gabriel was invited too, we discovered that it is hard for Indonesian people to say yes or no directly when invited to eat. After four coaxing invitations Gabriel eventually joined us. So we sat around the table: Merv, a New Zealander; Denise, a North-American Indian; Henry, one of the Canadian project workers from the plane; Gabriel, a local Indonesian; and us. An unlikely dinner guest list. Gabriel was delighted to find brown bread at the table – and promptly ate the lot! For desert, Maria proudly presented us with indigo gelatin and cream cracker pudding – this must be the latest Indonesian culinary delight.

Later, Merv drove us slowly through the noisy town in the dark rainy night to the Hotel Rabayu. We passed the office of MAF, the mission plane service that flies right into the dense jungle, to places that can only be reached by small, six-seater planes. Just what we might need to get us right up into the rainforest! At Hotel Rabayu we were shown a small, windowless, fanless room – no way I was going to stay there – no, we would boil to death! Merv then suggested Hotel Andhika. There, Thomas, the very friendly night receptionist, showed us to a room with fan, window, soft beds and complimentary tea – all for about £4 a night. That's more like it! We booked for two. Gabriel found us, having followed on his motorbike, and we thanked Merv for his kind help. Settled in our room guzzling the warm sweet complimentary tea, Gabriel confirmed our suggested trip up the Mahakam River. He is a Dyak man from upriver himself. Although he had never been beyond the rapids, he believes that the forest we are after is up there. He knew of a river ferry and suggested that he take us to find out about it. My bottom began to tingle with nervous excitement. A long way now from Jakarta where Ricky had thought we were on a wild goose-chase.

Fan still on full, we fell into a hopeful, heavy sleep.

This morning, room service – yes, much to Ricky's horror, I

ordered room service – brought us two boiled eggs each, toast, jam and tea. I fully intended to make use of this 'tourist' luxury while it was available. Gabriel arrived at 10 a.m. promptly and a three-hour search to change our sterling traveller's cheques began. Four banks and an international hotel all refused us. Without money changed we could do nothing. Desperately, just before closing time, we persuaded the manager of one of the banks we had tried previously to change our money. Later, we asked Gabriel to phone the operator for the MAF office number. By his gingerly handling of the phone, we realized he had never used one before. No reply. Needing to get information about something, we found our way to the MAF office: it was closed. In the heat of the afternoon (we always seemed to find ourselves doing important business in the hottest part of the day), frustration grew.

We went to seek Pastor Bong, head of the Catholic organization that operates upriver. As we arrived he was reclining in a long warm bath. We waited in the cool shaded quadrangle. When he eventually emerged he confirmed the existence of primary forest above the rapids. He offered to radio our arrival plans to Pastor Ranft there, whom he believed would help us. Good, we were beginning to get somewhere!

Gabriel met us back at the hotel at six-thirty and escorted us to the harbour where we found the *Nilam Cahaya*, a forty-foot long, two-tiered ferry boat run by a large family. We discovered it only leaves once a week – tomorrow at 9 a.m. People were already on board. We had to choose there and then either to buy places on the diesel-stained deck, or to stay on in the soft-bedded hotel with room service and the faint possibility of a mission plane later. It didn't feel like there was any option. What had we come for: a holiday in Samarinda, or an adventure in the forest? Nerves rattling we bought our tickets from the young captain and were told to board by 8 a.m. Done!

At the ferry we bumped into Gnow, a shy young friend of Gabriel, who is at Samarinda high school. He lives way upstream at Longpahangai, exactly where we want to go. His father, Bapa Ding, who has been to visit him, is travelling back on the *Nilam Cahaya* tomorrow. He would be happy to help us. We took Gabriel and Gnow to dinner, and then happened upon a pastel-coloured ice-cream parlour – mmm what a treat! It was Gnow's first experience of ice-cream and Gabriel, having lost his reticence of accepting our invitations to eat, ordered 'assorted ice-cream' – the biggest and most expensive on the menu. We made arrangements to meet him and Gnow and his father tomorrow morning at eight.

Angel Gabriel, as we now call him, will be there to translate; Bapa Ding, of course, speaks no English. The deal is that we will pay Bapa Ding's fare and food on the *Nilam Cahaya* and he will take us to his family's house, four days upriver at Longbagun where the ferry service terminates. He will cook for us and negotiate a longboat to take us up through the rapids to Longpahangai, another two days upriver. There we will find Pastor Ranft and, we hope, the forest that we are longing to see. Our fate is sealed!

So here I am, feeling extremely apprehensive, about to set off into my first jungle. Very relieved that we have our own personal guide who will help us out – but we'd better get learning some more Indonesian fast – I think we'll need it!

III

Nigel woke me in an early cloudburst and when we arrived at the quay, the *Nilam Cahaya* looked as if it had just had a mandi and was about to sink under the weight of passengers and cargo. Oil drums and roped-up crates were being hauled aboard and lowered into the hold through a trap-door in the open-sided lower deck. The deck itself was already deep in river people jostling with their bundles and boxes. Above, in the windowed dormitory, the more exclusive passengers were claiming their quarters. And above that, on the flat roof, more cargo was being tied down and secured. Once upon a time, this stalwart wooden ferry boat had been painted blue and cream. But years of ploughing up the swirling river had taken its toll; only the odd trace of colour remained. Though if you half-closed your eyes it still had the faint air of a Mississippi showboat. The proud young captain informed us in telegraphic English that the dormitory was full. We would have to cram in with the people on the definitely-third-class lower deck.

Waiting for our friends, we strolled along the narrow quay in trepidation. Huge dull stretch of churning river: yellow water lapping against the cane posts and, on the other bobbing wooden vessels, glum, squat-bodied boatmen, yawning and stretching beside smoking fires. Gnow arrived first with his father. We were presented and little Bapa Ding bowed ceremoniously. Dark, chiselled features; caverns for eyes, and elongated ear-lobes with large empty holes. Helpless, we faced each other – not a single word in common. But Angel Gabriel arrived on cue and clarified the deal. Bapa Ding bowed again. Yes, he understood his duties. Yes, he would ensure that we reached Longpahangai in safety. Gabriel was satisfied. With decorous solemnity, we all shook hands on the agreement and said our farewells to Gabriel and Gnow. Soon the juddering ferry set off and, wedged amongst the other passengers, we watched the dome-roofed mosques and jumbled buildings of Samarinda slip away. Ahead, the Mahakam was a vast and crumpled muddy sheet, and above the sun was already hot.

Lunch stop at Tenggarong, the last town accessible by road, was not quite what we had expected. A swarm of canoes bombarded us with their tiny floating kitchens and the straw-hatted cooks, balancing precariously, waved their ladles at us. Frantic activity, frantic shouting, but not a single piece of recognizable food. Thankfully, Bapa Ding took calm command and negotiated some little palm leaf packets which were filled with sticky rice and strong-smelling fishbones. The need to learn Indonesian fast was becoming urgent! Against the clawing lethargy of the long oppressive afternoon we took out the dictionary, determined to make a start. Our incredulous neighbours helped us. 'Selamat pagi' (good morning); 'selamat tidur' (good night); 'ya' (yes); 'tidak' (no); 'barapa?' (how much?).

In the evening I sat up on the roof; coolish breeze at last caressing my bursting temples and the low sun paling between stacks of splintering clouds. Behind, the looping river also paled and, either side, the heavily-foliaged swamp trees guarded the empty swampland beyond. In a lurid sky, the first stars appeared. Tiny beacons of hope for the unknown days ahead? Later, Nod and I sat with the young captain as he steered the boat into the night. His name was Supri, and he had a supremely winning smile. His narrow, soft eyes shone with comradeship as he passed us fleshy fragrant chunks of a giant jack fruit. And then, with a cigarette in one hand and a Coca-Cola bottle in the other, he lay back, champion of the river, manoeuvring the shuddering boat with a single bare foot. Dim, yellow searchlight splashing eerie shadows. Roar of the engine bouncing off the trees with a clattering echo.

Behind us, we had lost our sleeping place. The floor was totally covered with dreaming bodies. So, with casual grace, Supri cleared a space in the deep square pit beneath his feet. It was hard and hot and oily and I didn't dare stretch my legs for fear of getting them caught in the massive knobbled steering wheel. Nod gave up and went to squeeze himself beside Bapa Ding. But I tried to relax and let the thudding vibration of the engine massage me. At midnight, one of his brothers took over the shift and Supri came and curled up beside me. We had been taken under the young captain's wing.

Up on the roof with the first light, aching all over. Urggh! That new, uninvited travelling companion, fear, had got hold of me. How would we keep up our strength? Our health? The river was like a great magnet drawing us further and further into an unknown furnace. There was no escape, no turning back. We were pawns in a dangerous game and we didn't know the rules. By 8 a.m. it was already too hot to sit in the open. The sun was also a magnet, scowling, ferocious, eager to suck out my brains. To quell my fear, I called Nod. Better get on with the practicals of the day. Ferry life had its own rhythm, its own order: a lazy soothing rhythm, a stabilizing order. Imperative to hold onto these and not let the edges of my mind go astray.

Behind the toilets at the back of the boat was a narrow platform. One side was piled high with hapless chickens in cages, waiting to stick out their scraggy heads and give you a vindictive peck. The other side had a bucket on a string. Stripping to our underpants, we lowered the bucket into the river, drew it up and sluiced ourselves down with the warm muddy water. Grinning villagers, also washing, waved from a wooden jetty at the river's edge; while behind us, in the tiny workspace, Supri's mother was rinsing a mountainous pile of clothes (she had seven sons), and his father was plucking and gutting two of the chickens. Some of the washing was already hanging up, billowing into our faces, while the mixture of soapy water and chickens' blood trickled away in rivulets under our feet.

Mandi completed, it was time to practice Indonesian and make friends with another Thomas, his pretty wife and two young boys. This Thomas had his own small business in Samarinda and was on his way to visit his family. We were invited to stay with them on our return. If we prepared an offering of eggs and rice, his grandfather would manifest a ghost for us. Then Supri called us for lunch in the 'Restaurant', the cubby hole on the upper deck behind the dormitory. 'Kamu lapar?' we practised on Bapa Ding: 'kamu suka makan?' (Are you hungry? You like to eat?). He looked blank; we must have got it all wrong! Oh well, back to sign language. We salivated and rubbed our stomachs. That he understood. The gutted chickens were tastily cooked and mama nodded with a tinkling laugh as we licked our lips and savoured her food.

Soon after, we reached Longiram, the last little busy riverside port: bicycles, mopeds and a few small shops in bamboo shacks.

As we approached, the *Nilam* dwarfed the crowded quay and we were bombarded again with the floating kitchens. This time, scurrying vendors also poured onto the boat. Bapa Ding was agitated. We must buy bread. Last stop for bread before Longbagun. It was also Thomas' debarkation point and, as we pulled away from the shore, he called out for us to go to the pastor – the pastor would help us find his village!'Look!', Nod whispered excitedly, rousing me from an afternoon stupor. Some Dyak women had arrived on board. Their arms were covered with intricate tattoos, fashioned like delicate lace, and their ear lobes, weighted with clusters of large metal rings, stretched below their shoulders. Seeing us staring, their eyes flashed away like startled humming birds and their heads dipped behind the colourful circles of their parasols. Nod was transfixed. I think he realized for the first time that we really were bound for somewhere*other*.

So did I. And on the roof again in the evening. It was wide and high and the huge pale river and the huge pale sky were both flying through me. Every cell of my body tingled. Fear was gone and the taste of the wild was back. Down mid the looming shadows of the snoring deck, Supri had secured a sleeping space: a narrow platform above last night's pit. Just room enough for both of us to stretch out. There was no evening stop, so we had to make do with the bread and fried bananas that we had bought at Longiram. River banks pitch-black. Mystery and mud. And then, shrill villagers, calling, running, splashing their flaming torches across the trees. Driving with his foot again, Supri switched on his cassettes of Indonesian pop full blast. The bland western tunes and quasi-oriental rhythms pounded through our heads. At change of shift, he joined us again. I had a bit of a crush on our dashing chaperone and I wanted to give him a hug, but better judgement counselled me to turn away.

By the third day, we were both feeling rough from too little sleep and too much diarrhoea. I had spent half the night crouching over the square hole that was the toilet, torchlight catching the white of the foaming river just a few inches below me. But, apart from a mandi and our Indonesian class, at least there were no demands on us – except somehow to stop the elastic hours from stretching too intolerably. Humid heat is not invigorating, it's exhausting. But the signs of change encouraged us. The river was narrower and the first forested hills began to emerge out of the swamp. The banks were steeper; the trees were bigger; the villages were smaller and further apart. There were also many logging stations now. The narrow, corrugated offices on wooden jetties and the bays of floating logs – some over 100 yards long – were ominous enough; later, when we met Jaspar, he was to tell us how he had wept to see what lay behind the trampled gaps on the bank. Huge bulldozers and trucks go inland for up to 70 kilometres, smashing and destroying everything en route.

Together on the roof in the evening we were suddenly confronted by the grimmest-looking Dyak man who sprang out of the gloom brandishing a knife. Captions describing the 'Wild Men of Borneo' flashed through my mind. Was he coming to cut off our heads? Instead, he cut into a large, spiky, oblong, olive-green fruit. An overwhelmingly fetid stench issued forth – a cross between bad eggs, over-ripe pineapple and urine. The fruit is durian, much loved and prized by the Indonesians, though it is forbidden on aircraft because of its smell. Keen, greedy eyes, all fierceness gone, he handed us a generous piece each. The white flesh is divided into sort of packets with a smooth black stone. The texture: soft chewing gum and damp tissue paper. The taste: sickly-sweet, slightly rancid. Nod's reaction was extreme: he retched. And afterwards his sensitive nostrils picked up the smell from several hundred yards away. One whiff and he was off in the opposite direction!

At dark, Supri and his brothers moored the boat for the night stop. The passengers had thinned and we were allocated places in the dormitory. Unprecedented promotion: for our third night we would actually get a bed! But it was even hotter than below. From the map, we estimated we must be bang on the equator. The hottest yet. We sat out on the tiny deck behind the dormitory. Gasping. Not a breath of wind. If only the boat would move! The stars were burning holes in the black syrup sky. People were fanning themselves with anything they could lay their hands on. It was an effort even to raise an arm. Supri's ample auntie, who was in charge of the dormitory – and even had her own tiny cabin (unsurpassed luxury), was the only one with any life left. With a stylish lilt of her silken shawl and a gay tilt of her Coca-Cola bottle, she presided over us, fanning the easy comradeship. But even her puckered smile failed to lighten the weight of our eyelids and we were just about to lie down when some of the men came and told us there was a festival in the village through the trees. Furthermore, it was a special village, one of the few left in Kalimantan which was in a Longhouse.

We followed the men up the muddy bank in the dark and there, murkily lit by a few bobbing lamps, was a long, long, *long* – Longhouse! Raised on stilts, it seemed to go on forever and held, they told us, no less than fifty families. Oh, we'd heard of Longhouses, but never ever imagined them to be *this* long. With the increasing upheaval of the Dyak tribes, this community had migrated here from far upriver and built it on their arrival, just a few years before. Roofed but open-walled, a wide and stilted verandah stretched the length of the building. And from this, at regular intervals, narrow doors led off to partitioned sections, one for each family.

Along the central portion of the verandah the festival was in full swing; coloured lanterns, pulsing movement, distorted flickering shadows cast up on the bamboo walls. We were ushered to squat on the edge of the celebrations. And though the villagers took little notice of us, we were offered sweet black coffee and bunches of rambutan, the fruit with spiky, red-pink shells that we had eaten in Samarinda. There seemed to be a fancy dress parade in progress. Slow dancing up and down in a long follow-my-leader train. Some of the men were in drag with comic wigs. One was outrageously pregnant. Others were dressed as animals and strutted accordingly. The children, rows of bright, excited eyes, were doubling up and rolling over with delight. On and on the parade. A single repetitive step. A single repetitive riff. And on and on the children were laughing.

Next, the dance of the eagle; a costume of long coloured feathers which was passed on from one to the next as both men and women took their turn. Some doubled up like the children. The women had to be egged on. Some hardly managed at all – because of our presence? Shyness, in front of white strangers? And then the dance of the warrior. More feathers and a headdress. The young men were keen to have a go. Some were splendid. Muscles taut. Sharp scooping turns. Daredevil lunges. Spray of sweat beads over the hollering crowd. But the music was from a tinny cassette. The feathers were shabby. And under their costumes these guys were wearing sneakers and jeans. A paradoxical mix of old and new. Yet the trees of the encircling jungle, lapping against the burning stars, and the long long Longhouse itself felt eternal . . .

Some of our men had already left and we began to get scared. Supri had promised the boat wouldn't go without us. But what if he'd forgotten? What if it did? Day stop, night stop, nothing seemed to go to plan. In rising panic we dashed back and balanced along the plank to the safety of our last night on the ferry.

From Nigel's journal. Longbagun. Thursday 14 January.

Midday at Longbagun, sitting at the long table on the verandah. Rick has gone to rest in the room we call the oven, it gets so hot. Bapa Ding just made us noodles, rice, sardines, eggs, melon and raw bananas – so we will be well fed!

We arrived here yesterday at 3.20 p.m. Supri proudly announced that we were: 'On time'. Bapa Ding brought us here to the 'meeting-point house' to await a passing longboat to take us on up to Longpahangai – it could be one day or two . . . or three or four . . . or five! It's a large wooden house; it has a wide verandah with this fifteen-foot long table and benches. The main room is high-ceilinged, wooden-floored, with another long rectangular table and, sitting on it, two oil lamps and a large fly-cover for food. In one corner there's a fire built on a high platform with heavy black smoke-and-tar-charred pots hanging over it. When lit it adds to the already stifling heat. We laid our ground sheets out on the floor (why didn't we bring those foam camping mats?) and Bapa Ding rolled out his rush mat.

On the way through the village to meet the *Kepala* (head of the village), we saw people working stripping rotan, and a man repairing his wooden boat, upturned on blocks. At the back of the leader's house where we drank a glass of hot sweet tea, an old lady shuffled about almost bent double, with hanging saggy bare breasts and earlobes stretching right down beyond her shoulders, like the women on the ferry. She smiled a cheery toothless smile. Bapa Ding was on the hunt for food and bought the noodles and rice that we ate today, fulfilling his promise to feed us.

It's hot, hot and so humid, sometimes it's difficult to breathe. As soon as I move sweat pours off me. Always hoping for a breeze. The rain when it came yesterday was a welcome relief. None today so far; although plenty in the night. Some of Ding's family live here. We talked with his nephew, Savang. He is strong, well-built and makes me feel puny alongside him. He likes to hunt and showed us a gun that he shoots birds with. He mentioned going to play football at a village downstream. We may go with him and look for Jaspar – the VSO worker. It would be good to do something. I wonder how long we will have to wait. Killing time in this heat.

From Nigel's journal. Friday 15 January.

We had heard that Pastor Ranft's boat was in the area and there was a possibility it would be going upriver today. It arrived! Bapa Ding was excited. We could go! The boatmen ate supper with us last night. They sat around the lamp talking quietly with Bapa

Ding. He told them the story of our trip and how he has taken us on. We were lying on the hard floor listening.

We got up this morning at six looking forward to the next stage of our journey. An uncomfortable night on the floor, no soft bed and no fan here, and a puppy slept on my feet. The pig outside in his pen chased his food bucket around and two heavy rainfalls pounded on the tin roof, which kept me awake most of the night. Just as we were packing, Bapa Ding said, 'Tidak, tidak pergi!' (no go). With all the rain, the river is too high now for so many in the boat: it went without us. Deflated, I bathed in the early morning drizzle and washed some clothes in the muddy Mahakam. After the disappointment with the boat and another long slow morning, Savang agreed to take us to Jaspar's village, Ujohbilang, the district centre. His football match was on. We climbed into his longboat and, enjoying the cooling breeze, motored downstream for about half-an-hour; relieved to be doing something. He showed us the steeply-angled football field and invited us to play – not in this heat, thank you!

We asked for Jaspar's whereabouts at the 'Palace of Teachers', a clean, lino-floored house, hoping that he could shed some light on our forest search. The English teacher, suddenly faced with real English people, became incredibly self-conscious and could hardly speak, his colleagues giggling behind him. Jaspar himself then arrived, a tall, lean Dutch man, having heard that we were looking for him. No, he hadn't received Mark's message, but was happy to see us, starved of European company. He took us in his longboat even further downstream to his house and project. He was trying to introduce a permanent rice variety – but the locals had yet to be convinced that it would work. We walked along barefoot behind him in secondary forest. The area that had been cut appeared to be growing back vigorously, the trees and undergrowth tangled and thick. Jaspar, however, informed us that it would never be as rich as the original primary forest. Happy to be out in the open again after the 'prison' of Samarinda, the ferry and the house, our sense of freedom was soon curtailed by Rick stepping on a stinging ant. We realised that we were in foreign territory!

After supper Jaspar returned us upstream to find Savang. It was dark. Jaspar handled his longboat badly. We rocked from side to side, almost toppling over. I felt completely insecure. Were there crocodiles waiting to devour us? At last we reached the safety of the bank, lucky to escape with our lives. We found Savang, who had won at football and had decided to stay the night in Ujohbilang and get drunk – we were stranded! What to do now? Luckily, Johannes, Savang's uncle whom we had met in Longbagun took us under his wing for the evening. By then it was late, I was very tired and getting scared. He took us to a relative's house where once more we sat on the hard floor. There he related the story of his twelve incredibly hard years driving a logging truck. Long twelve-hour days driving sometimes 70 kilometres from the place where the trees were cut to the bank of the river, through thick mud and deeply-rutted tracks, often getting stuck and having to dig himself out. The strain and pain of the work showed in his eyes and body, as he told the story. He was not happy cutting and logging those trees, but what could he do? He had a big family to feed and no other means of earning money. He took pride in being with us and sharing his story. It gave me a first insight into the other side of the forest too.

Next stop was the café; an open-sided verandah attached to a house with rough benches at tables and a rickety floor and roof. There Johannes bought us sweet tea and bread cakes. The young woman server giggled nervously as she poured the tea, hardly daring to look at us. I sat for a moment in a wonder, catching myself in the realization that here I was, three days up a remote river in Borneo with no tourist hotels or bungalows and no place to stay for the night, and yet *trusting* Johannes – this must be adventure! On the way through the long village to yet another relative's house where we were to spend the night, we passed the *Camat's* house (the local government representative). Outside on the grass was placed a television. People were sitting around watching Dynasty! I thought, how on earth do these people relate to shoulder-pads and swimming pools – what plastic dreams were being planted in their minds? The TV was a present from the government for voting them in: reward or bribery, I wonder?

Nigel's journal. Saturday 16 January.
This morning we found friend Savang, who eventually took us back 'home'. As we pulled into the quay, Bapa Ding was anxiously waiting. *'Pergi Longpahangai jam sepula'* – (We go to Longpahangai at 10 o'clock). It was now 9.30. Another boat had arrived and was headed upstream.

In part panic and part relief, we packed very quickly, rolled up the ground sheets, filled the precious water bottles and rushed back down to the quay. A narrow wooden longboat that stretched for about 20 feet drew up. I thought it looked like a huge coffin and wondered about our fate. Would this get us through the dangerous rapids? Would the single outboard motor be strong enough to take us up? My heart sank when I saw, along with the three Dyak crewmen, another Westerner. I didn't want other white company. This was to be an adventure with the local people for just me and Rick. I reluctantly and resentfully introduced myself to an American anthropologist who was working with the Indonesian government. We bundled our baggage into the longboat and sat at the back, as far from him as possible.

We stopped again a short way upriver by two shacks perched high up on the steep slippery bank, and sheltered from the baking sun by a spiky bush hanging over the sandbank. The three men scaled the bank and slid down again with a carcass of wild pig which they dumped in the prow of the boat. Tonight's supper? And off we went again; happy to be on our way finally to the forest. Hot, hot sun, muddy river rushing under us and the surroundings getting more and more remote and wild. This is it now. This is what it's like to travel in the wild. Despite the discomfort, I liked it!

The three crewmen were from the remotest part of the river, close to the Sarawak (Malaysia) border, and were taking drums of petrol and provisions to their people. They had never carried Westerners before and were as shy of us as I was of them. We had to cover ourselves completely from the vicious sun and poured hat-fulls of water over us to keep cool. Even though Pastor Bong (in Samarinda) had said there would be no more logging stations after Longbagun, they were evident from the huge swathes cut in the banks and muddy, slimy tracks that had been made by huge logs being rolled down the banks. Rick, in his tense panic remarked, 'Maybe the primary forest has all gone'.

Between high cliffs and past huge waterfalls, we crossed the dangerous rapids. The driver's concentration was incredible as he steered and manoeuvred us through the narrow gaps of rushing water, zigzagging against the hurtling current: missing the jagged rocks and massive boulders by a hair's breadth. One mistake and we would all be plunged into the swirling river and swept away. At one point, the force of the water was so great, the engine almost gave out. At another, I saw a huge watersnake sitting on a large rock willing us to capsize. Several times we had to stop, unpack some of the cargo to lighten the load, and ferry it and us in two or three journeys. We began to understand why the local people never say, 'When I see you again'; they say, 'If I see you again'! We also passed a holy burial mountain and saw carved coffins high out of reach on sheer cliffs. Bapa Ding's grandfather was resting up there.

At dusk we pulled onto a sandy beach. We hadn't passed a single village all day. Two families from upstream had already arrived to camp; the women had intricately tattooed arms and ankles. Using their open fire, Bapa got to work and cooked our supper, while the boatmen roasted their pig. The sleeping place was a shack, with no walls, on eight-foot high stilts. Floor and roof – that's it! First no beds and no fans – now I didn't even have walls for security. We climbed up, a precarious operation, which entailed walking up a coconut palm trunk that had rough-hewn foot-holes. At supper, sitting on the sandbank beach, Don, the American anthropologist, who could speak fluent Indonesian, said that he and the crewmen had decided to sleep out on the beach. Rick and I were keen to join them, but Bapa Ding was adamant that we didn't. He shook his head hard and wrung his hands, very upset. He was our guide, we must listen to him. So off up the pole we went. As I lay down to sleep, the jungle was inches away: monkeys screeched, bats peeped, frogs croaked, lightning flashed sharply, momentarily lighting up everything. I wondered what would reach out and get me in the night. Later it rained – and I mean *rained* – miraculously we stayed dry. But Don and the crewmen staggered up soaked and shivering. Bapa Ding had been right!

From Nigel's journal. Sunday 17 January.
I must be getting used to the wild and hard conditions, or my fear knocked me out totally, because – I slept well. Up at dawn and a good breakfast, then back in the boat for the last stretch of the journey and the most dangerous set of rapids. We came upon the sound of them – they roared. Seeing how hard and fast the river was hurtling down, the driver decided that, for our own safety, this time we should get out and walk round them. Rick, Bapa Ding and I trudged through thick heavy mud and undergrowth high up on the bank. We saw the driver and Don pushing three times through the rapids with the loads. Don was exhilarated from the experience and I was jealous and disappointed that I hadn't taken the risk. But next time . . .

IV

And so, eight days after leaving Samarinda, we finally reached Longpahangai. From our cramped perches in the over-full longboat, both Nod and I had been gratefully watching the gathering clouds. Little by little they had bandaged up the sizzling sun and now it had become so overcast that it was even dreary. The ramshackle outpost with its narrow moorings, floating rafts and notched coconut poles, straddled the sheer muddy bank, steeper and more precarious than ever. The slit eyes of the agile boatmen twinkled as the two of us and Don cumbersomely clambered up to safety. Then they were off, keen to reach home before nightfall. Bapa Ding was also keen to get home; he pointed out the direction of the mission and disappeared.

The village was strangely empty and strangely silent. Along the dirt path, our presence was only marked by the odd dog whining amongst the rank weeds, and the odd dour face peering at us from the double row of skewhiff houses on broad stilts. Don had planned to go and announce his presence to the Camat (the local government administrator), but now he changed his mind, and, uninvited, attached himself to us. I was uneasy and I knew Nod felt the same. After all, we had made a special arrangement via Pastor Bong. But talking as always in fast-blurred circles, Don deflected our concern. His will was not to be contravened.

The church and the mission stood at the top of Longpahangai and both looked down on the river. Their walls were weatherboard, once painted white. The church had a short stubby spire, and the mission, a generous verandah which stretched its length and continued round along the end beside the church. True to our apprehensions, Pastor Ranft was not a little put out to be confronted with three visitors instead of two. He was Dutch, slow-moving and very fat. Draped in a grey sarong and wearing huge creaking sandals, his big face was as worn as the weatherboard. His thinning red hair hung dank and his pale grey eyes retreated behind pallid lids. 'I expected only two; I have only two guest rooms.' 'That's OK, that's OK', Don blurted several times, 'I'll sleep on the floor; that's OK'. Pastor Ranft's creaking sandals led us down the narrow passage to our 'cells'. They were high-ceilinged and airy. A small bed with a quilt; a window looking over the balcony and down onto the fast-flowing river. 'It is lunchtime, you are hungry?'

As we were ushered in to the dining room, two local girls were hurriedly setting our places. Dropping the cutlery in their haste, and averting their eyes, they tiptoed out even more hurriedly. Pastor Ranft bade us sit. The food lay protected from the flies under two large, dome-shaped lids; between them, an ants' highway crossed the cracked and faded plastic table-cloth. Pastor Ranft said grace and a cock crowed in the yard. Then he lifted the lids: a bowl of gooey rice, and a plate with lumps of dark, old-looking fish.

After the meal, Pastor Ranft brought out some hand-drawn maps. He showed us three areas where he affirmed there was still primary forest. One was further upriver. One was quite a way along a tributary. The third was closer, reached by backtracking a little way downriver and then veering out overland. I tried to temper my manic excitement. I tried to ask practical questions. I knew I should get my notebook and write down the details. But my body was still swaying from the boat. My stomach was lurching from the old-looking fish and Don kept rattling on and steering the conversation off course. 'There'll be time later' I tried to reassure myself; 'plenty of time'. But I still resented Don's presence and I knew that Nod did too.

Back down the dirt path, Pastor Ranft took us to meet the Camat. A young, friendly man in a clean, ironed shirt, he invited us into his tin shed and we sat at his small makeshift desk. Pastor Ranft explained our mission. The Camat understood. He would help us. It was his duty. He would take us to meet the Kepala (the head of the village). The Kepala would find us guides. After profuse thanks all round, Pastor Ranft excused himself and went back to the mission.

Most of the houses in Longpahangai had matted thatched roofs; the Kepala's was one of the few that boasted corrugated iron. It was set back between dark trees and the room we entered was also dark. No furniture. Bare floor. We sat cross-legged, and the Kepala entered from behind a screen. He had a sour, mask-like face, its mouldings not given to smiling; but he mirrored the Camat's formal politeness. Don, with his fluent Indonesian, took over the story. A lengthy discussion followed and Don negotiated the terms. We would go to the third area on the Pastor's map. It would be a two-day expedition. A short journey downriver by *chas* (small canoe) and then eight hours walking and we would come to trees five times the width of a man's outstretched arms. '*Bagus bagus sangat bagus*' (good, good, very good). '*Kapan pergi anda?*' (when do you want to go?). I said that we needed a day of rest first; a day to settle and prepare. The Kepala almost managed a smile and bowed his farewell.

In the sallow glow of the darkening evening, Nod and I strolled through the village. It was his turn to feel afraid. It had been rice and lumps of old-looking fish again for supper and he craved something sweet. Something for comfort. At a lop-sided shack of a shop, close to the water's edge where we had landed, a skinny toothless woman looked at us blankly and shook her head. All we could see were tiny packets of dried biscuits and small cartons of green bean juice. We bought some. And sitting on a fence in a deserted spot where a muddy stream crossed the path and the rank weeds grew ten feet tall, we made the most of our meagre feast. The biscuits were stale. The bean juice was warm. But they did contain some sugar and they were a change from rice. It was also a relief to be alone together.

Don had gone to meet the Kepala again, to continue making arrangements. He hadn't heard my request for a rest day and the Kepala had started making plans for us to set out in the morning. I had had to underline my anxiety: 'We must have a day's rest. We are not used to these conditions.' 'OK OK OK', Don had rattled on, 'I'll see what I can do'. He prided himself on his knack with these people. He and the Kepala were becoming mates: 'The Kepala's OK, he's OK'. And so he had sped off to discuss it all again. Locked in his anthropological head, he had become wearing company. He talked incessantly *at* one, not *to* one, and never stopped to listen. His logic was hard to follow and sometimes he seemed to contradict himself. He had been in Indonesia a long time. Originally he had come as an anthropology student, but now he was working as some kind of economic adviser to the government. He also had a wife somewhere, and seemed to be making good money. But he was vague as to why he had journeyed upriver, and his attitude to the forest and the Dyak people was also vague. Throughout our several days together he only came out of his insular head once. While 'mandying' in the river, he actually asked Nod a question or two about acting, and momentarily got interested in the idea that an actor has to use different techniques for stage plays and for films. Now he had decided to come to the forest with us.

We felt very small and transitory as we crumpled up the biscuit wrappings. Two timid aliens in the vast and thundering heart of Borneo; a thunder that was more a pulsing than a roar. For, despite the whispering undergrowth and the doleful murmurings of the river, there was a huge and slightly fearful silence blanketing everything. In faltering tones that revealed my own misgivings, I thanked Nod for coming with me; for braving the rapids and the heat, the hard floors and the lumps of old-looking fish. He had relaxed a little now, and in the dropping ochre light we headed back to the mission.

I must have slept well. I woke feeling good. The cocks were crowing expectantly and a shaft of early sun was dancing on the whitewashed walls. While Don grunted in his fretful sleep, I did my ablutions in the collapsing wash house at the end of the corridor, and then had a meditate. Optimistic and as expectant as the cocks, I only prayed that we would get our day of rest. My prayer was answered. The Kepala arrived, almost friendly and even almost effusive. The expedition was planned for the morrow. All was in order. The guides had been chosen and the fuel and supplies were being organized. Hurray! Well done Don. The long discussions had paid off.

Then Bapa Ding arrived. Our social calendar was getting hectic. We received him on the verandah, offered him lukewarm tea from the old plastic thermos flask in the dining room and sat with him at the large, low table, facing the church. Bapa Ding was clearly overjoyed to be home. The journey downriver to visit his son and the strenuous task of looking after the mad Englishmen had taken it out of him. He was also not a well man. Sometimes in the night he had rolled on the floor, moaning in pain and clutching his stomach. His cheeks were hollow and there were dark rings under his eyes. But he had unquestionably fulfilled his part of the bargain. His attentiveness and concern for our welfare had been unerring, his sense of duty, impeccable. Yet, the contact between us had remained formal; he had given us no clues as to what he thought and felt. A secret man. A closed volume. Dark shadows guarded the wisdom in his deep-set Dyak eyes.

The only gift we had to give him was a small, leather-bound New Testament. We had been worried because it wasn't a Catholic one, but Pastor Ranft had assured us that was not a problem. Bapa Ding accepted his gift with a low magnanimous bow. But Pastor Ranft, passing by, was unexpectedly abrupt, and creaked away down the corridor, inferring he was far too busy for idle chat. Perhaps Bapa Ding didn't go to church. Perhaps he wasn't a Christian. We never found out. We never saw him again.

Next, for the most vital part of the day: to practise walking in the heat in our jungle boots. Don came with us and we set off up the unkempt track beyond the mission. It skirted the river and was shaded by the boughs of the encroaching jungle. Soon it changed direction and took us up onto a hill on which stood the surprisingly large district school. In bashful confusion, a female teacher

Passengers on
the *Nilam Cahaya*.

Jau, the paramedic at
Ujohbilang.

The intrepid duo:
Rick *(left)* Nigel *(right)*

silently pointed us onward. We descended through white-stemmed trees under which there were pineapples growing and, finding ourselves back in the village, returned to the mission on our well-known path.

We completed the circuit twice in an hour. Within the first hundred yards, we were agush with sweat, and apart from what I've described, I saw little else. My uninvited companion, fear, was having a field-day, and I was having to give him a severe talking-to. It was my boring old varicose veins and a certainty that I hadn't broken in my boots well enough. Would they swell up in the heat? Would they explode? Had I tied my boots too tight? Would I get blisters? I remembered the Angel Card: *release* the nonsense; breathe out the fear . . . I wasn't breathing, I was panting.

After lunch Don announced he was feeling ill and we continued our gruelling exercise without him. This time we found our way into the steep rice fields. These were often almost sheer; small patches stolen from the surrounding forest. From their top ridges we caught glimpses of hushed blue mountains brimmed in white clouds. Back at base, I ripped off my boots. My legs looked fine. My feet were unscarred. Not even a sniff of a blister. Yippee! I had passed the test – and with distinction! I recklessly cavorted down the coconut pole and glibly submerged myself in the river. Nod warned me not to let go of the raft. The current here was much faster than at Longbagun. We had also been told that, just the month before, two Frenchmen had been taken by crocodiles whilst trying to swim to the opposite tree-covered bank.

After an hour of lifeless luxury on my quilt bed, I ventured out in the dusk for another mandi. But I stopped short at the top of the bank. Pastor Ranft was down on the raft, naked, washing himself. A colossal shapeless blob, he glistened palely in the gloom. Sensing that he would hate to be observed and have his privacy impinged on, I would have turned back. But I was too late; he had seen me. So, nonchalantly, I descended and joined him. He left fast.

Later, in the corridor, we met Pastor Lahagir, Pastor Ranft's assistant. He was a reticent, bespectacled man in a blue-check sarong. He whispered a genteel welcome and even volunteered a sheepish smile as he slid past us into his room. He didn't join us for supper, and subsequently declined from ever sharing a meal with us. In the dining room, we waited with bated breath as Pastor Ranft lifted the dome-shaped lids. The food had been the same so far at every meal, including breakfast. We continued to live in hope – but no, there it was: the same gooey rice and the same lumps of fish, looking even darker and even older, if that were possible. Pastor Ranft apologized. Fruit and vegetables were hard to come by, and to drink, he could only offer us tea. No coffee. All supplies had to cross those fearsome rapids. This made prices prohibitive; for the mission had dwindling funds and times had become hard. But at least our repast was sanctified, and after it, we adjourned with our mugs of weak tea into his study.

It was a large room; one side for his messy desk and the other for wicker armchairs with faded cushions and drapes. There were old curling photos on the walls and pictures in pastel shades. The atmosphere was musty and lonely, as if the room had seen more optimistic and more radiant days. Pastor Ranft had been in Longpahangai for over twenty years, and he showed us his scrapbooks from the early pioneering times. Detailed, hand-written notes and photos of young Dyak women with their long earlobes and tattooed faces. He was also an artist and a musician. The pastel pictures on the walls were his own. And his cello, in a worn case, leant against a corner. But the pictures were old and the cello case was coated in dust. Of late he had not felt the inclination to paint or to play. Coaxed very gently, Pastor Ranft was pleased to speak. But his pale grey eyes were hard to catch. They preferred to share their weariness with the invading cobwebs. His next project was the building of a community centre. This would have workshops and a youth training scheme. He showed us his own hand-drawn plans. But his presentation lacked enthusiasm and was imbued with little confidence. This was the modern approach; what people did these days. But was it what he really wanted? And was it even appropriate? There was disillusionment in those creaking sandals. Had he been in this self-imposed isolation cell for too long? Had his fire been quelled by the damp humidity? Had the Holy Ghost even abandoned him and moved on? Nod felt more generously-disposed towards him than I did. For me, there was a question-mark in the air. Something, somewhere I couldn't quite trust . . . But at least we had talked and spent some time together.

From Rick's journal. Tuesday 19 January.
We get up early. Feeling tense and scared. Don has decided not to walk with us; he is leaving with the Camat who is taking the government boat downstream on business. Pastor Ranft is also leaving, upstream to Longlunuk, another of his parishes. I offer

him money for our stay. He grabs it – too fast – and wishes us luck. We take our small knapsacks to the Kepala. Our guides are his son, Antonius – square, guileless – and his son's friend, Bero – slimmer, darker. Both are slow packing up. Doubt slips into my mind.

The four of us set off for the short trip downriver in the chas. Then our guides drag the chas up the bank to hide it in the trees and we start walking. Steep ascent. Slippery track. Tall, slim trees. Sweating buckets. We stop on a ridge. The river is already far below like a sluggish reptile creeping through the jungle. Then we leave the track, diving down into the steep steamy undergrowth. Bero leads, slashing our way and cutting notches in the stems as markers for our return. We walk for three hours. Only stopping to pick off the leeches from our boots and trousers. Hand-sized, luminous-blue, butterfly-like creatures flap silently around us, and at one point I nearly put my hand on a 'stick' that turns out to be a giant insect. We stop at eleven o'clock for lunch. Too soon. For too long. I am suspicious again, full of agitation. Something is wrong. They have difficulty making the fire; difficulty cooking the *mie* (noodles). They are like amateurs. Boy scouts. Nod says relax; trust them. I try to. But . . .

We walk for one more hour. Antonius and Bero decide to stop and set up camp. It's only two-thirty. When we ask them to continue, they just laugh and point to the trees around a stagnant creek. 'But these aren't what we're looking for. They are only the width of *two* men's outstretched arms,' we explain in rabid sign language. Their eyes slide away. They have come far enough. They don't know where the big trees are. So, in well-controlled but strong tones, we order them to take us back to the village. They are reluctant. We are determined. They resist but, despite their glimmering machetes and our puny little sticks, we insist. In a heavy cloudburst, we retrace our steps. Three hours fast walking. We have been fooled. Tramping my fury into the sodden ground, I rehearse my Indonesian speech to the Kepala a thousand times. We stop at the first ridge overlooking the river. I repent. Rage won't get us anywhere. So we share a joke with our guides, and a cigarette for comfort and peace-making. And then, with legs like jelly, on for the final descending lap.

We reach the Kepala's house just before dark and, with little Pastor Lahagir as translator, an extraordinary meeting ensues. While maintaining respectfulness and the appropriate decorum, we forcefully express our extreme dissatisfaction with the out-come of the day. But the Indonesians don't answer questions and the leader talks in convoluted circles; a misunderstanding; he doesn't know where the forest is either; perhaps it is too far away; perhaps it is all cut down. Then it starts to rain. Harder and harder and harder, beating down on the tin roof, till we have to move in closer and closer on the bare floor in the empty room in order to catch the interpreter's hesitant words. Finally, we literally have the Kepala against the wall. The mask of his face is rigid. Honour is at stake all round. Suddenly, the single electric striplight goes out and for a moment we are all plunged into darkness, still talking.

A long debate over payment follows. We'd paid for food, cigarettes and petrol for two days; also agreed on a daily fee for each guide. The Kepala wants the money in full. No way! He is adamant. So are we. Eventually, a compromise is reached: we will pay one day's fee for each guide and get half the money back on the food. Bero has disappeared and Antonius looks shame-faced. Coffee is served. The Kepala will look for older, more experienced guides and bring us the news tomorrow. We all shake hands. So we did pretty well. We kept our cool and held our ground, but the Kepala still holds the reins of the forest. We stagger barefoot back to the mission in the slooshing rain; we are the losers all right. Pastor Lahagir is very apologetic, and completely bewildered. He will put off his journey to a funeral tomorrow, so we can stay longer. On the dining table, under the fly-covered lids, something new: old-looking lumps of *meat*. As vegetarians, this would be unthinkable at home. But tonight we would guzzle up anything. Early to bed. Whole body aching. Sleep, please come fast. Blot out the horrible disappointment.

From Rick's journal. Wednesday 20 January.
Day of rest. My lips have swollen up. A belated reaction to the intense heat on the river? The Kepala arrives after breakfast. As we feared, no one will take us. No one knows where the big forest is. The men need to work in their rice fields. Also, the river is too high. He is brief and sour; keen to wash his hands of us. But with Pastor Lahagir as interpreter again he does help us make a double programme for tomorrow. Either we will go for the six-seater plane expected at the tiny airstrip upriver; or he will find a boat to take us back downriver. He will make enquiries. Make sure we get a fair price. But we can't trust him. So? What? How? Where? We must watch out for a passing boat ourselves.

Snoozing and reading Somerset Maugham. Feeling the desperate frustration. The forest so near, yet out of our reach. Luck turned against us. Why? My yearning mind plots a new plan: we'll go upstream to Longlunuk, to Pastor Ranft. We'll talk to the Camat there. Talk to the Kepala of the village there. They may be more helpful. They will be more helpful. We can't be beaten. Not after all this. Stroll in the evening taking photos. Clearer. Determined again. A tree with vermilion flowers. Bushes with lemon-yellow tongues. A woman struggling in a canoe against the current, clinging close to the bank in the shadows from the overhanging jungle drapery.

Later, talk to Pastor Ranft on the walkie-talkie radio: the Kepala in Longlunuk is away. There is no Camat there. We can't stay at the mission because it's too small. 'Over to you'. Crackle. Crackle. Hopes dashed again. He's no help at all. Voice as thin and pale as his eyes. Sorry about our failed expedition, but too lethargic to do anymore. Keen to be rid of his non-Catholic guests.

From Rick's journal. Thursday 21 January.
Pastor Lahagir has arranged for a boat to take us up to the airstrip. The boatman arrives after breakfast. We are ready and packed. He explains that the river is too high and dangerous to use a chas, so we will have to take a longboat. He wants to charge us a lot. If the plane doesn't come, the round trip of less than two hours will cost more than the fare for the four days on the *Nilam Cahaya*. Pastor Lahagir agrees it's too much. We send him packing! Talk to Pastor Ranft on the radio again. Crackle. Crackle. 'Over to you'. Hum-ing and ha-ing. There's only a 50:50 chance that the plane will come. We must understand that petrol is very expensive here. Yes, the high river's a problem. He is leaving for another village at lunch-time. Again no help.

I go with Pastor Lahagir to seek the Kepala. We pass a group of surly men lounging on their verandah. Can they help us? Maybe. They work out their price for the journey. It's less than the first man's offer. Encouraged, I haggle further. We almost clinch a deal. But now they want the full cost of the fuel in advance. And if the plane arrives? They'll reimburse us. Oh yes? Shifty eyes are scrutinizing the warped floor of the verandah. I demand they only charge us one trip at a time. But then they'll be out of pocket. And what about us? This new deal works out at *twice* the first man's offer! I appeal and am met with stony faces. At my wits' end, I reject their offer and turn to leave. The silent woman in the corner points to my swollen lips and my ankles. She shakes her head. The tiny scars where my boots rubbed are suddenly worse. Going septic. Covered in flies. The men laugh.

Back at the mission we try to get hold of the original boatman. Maybe he wasn't ripping us off after all. But he's already left for his rice fields. And it's too late anyway. Pastor Lahagir gets a headache. Nod binds my feet. They're bad. Start taking antibiotics. Why did I suddenly get careless? Up until now we have been so scrupulous with the smallest cut or sore – and now I've been running around barefoot, in the mud, not even noticing.

Feeling drowsy. I watch the evening river from my window. Plan one more bid to get to the forest: Bapa Ding – maybe he'll help us? Nod says: 'No'. Look at me; a wounded soldier. He's right. I couldn't walk anywhere for several days. And even if I could, we stupidly never noted down the key areas on Pastor Ranft's map, so we have no proof of what we're after. So, nothing to do but pray for no more rain tonight and thank god for Pastor Lahagir looking after us so well. Since Pastor Ranft's departure the meals have been getting better: green beans, bananas and even a hard mango. Sweet coffee, too. But Pastor Lahagir still refuses to eat with us and the two shy girls still tiptoe out as soon as we enter the dining room. Later, news comes that there is a teacher who needs to get downriver because his father has died. There is also a boatman who is taking a load of empty barrels downstream, but it seems he is not trustworthy. So the teacher is our best hope. We'll try to find him tomorrow.

In the evening I hobble out onto the balcony, and, in the listless dragging hours, we spend a long time discussing the turn in our luck. When did it change and why? Nod feels the spanner in the works was Don. With his fluent Indonesian, he had seemed to me to be the next twist of fate, but actually it had meant we'd abdicated our responsibilities and handed all our negotiations over to him. If we'd done the negotiating, would it have turned out differently? We always try to reach out to people simply and honestly; trusting our instincts, our intuition; taking heed of our first impressions. Our first impression of the Kepala was of a devious man, dealing for his own ends. Nod's first response to Don was a sinking heart. Why had we ignored these feelings? And for whose ends had Don been dealing? What was he doing upriver anyway and why did he leave so suddenly with the Camat? Had he positively blocked our endeavour? And if so, why? The circuit of questions keep spinning round. No answers. Only more questions. Easy to see how people go mad when cut off from all their points of reference, all their support systems. Reality starts to split. Paranoia starts to loom up.

❖ ❖ ❖

That night I thought I heard Pastor Ranft's creaking sandals in the passage. I also felt the men on that warped verandah leering down at me. What did these foolish white men want? To them we were the ones with ulterior motives: prying into their lives; prying into their forest. Their black, distrusting eyes, didn't like it one little bit. They lived by laws and traditions of which we had no inkling. And they had no intention of letting us in. They had been interfered with and messed about enough. Greedy prospectors. A despotic government. Shockwaves from the oil and logging boom that had caused pandemonium downriver. Not to mention Pastor Ranft's threatening heaven and hell. So what could the two white nutters expect but to provide fodder for their empty pockets. Earlier we had been invited to some ceremony in the village; but how could we go and socialize with the people who were trying to rip us off? Wouldn't it make us look even more stupid? Besides, my feet were bandaged and Nod had no heart for gregariousness alone. What a mistake. It would probably have been the very way to bridge the great divide.

Morning brought another disappointment: the bereaved teacher would not be going downriver until the end of the month. And so we had no choice but to set up our river watch: 8 a.m. to 2 p.m. No one, we had been advised, would begin the downriver journey later than that. We tried to make a constructive day. Meditating. Reading. Writing. This was the day of Nod's letter to Ray. And I wrote to my almost-forgotten family.

Dear Mother and Father and all,
We are marooned in the heartland of Kalimantan, home of the Dyak tribes. Until recently, they were the famous Head Hunters of Borneo, displaying the heads of their enemies as trophies of their valour and invincibility. Under the very thin Western veneer of jeans and T-shirts and the odd pop-blasting radio, they are still a wild, remote people (though no longer head hunters, we hope!). Still spearing food in the jungle. Still adhering to their traditional farming methods: they till their small rice fields for only three years and then 'slash and burn' a new patch, leaving the old one to re-establish as forest. Their myth of creation is about hornbills and watersnakes and the earrings of the moon – as fluid as the river itself. It is said that they only accepted Christianity because it still allowed them to eat pig. . . . .

. . . . And now we are marooned. Sitting on the verandah of the mission, looking down at the fast-flowing muddy river.

Sweating in the high humidity. Silence broken only by the crowing cocks and the songs of the highly-coloured, tiny jungle birds. Waiting to hail a passing boat. But even if one comes will it stop? The Angel Card I chose to help us on our journey was Release. So we release our fear, our disappointment, our frustration. And we wait . . . waiting, waiting for our luck to change . . .

It didn't. Not that day. Not a single boat passed. The vapid sagging afternoon mocked us as our industrious efforts slowed to a standstill. Humidity and apathy became the same word. And the claustrophobic silence in my cell crunched and fuzzed around me in big boots. No wonder Pastor Ranft's fire had been quelled. Ours had almost gone out in a few days. But at least my ankles and lips were getting better. The antibiotics were working fast and the wicker chairs no longer felt as if they belonged to a geriatric convalescent home.

'Where is the Pastor?' Evening had brought a stranger onto the verandah. A tall, broad man with a mellow voice. His features were different from the local people; longer, narrower, and his deportment was impressive. Sensing he might be a potential ally, I explained our situation to him in full. Lo and behold, he knew most of it already! Lo and behold, he was Gabriel's uncle! His name was Benedictus and he had come on yesterday's plane (so it had arrived). He was on business hoping to see the Camat. But even Benedictus was unsure what we meant by primary forest. Could we give him an image of it? Could we share our picture? We used the Kepala's expression: trees five times the width of a man's outstretched arms. Now Benedictus understood. Yes, he had seen the big trees, from the plane. Our best bet would be to return to Longbagun and then take a chas up to the two major logging stations just below the rapids. He gave us their names: P T Roda Mass Timber and P T Surapati Timber. The surveyors there would know all the details of the forest. We could sleep in the dormitory and drive with the big trucks 20 or 30 kilometres to where they were logging. It had never dawned on us to do this. What irony! To reach the *Great Forest* with the very people who were annihilating it. The idea filled me with horror. But Benedictus was a realist. We needed help and so we should go to the people who had the know-how and the transport to provide it.

After supper we sat out as usual pondering our fate. It was the only entertainment that we had and Benedictus had injected it with new life. His logic was sound and, although the idea was abhorrent to us, we would follow his advice. We also had obligations to fulfil downriver and now we were glad that we hadn't opted out of them by taking the plane. Supri would be expecting us on the *Nilam Cahaya*. Thomas's father would be waiting to summon up that ghost. And a charming loquacious fellow, another Ding, who had travelled up with us on the ferry, had implored us to visit him in his 'humble little village' on our way back. Under a big equatorial moon, hope at last. The surrounding sounds of the night softened. In the limpid moonlight, the forest felt breathlessly close; it was as if I could have just reached over the river and touched it. The ancient trees, the coiling orchids, a last bastion of untainted, primeval life. Nod and I felt close, too. We would complete the natural circle of our trip. And – would we make it to the forest after all?

V

From Nigel's journal. Saturday 23 January.
On the morning after the visitation of Benedictus I woke feeling odd. Rick gorged himself on some more dried old fish, but I ate little breakfast. We set up our verandah watch. But I had to lie down. Oh no, I had a fever . . . Then the sound we had been waiting three days to hear came into the faint distance: a longboat full of rotan and four men and empty barrels. Frantic we jumped up, waved it down from the verandah and it stopped. We ignored my rising fever in our panic to get away, and despite all our previous shenanigans, we allowed ourselves to be horrendously ripped off for the journey downstream. We thanked Pastor Lahagir for his help and kindness. We offered him some money but he refused saying, 'Oh no, we never accept money from mission guests'. Partly relieved to be rid of us I'm sure, he helped us carry our bags down to the waiting longboat. We ran at top speed, terrified that it would go without us. My head pounding.

On the boat I was in extreme discomfort, with rotan sticking sharply into my aching back and bones. Eventually we stopped at a small beach to rearrange the cargo for our passage through the rapids, and I was delighted to see the most spectacular collection of butterflies I have ever encountered. At least ten species on a tiny sandbank: yellow, violet, big orange, little orange, turquoise, velvet blue, green and black. A splendid treat.

The journey downstream was much faster than going up. Because of the lightness of the longboat, and the swiftness of the current washing us downstream at triple the upstream speed, it only took five hours. We even went through all three rapids with comparative ease. We arrived, relieved, at Longbagun and walked along to the familiar meeting-point house. Savang, the renegade footballer, was shooting birds; but we were welcomed by his sister whom we had not met before. She was a rather ungainly, large-featured woman, with nevertheless a grace and dignity about her. I collapsed on the floor.

From Rick's journal. Sunday 24 January.
Nod's fever continues. Family up with the light. Girl brings us tea. I go to buy food: biscuits, eggs, lychee juice. In stilted phrases, I enquire about a chas to take us to the logging stations, but I'm not understood. I return. Savang's sister offers us breakfast – rice and greens. Nod is bad. He can't eat or drink. Outside on the porch, women are stripping and cutting rotan, hour after hour. Some of the boys sit around the table. There is an easy laughing atmosphere between everyone. Lots of children come to stare anxiously at Nod. Once I count fifteen, standing in a row, all big-eyed and very serious. Later I read him a Somerset Maugham story; wonderful light relief after the long sultry day. Then enjoy the heavy grey dusk on the balcony, watching the heavy grey river. Here it is much wider and flowing much slower than at Longpahan-gai. Now I'm at peace. Singing and joking with Savang. He gets into dirty boy's talk, teaches me the names for cocks and fannies in Indonesian. But in the night, my head is racing again. The timber company plan is collapsing. How can we set off to the forest with Nod in a fever?

From Nigel's journal. Monday 25 January.
After an uncomfortable night with big sweats and a long day and night of more sweats, I felt better. But the hard floor had become unbearable; the lack of privacy awful: seven people sleeping in the one room, packed together like sardines. And the huge pig outside continued to kick his tray around his pen all night. In our desire to get away from the discomfort we made another mistake. We decided to try and find our merry loquacious friend Ding at his village the other side of the district centre, Ujohbilang. He spoke good English and we felt sure he would help us contact the logging companies. Rick found a man to take us downriver and, although I was not feeling too good, we were both anxious to move on.

From Rick's journal. Monday 25 January.
We set off. Nod very weak. But the relief to be away is immense; the meeting-point house has become a suffocation chamber to me. One hour in chas. Pass high white cliffs. We reach Longmalahan, Ding's village, and his pretty little house with blue, star-shaped windows. But Ding has gone back to Samarinda! Urgh! Nod sits on his bag feeling worse. We both want to give up. The watching villagers are baffled. Children crowd around. A pretty woman at the door looks shy, embarrassed. Ding's wife? Can't face Longbagun again and that hot, hard, crowded room. Finally we decide to go to Ujohbilang. Though we know Jaspar has also gone to Samarinda, at least there is that teacher who speaks English; he can help us and give us advice. I can use the time now to get to the logging company; even if Nod has to stay and rest, I'll go by myself. Somehow there has got to be a way.

But Nod stops me at the covered entrance to Ujohbilang. He wants to talk. Tells me he is frightened, feeling very ill. I've got to put aside everything else and help him to get better, this is absolutely the only priority. He's right. My heart plummets.

From Nigel's journal. Monday 25 January.
Of course luck was not on our side and no Ding. We sat on a log by the muddy Mahakam momentarily stunned. We didn't speak, just stared blankly. My body had reacted by breaking out in another fever. On the journey back upstream I realized I was very ill and that I must stop and recover fully before doing anything else. We arrived at the jetty. Rick was about to go rushing off but I stopped him, sat him down and made him see that priority must be given to my health, nothing else. He understood. He went off to the Palace of Teachers to get help. I stretched out under the canopy of the landing stage hoping nobody would come by wanting to speak.

Then a man who spoke English approached. A tall, slightly-built man with high cheek bones, unlike the strong stocky men we had become used to. His name was Jau. I explained that I was sick, needed help and a place to stay. At that point Rick came back – no luck, he had not been able to find anyone. Jau invited us to wait at his house. I summoned up some more energy and we walked right through the village and into the wooden house beside the one where we had spent our stranded night before. It was almost empty. Small table. One chair. Bare lino floor. Jau told us he was the village paramedic. I collapsed on the floor again. I thought I had malaria, typhoid, cholera, or even a combination of all three!

My temperature was 40 degrees – this was serious. I knew there was going to be no way I was going anywhere else until I was completely better.

Fortunately Jau understood and took on the job of taking care of me. I sweated lots and lots. I ate little, feeling nauseous at even the thought of food – particularly rice. His wife Emiliana, an extremely shy and pretty young woman who had never before spoken with white men, made me rice porridge. I threw it up!

From Rick's journal. Monday 25 January.
Siesta time. Jau tiptoes out and leaves us to rest. What an invasion: two sprawling giants! Nod is silent. Fever still rising. And now my head – in a different way – is banging too. I feel so helpless. And everything is going from bad to worse. We should never have moved a second time. Shunting around in the midday sun. Are we going insane?

Later I go and wash our clothes in the river; all Nod's things are dripping, soaked with sweat. On the tilting raft other people are washing too. It's just part of a normal day; kneeling and bending over the sluggish water. After Jau and Emiliana have gone to bed, I enjoy two luxurious hours to myself: limber, yoga, meditate. Then give Nod a gentle massage, and sponge his burning head. Tonight I face an extra hard floor. I try to make it bearable for him by placing everything we have, clothes, towels, everything under his sheet as a mattress.

From Rick's journal. Tuesday 26 January.
Nod feeling a little better. He craves fruit so I go with Jau to look for some. Pass a tree of ripe papayas and Jau negotiates with the old hag leaning out of the window. A hook is brought on a long pole and Jau dislodges two large fruits. Next we go to a fine-looking robust woman in a big house who offers us a huge bunch of bananas – at an unnegotiable price. Finally we visit Jau's aunt in a little shack at the back of the village. She makes us coffee and cuts us a fresh pineapple, while her daughter-in-law crouches on the floor, suckling her sickly baby.

Then a long session with Jau and the dictionary; our mutual language classes. Meanwhile, Emiliana makes us supper. She squats in the narrow passage opening onto the back verandah. Blackened pots and a small curling fire. At first she prepared us tinned meat, but was very relieved when I reassured her that we would eat the home-grown beans that she normally cooked. I tell Jau the story of our thwarted attempts to reach the forest. Like everyone else he just laughs! Indonesians always roar with laughter at misfortune! We are good friends now and chatting together; he gets as high and animated as I do. Even Emiliana has begun to chip in a little, edging forward out of her corner.

But Nod's fever reaches a crisis point. He stops us, needing my full attention, my full help. I hold his head. Silence. Nightfall. Emiliana and a neighbour are squatting in the dark corner. Hushed. Watching. Eventually the fever eases a bit.

From Nigel's journal. Thursday 28 January.
Rick proved to be a good nurse. He tended me carefully, changed me, bathed me and brought me momentary relief with massage. He held my head one night when I was particularly bad and helped me to bear the pain. I felt I had a major battle on my hands and I was afraid that I didn't have the inner resources left with which to fight. So I resorted to good old observation. I observed my pounding head, with the steel rings burning through the back of my eyes. I observed my back aching like billy-o. I observed every muscle, bone, cell, my blood going frantic with the task in hand. I observed my extreme discomfort, not knowing how to lie on the hard floor, or how to bring relief to my screaming body. I observed my craving for all the comforts of my London lifestyle: food, soft bed, music, everything one relies on when under stress. And I observed my panic that there I was three days up a dangerous river and miles away from any fast form of communication. I seriously considered whether we should use our emergency insurance number and call in a rescue helicopter . . . but from where? I observed Rick, seeming infinite patience, knowing he was screaming inside with disappointment at not getting to the forest.

I allowed myself to be selfish. I demanded what I needed when I needed it. My temperature oscillated. My hopes lifted when it fell and I was plunged into panic when it rose again. I only just held onto my two guiding angels – Trust and Patience – only just. The idea of getting the *Nilam Cahaya* kept me in focus – knowing we would have to be on it. Little by little I began to climb out. At one point I thought – *fever = rage.* I had never given full expression to my rage about this trip – I had buried it in my body. So I went through in my mind all the incidents and people that had made me angry so far. I pictured the events and people, breathed deeply into the pain, trying to get to the trapped energy. All of this I had read about and taught in my workshops. It began to work! The deeper I breathed, the more I released, the easier I began to feel. Ricky and I talked about it too which also helped. Suddenly I had brought myself through; some of my own festering seeds had been released.

We hear the *Nilam Cahaya* arriving. Hurray! I go to the river with Jau; but it's the *Almu-minum*, another boat. The *Nilam Cahaya* has broken down in Samarinda. I suck back another disappointment. I had been holding out hope for those hazy lazy days ahead with the supreme Supri and his lovely smiling family. So I go for an evening walk through the straggling village and along an overgrown track by the river upstream. Loud mellifluous birdsong. Tangled profusion of growth. I stop and look. This is still Borneo – whatever; still an amazing place. I am happy and inspired, for a moment at least. As I stroll slowly back in the falling yellow light, boys are dive-bombing into the river. Everyone is friendly tonight; or is it that I am easy?

I bump into Savang. Farewell handshake and, laughing, he's gone. After *makan mallam* (dinner) three men arrive for malaria injections. They are strangers from another part of Kalimantan and are on their way upriver to look for a special, highly-valuable black tree. Injections take place on the porch: trousers are taken down and Jau digs in the rusty needle. It hurts. Lots of nervous laughter.

In the dark I go to fetch river water for Nod to wash in. It hasn't rained and we have totally used up Jau's supply. As I return, a neighbour comes up proudly with something to show me. It is the severed head of a toucan. 'High price' he gloats. Because the feathers are used in their dancing, the bird is now very rare. The head is velvet-black with a gorgeous sheen; the enormous, preposterous beak is flaming orange. Blood is still wet on its dangling windpipe. It's a picture that somehow sums up our experience of Kalimantan itself. Awe-struck, we settle down to our last hard night in Ujohbilang. Nod has managed to keep his temperature at 36.5 degrees. We pray for his good health tomorrow. Our new plan is to go to Kutai forest reserve – the home of the orang-utans; the place the first Keith mentioned back in Jakarta.

Still on the *Almu-minum*. Almost at Samarinda – I think. We made our farewells to Jau and Emiliana, thanking them for everything, especially saving my life! Sadly we passed Ding's blue-star house and missed the invitation to meet the grandfather and the ghost.

Everyone has a different notion as to what time we get to

Samarinda. Jau thought Saturday night; someone else thinks Saturday 3 p.m.; another suggestion is Saturday morning; someone else has even said this afternoon. Whenever it is, no doubt we will be 'on time' again! In the night we hooked up with the *Little Nilam Cahaya;* it is a smaller version of Supri's boat. *Nilam Cahaya*, I am told, means *Jewel of the River*. We have been travelling in tandem, going at a fair speed as we're light. No long unloading stops. The villages are getting gradually closer to each other as we chug downriver. This is a sure sign that the longed-for soft beds, fans and tomato soup – my fail-safe health restorer – are close at hand.

From Rick's journal. Hotel Andhika. Friday 29 January.
We finally arrive at Samarinda just before midnight. Solid ground. And Nod has survived the journey brilliantly. Back at Hotel Andhika, Thomas, the ever-equanimous night receptionist, warmly welcomes us and puts us into the same room as before. A soft bed and fan at last! But I still feel far too strung out to sleep. Tomorrow Nod can rest, but I will get to work, to find out about the Kutai Forest Reserve. So far no one has known about it – but it is marked on our map. It must exist.

From Nigel's journal. Sunday 31 January.
Revelling in the luxury of the beds and fan. Luxuriating with room service breakfast of boiled eggs, toast and tea; I am ravenous, my stomach happy to absorb familiar food again.

Yesterday we found our way to the tourist office to get information on Kutai. We waited for ages to be seen. The office assistant, ecstatic to have some customers, not only joined us for coffee, but also begged us to let him come along! Eventually he issued the permits and directed us to the office of the Chief of Ports for boat details. We had another long wait sitting on a hard wooden bench. We were told the Chief was praying and couldn't be disturbed. When he emerged, he looked like he'd been having a long nap, not a long pray, and gave us no concrete information whatsoever. Confused, we returned to the peace and fan-cooled air of the hotel room. Napped soundly and were woken by a blast of loudspeaker chanting from the mosque opposite.

Tonight, on the balcony, serenaded by more mosque chanting, and rain streaming down, Thomas came to chat. We ate coconut cookies and *chocolate!* He invited us to go and visit his house and family tomorrow at four. A good opportunity to catch a glimpse of the real Samarinda.

From Rick's journal. Sunday 31 January.

In the gasping night our thoughts are sucked back to the Mahakam. It happens every time we try to slow down; my mind spirals into a whirlpool. What we discover is that we have both manifested our greatest fears. I didn't reach the primary forest and Nod got seriously ill. In our extreme culture shock after India and the bewildering days leading up to the trip, had we suppressed these fears? Eagerly we had noted the little twists of fate along the way. But, rather than twists of fate, had we just been clutching at straws? Still, we now have concrete information about Kutai. We have permits and boat times. If we take it steadily, there is no reason to fail again. And yet . . .

From Nigel's journal. Monday 1 February.

Last night I had a frightening dream. I woke up trembling and completely out of touch with my body. Rick made me do some hard physical exercises, then some yoga. It worked. I fell back into my body and back to sleep – but the fear was still there when I woke. This morning we had a violent row. I wanted to go with Rick to Balikpapan, the provincial capital, to confirm the Kutai details. He wanted me to stay and rest. We were both wild, we were both exhausted. We realized that we couldn't go to Kutai in this state. We have to get out of Borneo fast. I have to rest, and we are both on the very edge of our nerves. For a while we were both stunned by this ultimate disappointment. Like the moment in Longmalahan when Ding was not at his blue-star house, we sat, blank, silent. Our quest had failed.

At 4 p.m. Thomas knocked on the door. We walked through the hot streets of Samarinda and turned off the main shopping road, down a winding path to the river. Sounds of families: children laughing, playing; mothers shouting, calling. Houses on stilts with gang-planks between them, right on top of each other; just enough space to walk through in single file. It's noisy, claustrophobic. Small houses, glassless windows. Warm and friendly people watch us, laughing at Ricky's big nose, fascinated by my blue eyes and curly fair hair. Thomas's house sits on the edge of the jammed river bank. The river is muddy dark brown, used for everything. Children jump, splash, swim. Mothers wash babies. Women wash clothes. This river that is their life-line is also a killer. Thomas's mother-in-law recently drowned with one of her sons. They went missing at six in the morning, their bodies found floating face-down at four in the afternoon.

Thomas took us into his house: small rooms, some chairs, even a sofa. His children greeted us, delighted and shy. His small wife, a local Samarinda woman, cautiously brought us tea. He told us that he is from Malaysia, he has a Filipino father who owns a big rubber plantation; but he has no contact with his family back home. He left six years ago and has never returned. Something happened, the shadow of it is in him still, but he wouldn't reveal the story. He wants to return now but is trapped, no money for the air fares. He is worth more than his present job at the hotel, but that is all he can get. He showed us some books – two trashy brash American novels, and a book on meditation. Then it was time for his night shift and we walked back through the dark busy streets, past late-night markets, lights, incense, noise and chatter. I scuttled quickly past the ever-present reeking durian stalls holding my breath. Maybe it was that on the ferry that made me sick? A good respite from our own hassles. A good chance to see another life.

Nod and I left Samarinda on Tuesday morning at 7 a.m. bound for Bali and Lombok. It was strange to discover that after all the trauma I nevertheless felt a twinge of sadness leaving our stifling little room that had witnessed so much emotion. And Thomas, sad too, bidding us a fond farewell. The only uncompleted business was Gabriel. Thomas promised to deliver our letter. We only had his school address and had not made the effort to find him. Better not tarnish his wings with our dispiriting story of defeat. Better a letter just to thank him for his help and to wish him well.

We took a ferry across the river and journeyed by minibus for two hours over the devastated coastal hills and into the ugly, oil-rich port of Balikpapan. Our chief aim now was to find a beach to crash out on. We had hoped for a quiet week by the sea in India; now it felt like a must. Nod was not the only one who needed to recuperate. And we also both needed to slow down, to take stock; otherwise we would just repeat the same mistakes. Originally we had planned to cross from Kalimantan to the exciting neighbouring island of Sulawesi, but now we settled for a less adventurous agenda. We placed our bets on Lombok, the small island east of Bali, having been told it was beautiful, easy to reach and still undeveloped. It was also directly on route for Australia. But to conserve the little energy we had left it was essential that we get there fast. So we stormed the local Garuda office, our intention as determined as an ambulance siren, to change our next destination. The staff scrutinized our special-price tickets and refused our request. We demanded to see the manager and were begrudgingly ushered into his office. Flattery and pleading eventually worked! A discretionary courtesy. The tight-lipped staff issued new tickets and we boarded the 3.30 plane to Bali.

Huge storm, thunder, lightning and torrential rain. We bumped and fell our way out of Borneo. A crazy, one-armed, Irish road builder talked at us non-stop and told us Indonesia was great – 'no rules'! To us it had so far seemed all rules, most of which remained incomprehensible. But then he must have managed to keep it simple – like Mark had advised in Jakarta. Somehow we'd got complicated.

Despite my pledge to avoid more adventure, I am ashamed to say that I still dragged Nod to the remotest corner of Lombok. Travelling by ancient, open-backed, goat-packed vans and jolting rickety horse-carts, we were finally dumped on the edge of a perfect azure lagoon. Our arrival coincided with a festival. Thousands of local Sassak people crowded the slopes around the beach. And at midnight there was a performance of a play depicting the tragic story of the fabled Princess Mandalika. But, while watching a blood-thirsty magic act, Nod was pick-pocketed. Cash, traveller's cheques and credit card all gone. That was not all: two nights later in the tiny *losman* (boarding-house), we were dramatically burgled. Complex involvements with the police followed; the army was even called in. When the culprits were caught we were asked to pass sentence. We chose to let the young thieves off with a warning, but the Chief of Police overruled us and ordered imprisonment.

We scurried back to Mattaram, the island's capital, and were hassling for a fair price for a *bemo* (public vehicle), when a dignified elderly woman and her grandson came to our rescue. Her name was Hadidjah, and it transpired that she was the wife of Max Arrifin the artistic director of the Princess Mandalika drama we had seen at the festival. We became their honoured guests and for three days we discussed theatre and art and life with them. A rich gift. And a restoration of our faith in a country where we had experienced so much frustration. With Max and Hadidjah we had a welcome glimpse into another Indonesia.

So we never got our 'quiet week by the sea'! It was probably better we didn't: the dramas kept us on our toes; concentrated. Only during the few lulls – indolent siestas in the rickety losman – did the disappointment start to grip and twist my insides. My only foil to these moments was the possibility of a trip to Papua

New Guinea; a journey into the primary forest there. But that was months away. Besides, our money had already run out and we knew even less about Papua New Guinea than we had about Indonesia. Still, deep down I was resolved. We would hold onto this glimmer of hope through thick and thin.

PART TWO

TREES OF PARADISE

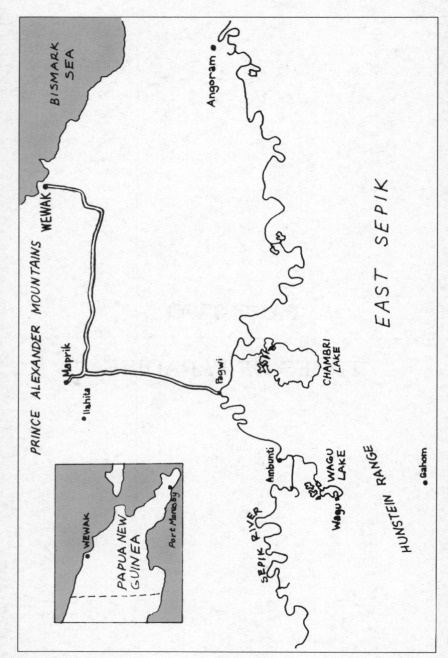

c/o National Theatre, Port Moresby, Papua New Guinea,
29 June 1988

Dearest Mother and Father and all,

Papua New Guinea – a fabulous, magical country! Dense jungle, impenetrable mountains, heavenly beaches and spectacular wild-life. Transport is still by small aircraft, most areas remain unlinked by road, and even the few 'highways' are unsurfaced tracks. It's a country of tiny villages, hundreds of languages, rich tradition, prevalent witchcraft.

A missionary at the airport told me: 'The Papuans are the loveliest people on earth, but also the most dangerous'. Law and order is breaking down in a big way, the expatriates are fleeing and there are frequent hold-ups on the roads and rivers by armed bandits. But so far I have only met the 'lovely' ones . . . An innocent, ancient people suddenly jolted into the grip of missionaries threatening damnation; colonials treating them like dogs; and now, the faceless multinational companies exploiting their resources. Little wonder they are turning to desperate measures . . . .

The villagers are the most delightful, engaging, generous, open-hearted people I have ever met. Stone age, golden age, a forest people, a bird people. Curious, fun-loving and oh, so gullible. I have fallen in love with them. I'll write again soon.

With love, Richard.

I

So yes, Papua New Guinea did happen. But first, the unexpected series of events that led up to it. Sandy, a young Australian who had done one of Nigel's workshops in London, had invited us to stay with him in Sydney. He had even sent a key, care of *Poste Restante* (P.O. Box), to Lombok; so, on Thursday 18 February, we arrived at Sydney airport already with an Australian home. Sandy is a builder. He had converted a small warehouse into the most original, beautiful house you could imagine. The centre was open like a courtyard, full of tall, large-fronded plants, and from it, the rooms opened off in textures of old brick, wood and coloured glass. The fridge was full of delicious food. Upstairs there was even a jacuzzi. Oooh, what luxury! We sank down on the wide bed in zombiefied amazement.

At the Actors Centre in Sydney, Nigel led his first Australian *Mastery* workshop and I assisted him. The Mastery is an intensive weekend course for people to expand their range of personal and artistic expression. We had a big group of enthusiastic actors, and the weekend was a success. Then we made the twelve-hour train journey to Melbourne to mount a second Mastery and stay with my long-lost Aunt and her eminent art-historian husband. It was in the state of Victoria that we met our first kangaroo, staring at us quizzically from a bank of tall dry grass; but soon our rigid flight itinerary demanded we pack up once again, this time for New Zealand. We spent a few days on the rolling island of Waiheke off Auckland, then we travelled down to the South Island and enjoyed a breath-taking trip through the Southern Alps and along the wild western coast. This was some of the most superb country I had ever experienced: endless, powerful, snow-capped peaks; vast empty beaches with the roaring breakers hitting the shingle and many, many sea-birds. It was so clean and so pure, it felt like genesis in action. There was only one problem: our money was running out. In Christchurch we ended up in a perilously tatty hostel. Still, it was worth it when we saw young albatrosses gliding over the cliffs at Dunedin and watched our first yellow-eyed penguins waddling up a windy beach.

Back in Australia, in Sandy's leafy house, we set up a money-earning programme. Another few Masteries and my first writing workshop which I called *Daring to Write*. We also mounted a rehearsed reading of my new comedy, *Further Education*, as a showcase for my work. But, during rehearsals, Nod started to feel sick; one day he would be fine, the next, he would feel bad again. On the morning of his birthday, 10 May, a doctor friend of ours came to lend us her car. She took one look at him and said: 'This is serious; looks like malaria to me'. I drove him to her surgery, he was deteriorating fast. She confirmed our fears and I rushed him off across the city to a hospital that specialized in tropical diseases. By the time we reached the hospital, Nod was in a serious condition. The doctors took one look at him and whisked him off for a series of tests and a frenzy of action. His Borneo fever had never been diagnosed and so it was not possible to confirm whether this malaria was connected with it or not. We had just begun to talk seriously about Papua New Guinea and though, in his inimitable way, Nod recovered amazingly fast, the doctors strongly advised him against going back to a malaria-infested country, at least for a while. But I had had enough of the city and I was longing to get back to the adventure of the wild.

From Rick's journal. Monday 16 May.
Warm Sydney evening. Bright lights coloured by the stained glass windows. Roy and Sandy across the dark patio, drinking beer in the living room, telling jokes, playing their music . . . All around, the city is roaring. And I am lost, displaced; gasping for space . . Above the rapids, up the Mahakam, camping on that wild beach; there I knew silence; there I knew space . . . there my heart was full of rejoicing. Nature thundering through me. Head intoxicated with the lightning and the fireflies . . . There I was tall and strong. There I was free. And now, back in the concrete and traffic, TVs, cut-throat competition and plastic filth, I am homesick for the sound of the pounding river. For the bird cries of the unknown...

That night I knew I had to go to Papua New Guinea anyway. It seemed selfish, but Nod understood. He would spend some time convalescing and I would go on the next adventure by myself. Trying to gather information on the Papua New Guinea rainforest in Sydney proved as difficult as trying to get the Borneo information in London. Once again my head was spinning in confusion, once again I seemed to be going round in circles. The couple we'd met in Suffolk who had spent several years in PNG had emphasized the importance of personal contacts and the need for a network of support. They had also told us that PNG had a National Theatre Company whom we should try to contact as they might provide the beginnings of the network that we'd need. So, on arriving in Sydney, I had sent them a letter of introduction and information on the *Mastery*; but I hadn't even been sure that we had the right address and so I had held out little hope of getting a reply.

But one came. Fast. On headed paper, with the logo of an exotic bird. It was from William Takaku, the Director of the Company. Yes, they would love to meet us. Yes, they would also love to do the Mastery. Nod phoned immediately. 'Hello' said a rich, plangent voice on the end of the line. It was William Takaku himself. Nod explained about his malaria and that I would be coming alone. William offered to meet me off the plane: 'Look out for the blackest man at the airport' he said. The first thread of the network had been sewn. What about the forest though? Again I had left it too late. Again my investigations were getting nowhere. An English contact who was manager of a plantation in Alotau, on PNG's eastern tip, had confirmed there was primary forest in his region. But Janet, an Australian who had just returned to Sydney after twenty years in PNG, recommended that the East Sepik Province would be more exciting. On the other hand, a friend of Sandy's had a contact in Mount Hagen in the Highlands. He was a German missionary turned coffee baron; he would be the perfect man to point me in the right direction.

Upstairs in the PNG High Commission I was shown a video of tribal ceremonies. But no one had any idea about primary forest. 'Isn't it everywhere?' asked the Tourist Adviser, an Australian. He recommended the Eastern Highlands. Yes, Mount Hagen, where the coffee baron lived, would be a good starting point. But really I should go to the Department of Conservation and the Environment in Port Moresby. In the Air Niugini office (Papua New Guinea's national airline), they knew even less. There were a few brochures on safaris and adventure tours. We had already extended our six-month plan for the overall trip, so I needed to leave by 4 June. If I wanted a cheap flight, I would have to book it there and then. So I did. Phew! I had a date and I had William to pick me up at the airport. But I still knew nothing about the forest.

In her open-plan office on the fifteenth floor of a huge mining company skyscraper, Janet counselled me. I had to understand that PNG was not like other countries. It was not geared up for tourists; the hotels were few and very expensive. The transport was difficult. Food was difficult. Everything was difficult. Everything could be dangerous. Janet's husband, Malcolm, was still in Port Moresby. He was an engineer. She would drop him a line about me. We could meet. He would be the one to help me get to the forest. Janet also had friends who ran the only reasonably-priced guest house in Port Moresby. I should stay there. I should telephone in advance to book a room and I should send them Janet's love.

There are few road links in PNG and to get a cheap deal on a domestic flight I also had to book it in advance in Australia. But I was still completely in the dark: Alotau, East Sepik or Mount Hagen? I settled for Mount Hagen and the coffee baron only because it was the closest to Port Moresby and hence the cheapest flight. Nervous, I picked up my visa and replenished my medical kit. Nod left for a prawn farm in Queensland and I sewed a secret pocket into my new trousers for my passport and traveller's cheques (I wasn't going to take any more chances). At the last minute, I panicked. Was I being stupid again? Hadn't I learned anything from Borneo? Here I was again, setting off with even less concrete information than before. Begrudgingly, I laid out the Angel Cards. What quality will help me this time? Which angel will help me reach the primary forest of Papua New Guinea? It felt like my last chance. It felt like time was running out. I tried to breathe. I turned over Humour. 'That's idiotic,' I thought, 'That proves these cards are a load of rubbish. Just ridiculous New Age superstition.' Still, I did surreptitiously look up 'humour' in my Pidgin phrase book and, for reference in times of need, I did print the following on the inside of my new notebook: 'The angel to help me reach the forest is Humour. In Pidgin: *sensa uma*. So don't forget it.' Actually I almost did forget it; partly because I hardly ever opened my notebook. It took all my energy to survive: the overwhelming humidity; the extreme conditions and the daily, unexpected twists that always meant a change of plan. Little time or space for reflection, little time or space for picking up my pen, on what was to be the most exciting, moving and heartwarming adventure month of my life.

On the Air Niugini flight from Sydney to Port Moresby, the plane was only about a third full. The cabin attendants were dressed in bright colours: orange, purple and green. Their wide smiles were genuine and the female voice that crackled through the intercom was soft and undemonstrative. 'Welcome aboard this bird of paradise flight to Port Moresby.' I felt a lump in my throat. Tears stung my eyes. There was a quality here that I hadn't met before. And was I really going to see a bird of paradise? Excitement tingled.

But why was I feeling so shaky? Why was I losing my confidence year by year? In the early days I had travelled without any fear at all. 'But now those days are gone, I'm not so self-assured . . ' the Beatles song rang in my head, and I literally wanted to call out 'Help!'

The steward looking after me was immaculately courteous. He was small and muscular with bulging biceps under his green, short-sleeved shirt. As if he had heard my silent plea, he served me extra fruit juices and told me to call for anything I needed. After the meal, when all the debris was cleared away, he came and sat down beside me. His excuse was that he thought I was someone else; someone he had been asked to look out for. Whether that was true or not, I'll never know, but we certainly both sensed a need to meet. His English was perfect, his accent soft, his manner shy. He had been a steward for seven years; he was tired of it now. His name was Campbell. He loved the arts. He loved the theatre. It turned out that he was a good friend of William Takaku. Campbell invited me to stay in his Air Niugini house. It would be no problem. I would be welcome. And, as long as I didn't mind cooking for myself, it would be fine. He would talk to William as soon as we landed and sort it all out. Campbell also told me about his frustrations with his work; how he hated to see his colleagues being abused by the passengers. The air attendants were frequently insulted. Twice Campbell had got so furious he'd pinned a passenger against the wall and threatened to knock him out. The only reason he hadn't been sacked was because he was such a good worker. Campbell then promised me that he didn't treat his friends like that. So I needn't worry. I would be looked after well and I would be safe in his house. Suddenly it felt as if I really was on a bird of paradise flight. Could this have happened on British Airways? I said goodbye to Janet's cosy guest house. I hadn't booked it anyway. Somehow I'd known I had to keep my options open.

In the stifling customs hall the queue remained static. Apparently the customs officers had arrived for work drunk and had all been sent home. There were no chairs so I sat on the ground. That's when the smooth-faced missionary in front of me said, 'The Papuans are the loveliest people on earth, but also the most dangerous.' I told him about Campbell. Should I accept the offer? The missionary retorted coldly, 'That's for you to decide.' Outside in the sweltering afternoon, William Takaku was waiting. And yes, he was the blackest man at the airport; not because all the others were white expatriates, but because he is from the island of

Bougainville in the North Solomons. His people are both culturally and racially different from the mainland Papuans. Dressed in old shorts and an undone shirt, William walked with wide bare feet and had a wonderful gleaming coconut grin. We climbed into the baking, battered pickup truck, and soon were bumping along through the haphazard streets of Port Moresby. Garishly painted stores with tin roofs, a market under a cluster of trees, empty undeveloped plots and small wooden houses on concrete stilts with gardens of palms and flowering shrubs. Trucks. Small dusty buses. And lots of people walking. Lots of children. Women with brightly coloured *bilums* (handwoven string bags), full of shopping strung across their foreheads, hanging down their backs.

Air Niugini Hill lay on the edge of town. It seemed to consist of several rows of large concrete bunkers built into the steep slope; first class, luxury bunkers though – they had verandahs, small gardens and a view of the open sea. The surrounding hillsides were undeveloped; rough bush and dry yellow grass. Below was a palm-fringed beach and beyond, green hills. Campbell's house was up a steep flight of steps. The verandah opened into a spacious room with minimal bamboo furniture. There was a small kitchen with a fridge, and upstairs there was a shower. I had my own bedroom with two beds in it. There were fans in every room and mosquito mesh at all the windows. As good as any guest house, eh? I wiped the sweat off my soaking face and William and I drank large glasses of iced water and made a sketchy plan for the next few days. Tomorrow, Sunday, there was to be a National Theatre performance on the beach. William also wanted me to help try to get some funding for the Mastery.

When Campbell got home he asked me shyly what I wanted to eat. Because of the ants, he kept everything in the fridge – rice, vegetables, bread and peanut butter. I suggested we cook together; but he got even shyer. I sensed he'd rather be left alone, so I promised to buy food and cook for him tomorrow. He served up the meal with style, artistry even, and great care: rice and vegetables, simply but tastily cooked. Campbell was from the East Sepik Province, the area that Janet had already told me about. He showed me on the map: it was up over the mountains on the north coast of PNG. His family lived in a traditional jungle village in the Maprik district. There were birds of paradise there and the primary forest lay close by. If I wished to, I could go and stay there; his brothers and cousins would look after me and take me into the forest. As we were talking, Mark, who worked in the reservations department of Air Niugini arrived and lounged back in one of the low bamboo chairs. Mark, also from East Sepik, had beady eyes, a naughty laugh and a well-coiffeured Afro hairstyle. He could change my Mount Hagen ticket, no problem; I would just have to pay the difference. I could fly to Wewak, the capital of East Sepik, and then catch a PMV (a public motor vehicle) to Campbell's village, Ilahita, four or five hours' journey through the jungle.

Talk about twists of fate, it was all happening as fast as the spinning fan. Here I was, chatting easily with my new friends; new possibilities were opening up; and I had only been in the country a few hours. All that crazy fear on the plane gone; washed away with my sweat. And I knew Campbell was right: I was safe. Not because of the high barbed-wire fence around the compound, not because of the armed security guards at the bottom of the steps; but because I knew I could trust these affable, generous, open-hearted guys. As I stretched luxuriously out on one of the beds in my room, Campbell came in and stretched out on the other one. Head still racing from all the events of the day, I got up and explained I was going to do some yoga. Campbell got up to join me; he would like to learn yoga too. There were three bedrooms in the house and I would dearly have loved to have the space to myself. But what could I say? Campbell was my host. Later I learned that he had come to keep me company so that I wouldn't feel lonely. It happened in several other places too. It was a gesture of respect; a way of looking after me.

Sunday morning on Ella beach seemed to be a social occasion: families strolling along the short quay, children paddling, dogs running and a few sailing boats out in the bay. But it was also a sad place. The water's edge was littered with old plastic bags, the smart, expatriate changing rooms had been burned down and around the Coca-Cola shack there were piles of rubbish and broken glass. Still, the scraggy palm trees gave some shade and the sea was a shimmering sapphire blue. The National Theatre performance was an impromptu affair. The actors arrived late on the back of a lorry and chose an open part of the beach. The play was called *The Conference of the Birds* in tribute to Peter Brook whose book William had read. The backdrop was the open sea, and very soon an audience began to gather, forming a natural horse-shoe shape around the area of sand that was to be the stage. By the time the actors had assembled their masks and headdresses and instruments, a good two hundred people plus children and dogs were eagerly waiting to be entertained.

The play was about a white plantation owner, a greedy man, who was planning to cut down the nearby forest in order to expand his money-making plantation. When the birds heard of this they called an urgent meeting and one member of each species flew to the grove where the meeting was to be held: a hornbill, an eagle, a bird of paradise and many more. The actors danced around on the sand, displaying their beautiful feathered masks and the audience roared in delighted laughter. How could the birds protect their precious home? How could they stop the greedy white man from destroying the beautiful forest? A passing family walked right across the middle of the stage. A wind-surfing board and its owner landed next to one of the birds. Children continued to paddle among the plastic bags. But the audience was not the least concerned. This was certainly live theatre, with a very live audience too. And what a spectacle, with the actors miming, singing and fooling against the brilliant sea and sky! William had connected the theatre and the forest. Here, environmental awareness and a spiritual love of nature were one: it was to be a lasting inspiration to me.

On Ella beach I also met William's wife, Puele, and their tiny daughter, Ani. They were sitting in the shade of one of the trees, unperturbed by the hectic theatrical events of the morning. Puele was much lighter skinned than William, and lighter skinned, too, than Campbell and his Sepik friends. She came from the coastal area below Port Moresby and her colouring and full-moon face looked Polynesian. After the performance I ended up in the back of the lorry with the company, squatting amongst the drums, the guitars, the masks and the actors' wives and children and babies. There was lots of merriment and laughter. Everyone was delighted that I had seen and enjoyed the show. But there was also tremendous shyness. Keen bright eyes were averted and brown faces turned away into the hot wind as we lurched through the dashing colours and the splintering sunlight of the ramshackle Sunday city. I think that's when it first dawned on me that these fun-loving and intensely human people just weren't used to being treated as equals by the arrogant and one-time colonial white man.

Back on Air Niugini Hill, William and I sat and talked. It already felt as if we had known each other for years. He spoke so profoundly that I found myself mentioning my meditation and its ideals. William was immediately interested. 'What is the name of this meditation technique?' he asked. It turned out he had taken a Vipassana course at the centre in the Blue Mountains above Sydney. There were just two Vipassana meditators in the whole of PNG, he explained: himself and another man from Bougainville who was important in the government, and whom I would meet later. That evening, we meditated together for the first time.

During the next few days we spent the mornings making plans and searching for Mastery funding. A formal meeting in a tiny airless office with a gracious, round-bellied bureaucrat in the Department of Culture and Tourism; a discussion with the actors in the company's run-down rehearsal studio; and a meeting with one of the directors of PNG's new TV station. For this, Puele had bought William a new pair of socks – he had acquiesced to wearing shoes for the occasion – and we waited for the director in the plastic Bamboo Garden cafeteria upstairs in one of Port Moresby's new concrete shopping precincts. But alas, the new socks didn't impress. The director, a young Australian, was only interested in cricket and flirting with his assistant whom he had brought with him as foil against the threatening thespians.

William also encouraged me over the Sepik idea: 'You will see the real PNG there', he said. But I was still dithering; still unsure. So I arranged to have dinner with Janet's husband, Malcolm, the expatriate engineer. We met at The Bistro, a fairly unfriendly restaurant without atmosphere. William, barefoot at the door, looked and felt out of place; he had brought his little Ani to see the *ples belong whiteman* (the place where white men go). A rugged Malcolm arrived with his special friend, the tiny Lady K, a Papuan national, well known at The Bistro. Lady K entertained me and most of the restaurant with the animated stories of her life. Snatched from the cradle, she had been married to one of the colonial administrators of PNG and, unprepared, had had to cope with the etiquette and the diplomacy of narrow white society. She had entertained in style, travelled far and brought up several children. But, after Papua New Guinea won independence from Australia in 1975, her gallant administrator had fallen on rocky times. He had turned to drink; they had become separated and now he owned a disco club and a video shop.

It was difficult to steer the conversation to the forest. Malcolm had planned to introduce me to the culprits themselves, some of his logger friends. Memories of Indonesia began to swim back. But he thought East Sepik was an excellent idea. He had not been there himself but was confident that I would find primary forest in plenty. He also affirmed that it was a better idea than the Highlands where, because of its altitude, the forest was relatively small. The Highlands had also become very dangerous. The famous bird of paradise sanctuary had just been closed down after tourists had been robbed and murdered on the approach road.

Lady K tipped her leftovers onto my plate to feed me up and announced confidentially that she was really a princess. When we parted, her fond farewell was unexpectedly intimate. Was I being seduced by a royal princess? Janet, back in her Sydney sky-scraper, had warned me that Lady K was a witch and had trapped Malcolm. Janet was terrified that if Malcolm tried to leave Port Moresby, Lady K would cast a spell on them both. Magic, she had told me, was commonplace in PNG. With nervous, diffident laughter, the Papuans refer to this magic as 'the Sanguma business'. When I told Campbell about my night at The Bistro he doubled up with laughter. Lady K was very well known. Lady K had also given him her intimate farewell on more than one occasion.

My intention was still to go to the Department of the Environment before I made a final decision on my destination; but communications were proving just too difficult. The phone in William's office was out of order. The public call boxes outside the big post office were crowded, noisy and erratic. Public transport was completely incomprehensible, and the humidity sapped me of my determination and will power. Against my limited energy and chronic indecision, Campbell's house was a sanctuary; a perfect haven where I could shower and rest under the fan. In the evenings I cooked simple suppers and sat out on the dark verandah wallowing in the balmy breeze, the hissing song of the sea below and the showers of cascading stars above. But now I really did have to decide. Campbell wanted to know. Was I going to go to his village or not? Yes I wanted to, I really wanted to; but as usual I was scared. I was suspicious too. Would his family really welcome me? Did he send everyone he met on the plane? Wouldn't they be sick of his western friends by now? Campbell shook his head and smiled. 'They will be happy to see you. They are my family, you are my friend; you are my *wantok*.'

There are over 700 different languages in PNG; *wantok* means 'one talk' – someone who speaks the same village language: a clansman, a kinsman, a neighbour. The wantok system also provides a unique and ancient system of support: a wantok is always looked after and safe. A friend can also become a wantok as an expression of love and respect, a bit like an adopted brother or sister. As Campbell's wantok, I would be welcomed and looked after without question by his family. But did he really understand what I was after? The concept of the primary forest seemed to confuse everyone; it was even beginning to confuse me too. It was time to get hold of my rattling head. Campbell was a deep and educated man, if anyone was going to understand my search, he would. He had spent some of his childhood years in Melbourne fostered by a white Christian family. He was the union representative for Air Niugini, a choice which barred him from promotion but which he embraced because of his passion for equality and human rights. He was also a member of the local group of Friends of the Earth. On his wall was a poster with a quote from a speech by Chief Seattle of the Suwamish tribe of native North American Indians: 'How can one buy or sell the air?' It was the first time I had come across it, though later I learned that it is much quoted. To help us both, I wrote out what the purpose of my visit to his village would be. It was the first thing I had written in my notebook. I showed it to him.

My dream for the Sepik:

I long to experience the village life of the local people, to spend some days with them, observing, learning, sharing, enjoying their honourable lifestyle.

I long to make a trek into the primary forest; to experience the power and splendour of tropical nature; to sleep out with the noises of the night; to reach as remote and undisturbed an area as possible.

I long to hear and see the rich variety of wildlife and especially to catch a glimpse of one of the birds of paradise.

I long to visit some smaller villages to which the only access is by foot.

Campbell read it slowly and then looked up at me. His deer-like and slightly furtive eyes were gleaming. 'Yes, you will find all that at my village. I will write to my sister Rosemary and my nephew Chris and explain it to them.' The decision had at last been made. Mark changed my ticket. I kissed goodbye to the coffee baron in the Highlands.

The next afternoon, which was my last day in Port Moresby, William took me in the company's pickup truck up through a spectacular gorge to one of PNG's few National Parks. Together with a group of his friends we walked along a muddy forest path in the thick dusk. We came to a tree on which there was a sign which said: 'The birds of paradise feed here'. My appetite for adventure was tugging at its leash. On the journey back there was a violent rainstorm and our poor companions on the back of the truck got totally drenched within seconds. In the cab, William told me stories. His rich bass voice and gurgling laughter took on a new kind of resonance amidst the sloshing water, and his deep eyes shone even brighter under the threatening black clouds.

Bougainville, his homeland, was truly a paradise island and his childhood had been spent in traditional manner in a small village on the edge of the jungle, and on the edge of the sea. His father had been a great fisherman who, every time he came ashore with his fish, not only brought good food to his family, but also to all the households in the village. But maybe his father had been too good. People had become jealous and, when William was still a small boy, his father had been poisoned: the 'Sanguma business' was suspected. After his death, William was flown to the High School up in the north of the island. He proved an exceptional pupil and, after graduation, he won a scholarship to attend the art school of the university of PNG in Port Moresby. There he excelled in the performing arts and was sent on a special bursary to study at NIDA in Sydney, Australia's top academy of dramatic art.

Once only William was given the funds to return home to visit his mother. On the last day of his holiday he misjudged the time. Suddenly he was late and had to leave in a hurry. In a rush, he packed up his belongings but something was missing, something had been misplaced: he couldn't find the key to his Sydney lodgings. Angry and het up, he had harsh words with his mother and sped off in a canoe to reach the road from where a truck would take him to the airstrip. As William paddled away his mother continued to search for the key and found it. Excited she jumped into her own canoe and chased William down the waterway. But she was too late, he'd already gone. Back in Sydney William received the news that his mother had died. His heart bled with sorrow. Their last moments together had been harsh and confused and he had not given her the loving farewell she deserved. From a small dugout canoe to a battered truck on a bumpy road, to a tiny six-seater plane, to the sprawling urban Port Moresby, to a huge sophisticated jet, to the vast concrete jungle of Sydney, William was well aware that he had travelled thousands of years in a lifetime. As he and many of his contemporaries were finding, thousands of years was a hazardous gulf to bridge.

While he was talking, I brushed my hand down across my ankle; I felt a rounded knob. It was a leech, swollen to slug size with my blood. William jammed on the brakes and screeched to a halt. We all pulled several leeches off our legs! Back in William's purpose-built government house, Puele had prepared me a farewell supper. We parted like old friends and they wished me a safe and successful journey.

The thirty-seater plane was full. We were welcomed aboard in English and Pidgin. We were served tea and biscuits and, later, biscuits and tea. The journey was in four hops: first up to a cloud-lost Mount Hagen, then over a sea of forest to the coastal towns of Lae, then Madang, and, finally, up the north coast to Wewak in the East Sepik. In my hand I clutched Campbell's detailed directions. I was to make my way to the main warehouse on the quay. I was to go inside and ask for Campbell's wantok. He would take me into town and help me find the right PMV for Ilahita, their village. But Wewak's small airport was even more humid than Port Moresby and the heat was palpably aggressive. Stealthy, shifty eyes scrutinized my every move; my courage slithered away like a faithless pet snake and I lost my nerve. There was no way I could face traipsing round in the midday sun. Thank god I had an alternative, though up until then I hadn't really considered it. One of the National Theatre actors had previously worked with the local company in Wewak, called the *Raun Isi Travelling Theatre* (*raun isi* means 'going about easily'). He had given me the telephone number and told me to ring Larry Lavai, the Artistic Director, if I needed help. So I did.

Larry's voice was languorous but reassuring. They didn't get many visitors. I should make my way to the post office and he would send someone to meet me. The mini bus was also full of stealthy eyes and the seats were ripped. We skirted a perfect, palm-edged bay: white sand and dazzling turquoise sea. We trundled past a line of corrugated warehouses; big potholes in the road. Outside the large, cream post office, Alex was already waiting: a skinny young actor with bare feet, a huge mouth and red betel nut-stained teeth. Leading me down the main Wewak street, he spoke in a whisper. Makeshift corrugated buildings, overhanging awnings, crudely painted signs; several all-purpose super-markets, a bank, an Air Niugini office, a Christian book shop, a smart new chemist and, under fat gnarled trees, the colourful market in full swing. More shifty eyes and dark-skinned men: lounging, squatting; easy, lazy; chewing, smoking, spitting. It felt like an outpost, a border town, as if the humid rampaging jungle was only just being kept at bay. A few dusty trucks, a few bumping cars, everything, everyone slowed down like a record grinding to a halt in the heat. At the end of the street we had to wait for another bus and sheltered gratefully under tall spreading trees together with women in faded florid smocks with tattooed faces, bundles of children and bilums full of coconuts and bananas. Squeezing into another rickety minibus, we wound our way down a leafy track that led to the Raun Isi campus.

A laid-back Larry with a wistful face took me into the kitchen. Most of the actors were out on research projects in the villages, gathering information on traditional dances and customs, but Alex and Norm had stayed behind to look after base. Lackadaisical bodies on broken stools under the noisy fan. High peals of shy laughter, beaming smiles and saucer eyes. I felt immediately accepted and at home. The Raun Isi campus comprised a couple of long, basic sheds a bit like Nissen huts. One of these served as the sleeping quarters for the actors. The other was divided up into the kitchen, which opened onto the rehearsal space, a small office and, behind the office, an even smaller room where Larry lived with his wife Alice and two baby daughters. A third, smaller shed served as toilets and washrooms and a fourth shed, collapsing fast, was used as a second studio. The area was surrounded by grass, tall palm trees and wide-leaved flowering shrubs. After a chat and a snack, Larry and Alex took me back into town to hassle for an Ilahita PMV. It was all utterly incomprehensible. No one seemed to have any idea where anyone else was going. The PMVs were like small cattle trucks with rows of seats on the back and makeshift canvas roofs and flapping tattered sides. I clung to the half shade of the trees. The heat had turned white. The dust seemed to be vibrating and I was beginning to see double. It became apparent that we were too late. The Ilahita PMVs had all left in the morning. No one was going so far so late. I would have to stay at Raun Isi overnight and we would try again in the morning.

The shower only gave a feeble trickle, but it was a trickle of bliss and, lying out on a hard narrow bed in the room of three of the absent actors, I was relieved. Enough and more for one day. For supper Alice cooked us chicken in coconut milk and large chunks of *kaukau* (sweet potatoes) and *taro* (a purple fibrous root). She was a full-boned young woman with a patterned tattoo on her forehead. She was also excruciatingly shy; she was obviously unused to big sweaty white men sprawling over the wooden table on the concrete floor in her kitchen. But overall, life seemed fairly westernized at Raun Isi. Until Larry picked up a bow and arrow and shot a rat while we were eating. Until I opened a drawer in my room and found it was full of eagles' wings. Until Caspar, a man from the Sepik River and a specialist in making costumes and props, proudly showed me the large scars across his back from his initiation into manhood. Until I dared to look more deeply into the eyes of these young actors and saw shadowed signposts pointing to a world about which I knew nothing.

'Ilahita? Ilahita? Is anyone going to Ilahita?' It was only 8 a.m. but apparently we were again too late: the Ilahita PMVs had all left at the crack of dawn. Eventually it was decided that I should go to Maprik, the District Centre; I would reach there by midday and there would still be time to find local transport for Ilahita. Yes please, anything; I was impatient to reach the forest. 'Maprik? Maprik? Anyone going to Maprik?' Plenty, plenty. Larry helped me up onto the back of one of the crowded wagons; at least the flapping canvas would give me some shade. Larry warned me that the road to Maprik was very dangerous; there were lots of hold-ups by *rascals* (armed bandits). OK, but what was I supposed to do about it? Larry and Alex waved goodbye and I pictured Nod's face beside theirs, fraught with alarm, as I flapped away into the searing, venomous heat-haze.

From Nigel's journal. Airlie Beach, Queensland. Sunday 12 June. Today I flew in a seven-seater sea-plane to the reef. Rick would have been proud of me. Despite it being smaller than the smallest of the Merpati planes in Borneo, I felt much safer. The huge floats have wheels under them for land landings and take-offs. I sat directly behind the pilot, seeing the myriad of clocks, dials, meters and digital counters; it felt like being in a big left-hand-drive taxi.

We land in the sea, a smoother landing than some of the Jumbos, and pick up two Japanese honeymooners from Hayman Island, an expensive, exclusive island resort, where I would be tempted to stay, if I had the money. We take off again, bumping and skimming through the waves, sea spray swooshing alongside. Then the first glimpse of the reef; a bit like glancing at an amoeba down a microscope. Bluest of blue sea; through it pink, green, grey, purple, then bright turquoise sea. Reminds me of dropping pancake mixture into a frying pan when it separates and bubbles. Off the plane into the glass-bottomed boat and scoot across the reef. Handed plastic shoes for our reef walk and snorkels, masks and flippers for snorkelling. We are allowed to pick up and replace but forbidden to carry any coral off. Large brown birds with three-foot wing spans and light underwings which reflect the turquoise sea wheel overhead – masked boobies. I jump into the sea. The reef drops 600 feet at one point and I drop into a new world. Waving, waltzing, weaving coral. And fish – tiny, brightly coloured, striped, crested, spotted, blotted, dashing and swirling past and around me in kaleidoscopic splendour. Then urgh! A four-foot large, round-bodied monster with a big lump behind its head and rounded fins that look like wings – it heads straight towards me. The sound in my snorkel of my breathing stops. The creature swerves at the last minute, my heart beats fast and I come up for air, treading water in my flippered feet to recover. A Maori wrass I am later told. This planet never ceases to amaze me: a whole new world I didn't know existed.

I'm glad that, after my 38th birthday present of malaria, I chose to come and recuperate in Queensland. Sometimes fate plays a strong hand. Here I am, sitting under these tall gum trees at sunset point of Airlie Beach – the gateway to the Whitsunday Islands and the Great Barrier Reef – whilst Rick, the explorer and adventurer, goes off to PNG to do it alone. In my present state this is good enough for me; though I do hanker a little for the rough remoteness that I have dipped into with Rick. As soon as the sun disappears behind the hill the lorikeets start screeching and squawking. They are vying for branches to sleep on and partners to sleep with: knocking each other off, hanging acrobatically upside down and crawling along the branches. A flash of yellow undertail as they flit and swoop and screech and squawk from branch to branch and tree to tree.

On this break to recuperate I've seen waterfalls cascading through dense forest, and firetails, with their red caps and bottoms, flitting about; the blue wren flashing its vivid blue head and tail; short- and long-billed curlews. And those splendid, noisy birds above me – blue head, red beak, yellow collar, red chest, green back and wings. Everything today seems to be in brilliant primary colours. Even the sunset tonight is brilliant scarlet red. And I sit for a moment and look and breathe and feel lucky. To be here. To be alone. To be nearly well again. To witness another wonder of the world. And I trust that Rick is safe and following his destiny. 'Better for him to die doing what he loves doing' is a thought I hold on to when I have a twinge of fear about him in PNG. Too dark to write any more – back to my 'unit'.

II

Maprik lies on the other side of the Prince Alexander range of rugged, thickly forested hills that separate Wewak from East Sepik's interior. Up a steep slope out of town and soon the tarmac ran out. Flashes of the dazzling sea far below and glimpses of the dramatic forest ahead. On the map, the Maprik highway had looked like a major trunk road, in reality it was a narrow winding unsurfaced track, in danger of being crushed out of existence altogether by the lush outpushing jungle either side. A precarious roller coaster – with collapsing bridges in the narrow dips and villages perched on the ups. Tin and corrugated iron gradually gave way to more and more bush materials, small trade stores and mission churches to occasional *haus tambaran*, the Sepik spirit houses, with their high swooping roofs and mysterious, intricately painted entrances. The local villagers wedged all around me were too shy even to acknowledge me, and I was too hot and uncomfortable to be able to spare much energy to woo them. Suddenly, through the flapping canvas I saw three scowling men jumping out onto the track ahead. My heart stopped – *rascals!* This was it. Would they take everything? Would they find my secret pocket? But the PMV didn't even slow down and, as we passed, their scowls were smiles, their machetes were being waved in friendship and they shouted jovial greetings to their travelling wantoks. I took a long swig from my water bottle.

It was already afternoon by the time we reached our destination: a few sleepy buildings, a school, a couple of churches, a large ugly trade store, a playing field and a peeling signpost to a hotel that no longer existed. No one had any idea about a PMV to Ilahita. I was pointed up a flight of crumbling steps to the police station. Inside, a large, overweight policeman was standing behind the dusty counter fanning himself with a tattered file. I was welcomed and invited to sit down on a broken chair, the only chair. Travellers were always welcome in Maprik; the policeman had even let tourists camp behind the police station once. Ilahita? Well, there were some local teachers who were supposed to be travelling in that direction. If I walked on along the road and waited under the trees they would take me. And so the mad Englishman was out with the mad dogs in the midday sun again, puffing up another hill. Not a single vehicle passed and there was not a single person in sight, until a small group of convicts came by, spades and shovels over their shoulders. One of them announced that he was

Campbell's cousin. But they were under the impression that the teachers had already left.

My friendly policeman was not surprised to see me again. Oh well, I'd better sit down and wait with him. Maybe I'd still be lucky, maybe someone else would be going. Flies made tracks across the dusty counter and the old wall clock jerked round: three o'clock, four o'clock. Oh well, not to worry. I could always spend the night in the police station. Four o'clock, five o'clock. Oh well, maybe there would be a PMV tomorrow. I was knackered, I was hungry. My strength was dropping with the click of every laboured minute and I dreaded the thought of having to sleep on that dirty, cockroach floor.Then, from nowhere, a younger policeman arrived. A discussion in Pidgin ensued. Something was afoot. The teachers were still here. They were stranded too. The young policeman pulled on his shining armour and marched out to start up his vehicle; he was going to take us on our way. Campbell had instructed me to spend my first night with his sister Rosemary in the village of Balif which lay just off the main highway and from which a smaller road wound its way just a few kilometres further through the forest to Ilahita. Rosemary's husband, Titus, was in charge of Balif's aid post. The policeman knew them well and would drop me at the door. The vehicle was a cab with a large metal cage behind it for transporting criminals; I and the two grateful teachers were locked up in the cage. Oh well, at least we would be safe: safe from those rascals.

Evening was already swallowing up the fierce afternoon as we bounced along the so-called highway and startled villagers stared up in amazement at the poor white convict rattling by. My exhaustion evaporated into the high pink sky. Birdsong whistled through me and the green translucent jungle spilled into my heart. I was getting closer. As we turned off left down the track that led to Balif, the light was already failing. I stood nervously beside the tiny aid post as a square, dark man dressed only in shorts approached. 'Are you Titus?' 'Yes.' 'I am a friend of Campbell, I have brought you a letter.' The strong handsome face broke into a surprised smile and two boys came running out of the trees to see who this stranger was. They all three led me over the rough ground to the house. My first bush house, made entirely from natural forest materials, on strong stilts with narrow wooden steps leading up to a shallow verandah. In a small empty room, Titus pointed to a narrow mattress on the springy floor and told me to *malolo* (rest). The taller boy brought me water. Then they left me.

'Richard, Richard', a woman's voice was calling. It was already pitch dark. I had fallen asleep. Pushing open the creaking, ill-fitting door, the woman appeared, dimly lit by the oil lamp she was carrying. In the shifting circular shadows I could just see her face. Beneath a broad forehead, eyes overflowing with goodwill; above a strong jaw, big lips spread open in a joyful smile. Due to Titus's extreme shyness, fears as to how I would be received had not quite abated on my arrival; but one look at Rosemary made everything clear. Campbell had of course been right. I was welcome, of that there was no doubt. Rosemary had read the letter and understood everything. She had also already seen me: working in a small coffee plantation some kilometres along the highway, she had been one of the startled villagers who had seen the white convict rattling by. Apparently I had caused quite a sensation. She had been very concerned and was now relieved that the mystery had been solved. She was so grateful that I had reached Balif safely. She was so thankful to Campbell for sending me to honour her humble household. It was a miracle that I had travelled so far across the world to stay with her and her family. Tonight, if her simple house was acceptable to me, I would rest with them. In the morning, yes of course, she would take me on to Ilahita. But now Titus had prepared supper, I must come and eat.

We sat in a circle on the baked earth. Titus, Rosemary, their three sons and me. In the centre of the circle, the small fire on which Titus had cooked. Surrounding the circle, the looming outline of the homestead and a thicket of trees. Above the circle, an awning of diamond stars. The blackness throbbed with crickets and the six eyes of the lean boys danced at me in the fireglow. I felt immense gratitude and immense privilege to be a guest in this ancient and splendiferous dining hall.

In the early morning, I washed with a bucket of water from the well and Titus proudly showed me the large, oblong yam house. Inside it was dark, only a little light penetrated thinly through the slatted walls. The area close to the entrance was used as a kitchen, and a few, simple, fire-blackened utensils were standing in ordered fashion on the baked earth. Behind, the fantastically shaped yams loomed up in rows like a grotesque assembly of trolls and goblins. These yams were of profound importance to Titus and later, at his request, I photographed him ceremoniously holding up the largest specimen. Before the yellow dappled light turned into the harsh glare of the day, I took a stroll through the trees and tall jungle grass. The muddy path opened into a clearing on which stood a couple more small bush houses. Stilts, ladders, everything made entirely of bush materials. Earth, scratching chickens and curling smoke. Shafts of sunlight through dark leaves. An old woman leaning at an entrance smoking a home-made cigarette and waving a bounteous good morning. It was my turn to be overcome with shyness. I wanted to but couldn't go on. I felt too crass, too clumsy to intrude. This was the real Papua New Guinea; just like William had promised me. The village, the forest, the people and a timelessness, as dreamy as the curling smoke.

Back on the shallow verandah, Rosemary's full golden smile melted my feeling of separateness. In broken English and with long, low, heartfelt sighs, she told me the story of Titus. His first wife had died and he had turned to drink. She had married him out of pity and he had treated her cruelly. Many times he had beaten her and even hit her in the face, always refusing to listen to the word of the Lord. Rosemary was a Christian. Her faith and love of Jesus were total and all-encompassing. She had prayed and prayed and borne her suffering in silence. Then one day it happened. For some unexplained reason, Titus had come to church. He recognized Jesus for the first time, and repented. He had never drunk again and from that day he had never raised his hand to her. Titus had become a good man. A good husband and a good father to the three orphaned boys they had adopted. As Rosemary spoke, true Christian love flowed out from every pore of her body and her eyes were glowing lamps of human joy and kindness. A strong, brave village woman. Her faith in Jesus was infinite, as was her boundless gratitude. To her, the Bible was everyday reality and Jesus' teachings were absolutes to be held and practised moment by moment. We had a good time together on that little balcony, waving to the odd passer-by, rejoicing in the wonders of the Lord, and listening to the natural sounds of her happy, harmonious, local, biblical world.

Ilahita is a large village, divided up into several areas. Campbell's family lived in Ilahita Two. As we arrived down the track, the news spread fast and soon the whole extended family were gathering to meet me under the large family house. Chris, Campbell's nephew, who was learning English at the local high school, pored over the letter of introduction and discussed it at length with one and all. Campbell's brother, Jeffrey, in whom I immediately saw a like-ness, was too shy even to look at me. He had no English and no schooling, Chris told me confidentially, but he did boast two beautiful young wives and several gurgling babies. Maksi, Campbell's older brother and the first-born, was away somewhere on the coast, but his wife Roha was there to greet me instead, with the sweetest smile and the roundest, soulful eyes. At first I got the impression she was Campbell's mother and couldn't understand how she could be so young; but then I began to understand that sisters-in-law, cousins and even distant relatives are all called mothers and sisters and brothers. And there were lots of them too; and lots of aunties and uncles. *'Mi hamamas lukim yu. Nem bilong mi Richard'* (I'm pleased to see you. My name is Richard). I said it again and again, as one after another came forward eagerly to shake my hand. Finally, Campbell's real mother appeared, giggling and nodding, a spindly elderly woman with a comic face and large, strong, wrinkled hands. Nodding and cooing she held my shoulders and looked up at me with a cheeky sparkle. Like Rosemary, she was so happy to see me and she was so grateful that I had come safely from so far away. But next time I must bring Campbell with me. Campbell had been away too long. She wanted to see her son again. I must tell him to hurry. I must tell him that she missed him, missed him every day.

Enjoying to the full his important position as holder of Campbell's letter, Chris reassured me that he understood its contents and that he and Jeffrey and Michael (a cousin), would fulfil Campbell's directions. Chris was a slim, springy youth, his face strikingly different from the other members of the family; his features were slimmer, sharper and his narrow nose was almost Roman in shape. He took immediate charge of me and led me up a steep ladder on the end of the house into the guest room, my room. It had its own entrance and it had a tin roof which made it unbearably hot but which seemed to fill the family with much pride.

The rest of that day is a bit of a blur. Chris and Michael took me *wokabaut* around the village and I seemed to meet literally dozens more aunties and uncles. I was invited up into several of their houses and I was presented with several large plates of gelatinous *saksak sop* (sago soup). We also made plans. The following day, together with Lawrence, an older cousin, they would take me to visit the jungle gardens where the villagers grew their daily food. Then the day after, or the day after that, they would take me to the forest and we would camp out and see the big trees and go to the place where the birds of paradise fed. This time I was not so surprised when both Chris and Michael came to join me at bedtime. Like Campbell, they were keen to learn yoga, but when I lay down to sleep, they slipped out for a last *wokabaut* or *spin*, as they called it, before creeping back to sleep on the floor by the entrance.

❖ ❖ ❖

From Rick's journal. Ilahita. 10 a.m. Tuesday 14 June.

At last I've given myself a day to write. I'm sitting in Chris's room, floor of bare plaited bamboo strips, three walls the same, the fourth of cardboard. Empty except for little wooden desk which he has made himself and some scraps of paper with printed English exercises on them. One tiny glassless window through which two boys are peeping at me. Village empty, everyone has gone to their gardens to work. Only Michael is sitting outside; it is his job to look after me today. Up the track, schoolchildren are shouting and singing. In the distance there is banging: someone is making a new house across the valley in the other section of the village. Overhead, in the tall coconut palms and breadfruit trees, there are parrots calling: loud shrill cries, strange, flute-like peals, then bouts of silence. A few morning crickets chirping and butterflies roaming: pearly blues, yellows and patterned black and whites. Ilahita is on the edge of the big forest; villages beyond here are reached only by foot.

Ilahita has two kinds of houses: a few, like this one, square, on stilts; but most are smaller, tent-shaped, with a framework of bamboo, a single room and a sloping roof of palm-leaf thatch that reaches down to the ground. Cooking is done on fires in front of the overhanging porches. Three small tins are placed in a triangle to rest the pot on, and small twigs and branches are economically fed between the tins to the small central fire. In the evening everyone sits round these fires, squatting on the baked earth, smoke curling up to the brilliant stars. Easy chatting, easy laughter; tiny naked children lolling on their parents' laps, babies sucking at bare elongated breasts. Everything is scrupulously swept and clean. Except for the villagers' clothes – an odd hotchpotch of handmedowns from the Australian mission. Shorts and threadbare T-shirts for the men, cotton skirts for the women or, more traditionally, lengths of coloured cloth which are wrapped around them and tied behind their necks. Often these clothes are just rags but they don't seem important. Of far more significance are the tattoos on people's faces and sometimes on their arms. A small people. Dark-skinned, broad, with deep-set eyes and wide noses.

Yesterday, the handsome older cousin, Lawrence, accompanied by Chris and Michael, showed me his gardens. Breakfast first outside his little house: slices of yam fried in cooking oil with salt, obviously a treat, and served on leaves for plates. Lawrence was as proud of his baby piglet as he was of his young new wife. We walked for an hour, up and down the steep hillside, a narrow zigzagging path through the jungle gardens. Some are meticulously weeded, some already in their last year of use, after which they will be left to grow wild for five or six years to give back nutrients to the soil. No rows of produce here, the crops are scattered, a luscious profusion of tapioca, pawpaw trees, pumpkins, *ibica* (the main green vegetable), tulip-trees (also used as a vegetable), *pitpit*, a wild form of sugarcane, and the vines of yams and *mami*, a large white root. In lower areas, often clustered around creeks and streams, are groups of sago, banana and coconut palms. Among the crops are coloured flowers, and everywhere lots of butterflies. Food is not a problem here. There is enough for everyone, they say; if a man is hungry, it is because he is lazy. Though from the runny noses, protruding bellies and blemishes on the skin of many of the children, there must be some nutrient deficiency. The diet is almost entirely fruit and vegetables. Tinned fish and corned beef from the poorly-stocked trading store are too expensive for most to buy. The yams and mamis are generally baked whole on the fire and then scraped for eating. Sago seems generally to be boiled in large gelatinous chunks with a mixture of ibica and pumpkin leaves. A large bowl is offered. You eat as much as you can then pass the bowl on to the next in line. Granny and children wait till the end.

Back in the gardens, we reach Lawrence's bush house, a simpler, open-ended version of his home. Michael scoots up a pawpaw tree and brings down several large yellow fruits. With his big-bladed knife, Lawrence peels the fruits and slices them up for me to eat. It's getting hot now and it's a relief to sit in the shade of the shack and watch them make a fire to bake some yams and pitpit. After sharing the bananas that Lawrence brought me yesterday, we have a snooze, lying on the dried palm leaves. Then Lawrence tells us about his time working in the Highlands on a tea plantation. He joined a gang of rascals led by a policeman and they raided a drinking club in Mount Hagen, holding up the barman at gunpoint. Soon after, there was an argument between the Highland workers and the Sepik workers. A Highlander was killed by a bulldozer and the Sepiks had to flee for their lives; the Highlanders came after them with spears and axes. Lawrence came back to the Sepik under police escort for protection.

Continuing our spin, we come to the garden of another village. Here we have to make a wreath of ferns and grasses for our heads to show that we are passing through in friendship. Up an overgrown hillside, through old gardens ready for cutting and planting again, we reach the village on a plateau. It is especially clean and pretty. The earth round the bamboo and palm houses is beautifully swept, and flowering shrubs and herbs are planted here and there. The village is almost empty. Just their green coffee beans spread out on sacks and palm leaves lying in the sun. This is their main cash crop; somewhere at the corner of their garden, everyone has a small coffee plantation. Each local district seems to have a depot from which the beans are collected by a regional truck. Just one smiling woman in rags is squatting, feeding her baby; and one very shy man, who offers us coconuts. Tying his feet together with a rope which allows him to get a purchase on the trunk, Michael climbs the high palm. The heavy coconuts drop to the ground and Lawrence fills my water bottle with coconut milk. This village is higher than Ilahita, reached only by a winding path. All around below the garden jungle stretches and, on one side, a forested range of mountains rises blue and hazy in the afternoon heat. But under the bending coconut palms it is shady, almost a hint of a cool breeze.

On the way home, Lawrence and Michael stop suddenly. There is a loud piercing cry from a clump of high trees to our left. It is a bird of paradise. My heart stops. We dive down the steep slope, racing fast to the deep stream at the bottom. The clump of trees are incredibly tall with loose boughs of thick foliage. The bird is crying again; it's somewhere up there. We strain our necks. Then tiptoe along by the stream. Eventually we see it. First just quick glimpses as it swoops between the branches. But at last a clear sighting: gorgeous yellow cascading tail like a frothy golden waterfall; then a wide white stripe and the rich reddish wings and upper parts. High in the tree, the bird is hanging half upside down. Still for a moment, and then off on its gorgeous wide wings. Its high repeated cry fills the steep narrow valley.

Above, there is a group of houses marking the beginning of Ilahita. People live there. Babies are born, children grow up and people die. Living, dying with that piercing cry in the air, with that magical tail flashing through the branches overhead. Ancient traditions, ancient customs, always inspired and adorned by those gorgeous yellow feathers; feathers that are the jewels of these people, their epitome of beauty. A social system venerating the family. Venerating old age. Venerating the great yam: symbol of potency, symbol of prosperity. Until the missionaries came. Made them throw away their grass skirts and wear handmedowns from the whites. Made them change their names at their baptisms so that everyone is called Rosemary and John and Paul. Except the older men who hold two names, their real name and their

Christian name. Just five years ago, they pulled down their temple that stood at the centre of the village and burned all their 'pagan' carvings. Only one or two have refused to be converted: silent men. How I should love to have been able to converse with them. Spirits who were somehow strong enough to withstand the 'word of the Lord'; strong enough to cling to the beliefs that had served them so well for thousands of years. No alcohol, no thieving, no adultery, no rape: all this had come with the whites.

However, one thing has remained unchangeable: they still love their yams. Everyone was so upset that I missed their big yam ceremony by just one day. Traditional dancing and singing and everyone's yams lined up and decorated, with people coming from all the villages around. Everyone mentions it again and again that I should have hurried, I should have hurried. The old men are particularly sorry. Oh, they can talk about yams for hours. They love showing them to me. They love cooking them for me. And one of Campbell's uncles, who called me his *pikinini* (child), brought me some special ones from his garden for Roha, Chris's mother to prepare for me. A gift of welcome and friendship. A gift from the yam people.

And so, in the evening as dusk falls through the rosy-cloud sky and we go out to watch the flying foxes waking up and flapping through the trees, the little fires are lit and the sago and yams and greens are boiled or steamed. A special treat for me: yam and mami soup, made with coconut; it is creamy and sweet. Once again, Roha prepares it with love and care, squatting over the pot. Her mother has come to visit from the next village: a tiny scrawny creature with high cheekbones and a sunken face; but her eyes are still bright and her body agile. In her colourless rags with her necklace of bones, she sits cross-legged on the dry earth, blending with it, part of it. Too shy to look at me, she moves to sit away from the hurricane lamp; scrawny outline in the shadows, hair turned almost yellow with age. A woman of the forest. A woman who knows all there is to know about yams and sago. A woman who knows the old myths, who speaks the old language. A woman who knows about daily toil on the steep, hot hillsides of her jungle gardens. When it's time to sleep, I ask Chris to teach me 'good-night' in the village language, and I shake her sinewy hand and say *'Owamb'*. She is sitting apart now, by her own little fire, a mangy puppy snuggled up to her. From the flames I just catch a glimpse of a sweet smile in her sunken eyes. My old mum of the forest. So beautiful in her own scraggy way. My heart breaks with tenderness for you, old woman. For a time when people were at one with the birds. For a time before the white man hurled his ignorance across the world.

In the dark yam house behind her, Chris shows me their original pots and plates, made either from coconut shells or baked, blackened earth. There are strange tools for the garden and several old bamboo spears. Also, two daggers made from cassowary thigh bones sharpened to a vicious point and decorated with intricate carvings; these belonged to Campbell's father. Campbell's family is part of the clan of the cassowarys, the giant flightless bird that inhabits PNG's forests. That's how far Campbell has travelled; speeding between Port Moresby and Sydney and Singapore serving gin and tonic for Air Niugini. No wonder I sensed that he was somehow lost. No wonder I sensed that his life was in confusion. No wonder, as he talked sometimes, I felt that the division between fantasy and reality had become blurred. No wonder he got drunk. No wonder he got stoned. No wonder he wanted me to hold him like a baby, tensed and freaked out with too much booze and marijuana on the last hot night in the concrete house, in the dangerous, violent city. Like William, Campbell has also travelled ten thousand years in a lifetime. A man who I sense is lost between two worlds. A man who reads the words of an Indian chief and dreams of returning to his village to revive the dying traditions, to protect the forest, to care for his people. To hold the bridge open and give both sides life. A man who stays on in Port Moresby and continues to drink.

I wrote my journal in Chris's room because the tin roof of the guest room made it totally unbearable between about 9 a.m. and 5 p.m. It was my one day for writing and rest: time for me to prepare for the big adventure the following day. We were to spend two nights in the forest: the first beside a large river and the second under the trees where the birds of paradise come to feed. It felt very special to spend a day at home in the silent village. The ground round the simple bush houses perfectly swept. The tall magnificent trees casting a dark tapestry of shade, between them a watery glimpse of the distant blue hills far away across the forest basin. And, up in the canopy, crimson parrots darting among the threads of sunlight. But it was also difficult. Ilahita was extremely hot and hard. To sit and write took all the willpower I could muster. To do nothing at all was almost as exhausting. Hour after hour, Michael patiently sat under the house watching over me and fetching me water when I requested it. He was so solicitous of his charge. But there was a sadness about him too. He knew that there was another world beyond those blue hills, a thrilling glamorous world; but it was not his fate to embrace it. Michael's parents had both died and so he was living with his cousins. Unlike Chris, who was enjoying further education, he was left to roam around the village.

Sunset is *waswas* (bath time). Either I would be taken down the steep path to wash in the muddy creek or I would be brought a bowl of water and I'd strip quickly behind the houses, warding off the ever-hungry mosquitoes. As the village filled up, and after Chris had come home, ostentatiously flaunting his school work, I suddenly jumped up and started doing a physical limber, in a manic burst of energy after the static day. Soon I was surrounded by a hooting crowd of children and half the youth of the village came to join in the mad prancing. These boys were always game to try new things. But the press-ups were too much for us all and we ended up a roaring, sweating pile of laughter. The white nutter had to go for a second wash, which pleased the lurking mosquitoes, and I was famished by the time Roha called us for supper.

Under the early stars, as we crouched in an arc around her fire, Roha apologized again. She had made me my favourite mami soup, but again there was no protein. She had no money to buy a tin from the trade store; she was so worried and she was so sorry. I could have bought one, of course, but I didn't want her to feel, or her children to feel, that her food was second best and so I reassured her that it was fine, that it was plenty and that I was fully satisfied. It was certainly prepared with the utmost love and the utmost care; if that could nourish, I told myself, I would be well replenished. As we were eating, a group of women walked by with a flaming torch and carrying bibles. They stopped and murmured quietly to Roha in their soft burbling *tokples* (village language). They were talking about me. Chris explained what they were saying. They were sorry for me, so sorry because I was so far away from my home, because I was so far away from my family. That's why they were so sorry, so sorry. Roha was sorry too and her tiny mother and Campbell's mother and all the aunties and cousin sisters. 'So sorry', the women repeated gently as they moved away towards the mission church, their spirits flowing out to me in sympathy and compassion.

I don't remember packing up or how I felt that night, except that Chris and Michael went for their customary last village spin. I pretended to be asleep when they got back, though, as always, I was still wide awake. I think I was kind of blank, kind of numb about the big walk ahead. I couldn't begin to face the possibility of failing again and I couldn't even dare to conceive that I might actually succeed: that my goal might be reached, that my long dream might be realized. And so we just got up in the morning and set off. Chris, Michael, Lawrence, Jeffrey (Campbell's brother) and two or three other cousins as well. Part of me was alarmed by the size of the party, but then these people always did things together, and the bundles of spears slung over their shoulders, indicated they were taking the opportunity of combining the *bikpela wok-abaut* (trek) with a hunting expedition. To begin with we had to walk back along the road towards Balif. As usual, the dreary old battle with fear started waging about a minute after I'd picked up my knapsack. My boots felt tight, my legs were already aching and my hips were locked and tense. Still, I had survived Kalimantan for god's sake, so what the hell was all the fuss about? My friends kept stopping and chatting to neighbours and mates at the side of the road. I suppose our expedition was 'Stop Press'. But the sun was already over the trees; I was already thirsty and just needed to get off that hot track and know we were making some progress.

The walk through the dank fertile gardens was more reassuring. A squelchy path through walls of pitpit, coffee bushes, yam vines and pawpaw and banana trees. People were already at work and they shouted greetings of good luck as we filed by. Beyond the gardens in the dark wet forest, I felt less assured. The trees were narrow-stemmed, the undergrowth was sparse, and we only came to one giant tree which they insisted I photograph. It was a living colossus: a massive haphazard circle of aerial roots twisting down to grip the mud like giant petrified guy ropes; and huge grey branches like the limbs of an upside-down elephant struggling to get up. But I hadn't crossed PNG to see one tree. 'Ricky, shut up – we have only been walking for a couple of hours'.

Along a fallen tree trunk lying beside a shallow river, the party stopped to rest. 'Which direction is the *bikpela bus* (big forest)?' I asked. They looked puzzled. 'The *bikpela bus*,' I repeated, 'which direction?' 'This is it,' Chris said, 'this is where Campbell told us to bring you. This is the river where we are going to camp.' I don't know what I felt. Maybe an ugly deformed hand gripped my gut and gave it a vicious twist. Maybe the gloating destroyer of a lifetime's dream hurled its deafening whoop of triumph at my broken ears. Maybe I just screwed the lid down tight on this unreal moment of disbelief. Maybe I just looked at the river which had turned a dull grey and said 'Oh'. 'This is it,' Chris repeated, 'this is the bikpela bus that we have brought you to enjoy.' Maybe I looked at the sky which had also turned a dull grey and said 'Oh' again.

What was the matter? Wasn't I happy? Had they done something wrong? The line of dark eyes along the tree trunk turned on me with concern. What could I do, what could I say? All the beauty and the wonder of Ilahita seemed to be gobbled up by the horrible flabby monster of failure. All the colour and richness of the last two weeks seemed to be blanched to nothing by the laser spotlight of defeat. Wearily, I turned the record back and placed the needle at the beginning. Pastor Ranft, Jau, Pastor Lahagir and all the passengers on the *Nilam Cahaya* came to join the line of eyes. The hunting boys were so sorry, they had just thought I had wanted some fun. They hadn't understood that I had come to Ilahita with a purpose. They only wanted to help me and now they were so sorry. Sparks of rage, shot through me like ripping firecrackers, but they fizzled out and died just as fast, as they landed in the pool of open hearts beside me. I think that moment must have been too much for us all after the build-up, after the enthusiasm, after the preparation and after the Stop Press boasting. So someone changed the subject. Was I a Christian? Did I believe in hell? If their parents or grandparents had died before they had heard about Jesus, did that mean they had gone to hell? Did that mean they were sinners? These questions weighed heavily upon the young men of Ilahita. I tried to answer as best I could, but I was in no mood for a theological debate.

In crocodile file we crossed the shallow river and made our way to a bush shack beside a clump of sago palms in an overgrown garden; there they told me to rest while they made a fire and cooked our midday meal: pitpit and taro, baked and smoked on the open jungle fire. Lawrence served me with touching chivalry and all the panache of a silver service waiter. They were all keen to feed me up, to fill up the holes of my disappointment. After eating, Lawrence and Jeffrey and the older cousins went off to hunt. Jeffrey's shyness had left him now, he was at home in the forest; his eyes as fast as arrows, his taut and perfectly proportioned muscles ready to spring into action at the slightest rustle in the undergrowth. Meanwhile, Chris, Michael and I lay down on the ground in the shack for an afternoon nap. In a moment they were both fast asleep, lying close together, backs curled over and legs pulled up, almost in the foetal position. So easy, so comfortable, yet ready at an instant for the unexpected with their large machetes close at hand. When they woke up and the hunters returned for a short break, I told them that I wanted to go back to Ilahita; there was now no point in camping out. Chris and Michael agreed to take me, while the others chose to stay on. They would wait for sundown and go night hunting; they would return in the morning with their bounty. And so, through a lacklustre afternoon, I dragged my boots, retracing our steps.

Everyone was of course surprised to see us. When they heard the news they were very sorry. Roha shook her head and sighed as she served up my mami soup. No one had understood and everyone was so sorry. I tried to make light of it. I told them I would just have to find the forest somewhere else. I repeated again and again that it had been wonderful to come to Ilahita, that I was very happy to be there. But they still shook their heads and sighed and Chris looked at me with cut eyes. He pondered the problem and explained. Tomorrow was Thursday. If I wanted to go back to Wewak and find another forest, I would have to go tomorrow. The Ilahita PMV only went on Thursdays and Sundays. If I waited till Sunday, it might be too late for me; and it would be very difficult to get to Wewak if I didn't use the PMV. Of course they didn't want me to go so soon, but if I had to they would understand. All eyes were on me in the firelight wondering what I was going to decide. At least have some more mami soup. It was a horrible dilemma. I loved these people so much and yet, and yet, my time was running out fast. If I was really going to make yet another attempt to find the primary forest, I would need every minute of Thursday to Sunday. And though I had loved my hot silent day in the village, would it be so lovely if I was burning up with the old disappointment?

Chris and Michael sat with me in silence on the ladder outside my room. They knew it was difficult for me. They were completely selfless in their wish for me to make the right decision. Their compassionate eyes were as bright as the forest stars. They didn't want to rush me, but I did have to decide. Chris would have to go and warn the PMV driver. Sometimes he left even before the light and so he would have to know that I would be going along with him. Oh god, it would mean leaving before the hunters came home. What would they think if I had just gone without saying goodbye? What would Lawrence think? Lawrence who had attended to my needs so well. And what would Roha think and Campbell's mother? Wouldn't they be offended? They had welcomed me with such open arms, could I just rush off so suddenly? And what about Rosemary and Titus? How could I leave without even saying goodbye to them? It would be so out of order, such bad behaviour.

And yet, and yet . . .

Chris and Michael knew the answer before I did. They were very sad but never once tried to dissuade me from going. Chris gently helped me. It was all right. Everyone would understand. I needn't worry. No one would think badly of me. But I still felt horribly torn: wanting to stay, wanting to honour these friendships, wanting to round off my visit in a gracious way; yet knowing I had to go. My quest was still too strong, I couldn't let it go. Sadly, we strolled through the dark village together and made the necessary arrangements with the driver. Sadly, we strolled back and they squatted on the floor of my room and watched me pack. We would have to get up very early. They would wake me up and take me to the PMV. Sadly, they went off for their night spin and sadly, I curled up to try to sleep.

In the white grey moments before dawn, Chris lowered my pack down the ladder. Roha was already up. In the early hush, she came over the earth to me and, holding both my hands, sang me a farewell song. As she sang, she looked directly into my eyes. Looking back into hers I saw no cloud, not even a flicker of hurt or consternation or begrudgement. I saw only a radiant spirit absolutely full of love, caring and understanding. Next time, Roha said, you will bring your mother and father. Next time you will stay longer. I had to turn away fast; I was fighting back a whole choking well of tears.

Chris and Michael were waiting and together we walked silently and sadly through the village once more. Chris, swinging my bag and Michael, holding my hand. Just before we reached the shack which garaged the PMV, one of the aunties came running through the half-light towards us. She was carrying a huge knobbled yam. Out of breath and hesitant with shyness, she presented me with the yam. She was so deeply sorry that I had not found what I was looking for but she was so deeply happy that she had woken up and caught me just in time. Again I had to turn away. It took all my power to hold down the tears. Phew. This had never happened before on my travels. I had often felt sad to leave wonderful people and wonderful places, but never this. Luckily the driver was already keen to set off. A quick hug for my two faithful friends and we were away.

Oh, you people of Ilahita, you touched me so deeply and you gave me so much. Please forgive me. Please forgive me for walking out on you so fast. Please know how much I loved you.

III

At Raun Isi Larry and the actors were pleased and relieved to see me safely back in one piece. About my failed mission they had little to say; they were more interested in planning a welcome home feast, and Larry took me along the road to the Sunset Market to choose what I wanted to eat. Just at the hour of sundown, the women from the surrounding settlements come with their garden produce and squat along the edge of the tree-lined road. In a PNG market there is no haggling, no shouting and no declaiming of wares. The women sit silently, with their little heaps of peanuts, betel nuts and baby tomatoes laid out on palm fronds in front of them; with their bundles of pumpkin leaves, ibica, tulip leaves and saksak piled up beside them. Each commodity has a standard price and it was left up to us to wander along the line and choose. The faces of the women were as varied as the pawpaws, pineapples and bananas: women from many different rural areas who had been drawn to Wewak for one reason or another. Local employment is scarce, and so they rake in a few *toya* (pennies) for their families tending small patches of garden, or picking wild produce straight out of the jungle. Tattooed faces and faded smocks, they squatted in motionless silence, just an occasional whisper, a shy laugh with a tilt of the head, a murmured order to a tiny daughter. Larry took his time and chose carefully, teaching me the names of the things I didn't know.

When we got back, Caspar, the prop builder with the initiation scars on his back, was already bending over an open fire out on the grass behind the kitchen. He was baking a *mumut* for me which he had caught himself: a large rodent creature, something like a cross between a hedgehog and a rabbit. He was baking it whole and the fur was singeing with a pungent stench. Alas, I have little memory of that feast, except that I had to pull the charred fur off my blackened morsel of meat. My head was already zooming. I battened down the hatches for the night and scribbled half-legible scrawlings across my journal: 'Have I really blown it again? Is it too late now? Should I give up? Is this my final defeat?' During the night there was an almighty cloudburst and torrential rain smashed down onto the Raun Isi roofs. I almost wished it would wash me away. The following days were a carousel with a leaking engine. But, as my blurred vision began to swim back into focus, I re-read my Jakarta poem and it refuelled my determination. I still had two weeks, there was still time. With help from Larry and the actors I forced myself into action. There had to be *someone* in Wewak who knew about primary forest.

The Raun Isi phone was only for incoming calls and so I had to traipse into town to do all my business from the crowded callboxes at the post office. Larry's expatriate friend invited me for drinks at the yacht club, but then, catching the desperate tenor in my voice, referred me on to another expatriate, who in turn referred me to Francis Iko, a West Sepik man who apparently had a lot of forest knowledge. I was also given the number of the Executive Adviser for Planning and Development in the province. He was friendly enough on the phone, if a trifle evasive: 'Oh yes, I know what you mean. The kind of primal forest like the Amazon. I really don't know actually. Maybe there's some left in the Angoram district. I suggest you go and talk to the Department of Forests. I'll give you their number.' And so I made appointments both with the Forestry Department and with Francis Iko. I also went to Air Niugini to check out flights to Alotau, one of my original options in Port Moresby. Maybe I should just pack up and get myself there; however much it cost, at least the plantation manager had promised that there was primary forest nearby. I would feel a little foolish, I had already written to tell him of my change of plan; but, what the hell, he would understand. Anyway I would telephone him. I found his number in the phone book. The directory for the whole of PNG is smaller than our local one for Bury St Edmunds at home.

In my over-activity to compensate for the dismal voice that wanted to give up, I almost passed out on the street. Alex was to-ing and fro-ing with me for moral support; so we went to the *kaihaus* (café) for replenishment. It was a very hot shed with a counter. I've no idea what we ate or drank, but it was clearly a treat for Alex and it kept me on my feet for a few more hours.

I found Francis Iko in a large warehouse by the sea. His desk was at the end of a big dark space, the only light coming from strips of meshed window, close to the high roof. 'How can I help you?' he asked in very broken English. A frog-like, barrel of a man, he looked as if he was about to roll off his metal office chair. He was from a 'backward' area of West Sepik, the next province. He confirmed that there was big forest all around. His people were not used to visitors. They wouldn't be hostile but then again they wouldn't know how to look after me. But I could base myself at the mission; I could set up a camp in the forest and do whatever I wanted to from there. There were regular flights from Wewak and so I could arrange for my supplies to be delivered. That wouldn't be a problem. I tried to pin him down to a precise spot on the map, but Mr Iko was not used to specifics. He also did not offer his family as contacts. The round black eyes in his loose black face were not unfriendly, yet they didn't instil much confidence. I thanked him and left.

The Department of Forests was situated within the complex of government buildings known as Kreer Heights on top of the hill overlooking the town. It was up the same road that I had travelled on my way to Maprik, but this time we took a local bus and it was Herman with me now, another actor who had just come back from his research work in his village. The forestry officer was another big man. He treated me formally, with some suspicion; but at least he really did understand what I was talking about. He opened a map and pointed to a place called Wagu: there I would find primary forest. Even on the map I could see that it was very different from Ilahita. Wagu was a village at the end of a large lake; there were no other villages nearby. But then the forestry officer changed his mind. No, Bisorio would be even better. Again he showed me on the map. It was much further up, close to the Highlands, and far away from the river and from any other communication system. At Bisorio, there was a very big forest. But the only access was by the plane of the New Tribes Mission, I would have to go and talk with them. Their base was just a few minutes walk up the road; he gave me directions. He also asked me to sign my name in the visitors' book: it was a small exercise book with only a few names filling half the first page. I wrote 'tourist' to abate his suspicions that I might be a radical environmentalist or a racketeering prospector. I thanked him. The audience was over.

The New Tribes Mission was a new, two-storey house up a mowed slope. There was a youngish white man with short hair and spectacles crossing beside a land-cruiser. 'Hi', he said, with an American accent. I introduced myself and Herman: 'Hi, Herman', he smiled on automatic. Unreal warmth in his voice; 'What can I do for you fellers?' I tried to explain it all lightly without sounding too intense. He wasn't keen to help. Bisorio had been set up as a mission, not a guest house. The people there were very 'primitive'; the area had only been opened up for a few years; there had already been enough visitors. Anyway it wasn't up to him. I would have to telephone the headquarters in the Highlands. If they agreed, I would have to wait for the mission plane. It only went there occasionally; there was no regular service. And anyhow what was wrong with the forest round Wewak? What he said was fair enough, his argument was clear, but his attitude was dismissive as if there were other, unspoken ulterior motives attached to his dissuasion of my proposed trip.

Knackered, I lay on my bed and flipped through my notes. I wasn't getting very far. I decided not to phone the mission headquarters, there was too much negativity in his attitude, and I didn't have the time to hang around waiting for the mission plane. There was no way I could risk going to West Sepik; Francis Iko had given me no clear assurance. And the news on Alotau was not encouraging: there were only three flights a week and they left from Port Moresby. So what were my options now? Option one: still try to fly to Alotau. For this, I would have to recheck the flight, the connections and the cost. Option two: phone William. Get in touch with a pilot that William and I had met while looking at a possible venue for the Mastery. He had offered to fly me in a helicopter to a spectacular airstrip deep in the thickest forest. We had arranged a provisional date on my return to Port Moresby; but if I went earlier, maybe he could take me there and leave me to trek. Option three: go to the yacht club; practice my most convincing expatriate chortle and elicit more names and contacts out of Larry's friend. Option four: go to Wagu, the place that the forestry officer had mentioned first; phone him again to confirm that it would still be his second choice and to find out the best way to get there.

The position of Wagu on the map still excited me but there was one horror in the way. Wagu was along a tributary off the great Sepik River, in the vicinity of Ambunti, the district centre of the Upper Sepik. The Sepik was the most publicized area of the province. When I had glanced at a travellers' book for PNG, there had been a lot of commentary about the Sepik River: it had become quite a touring centre and there were many tales about people being ripped off, charged exorbitant rates for boats, food, and accommodation. One of the very last things I felt like was tourist hassle; in my tiredness and low spirits there was nothing I dreaded more.

It started to rain again. Though there was mosquito net at the window, they still managed to get in around the ill-fitting door, and now there was one that I couldn't catch, testing my tattered nerves with its evil wiry scream. Norm, one of the actors I had met first, lived next door with his teacher wife and little daughter Scarlet. He had a few cassettes which he played repeatedly. They were some of my old favourites – Dr Hook, The Eagles – and their familiarity was usually a comfort as the drumbeats of their rhythms vibrated through the narrow wall partition. But at that moment, even 'Sylvia's Mother' failed to buoy up my plummeting spirit. In fact I tipped into the worst despair of the trip. Metaphorically, I threw all the options on the floor. I had had enough. I had failed and I couldn't do any more. Round and round went the droning record. And when I tore it out of my head and smashed it on the floor among my futile options, there was another one below it playing the same identical dirge.

I don't know how long I stayed there, indulgently soaking in my misery – the martyr lying on his self-sharpened bed of nails. But suddenly I stood up. I don't know how or where it came from, but suddenly I had an urge to go and chat with the actors. At least it might clear my head: distract me, divert me. A group of them were sitting round the kitchen table; I joined them and I found myself telling stories of the Mastery. They were fascinated, intrigued. I stood up and demonstrated one of the emotional exercises. They howled with laughter. They doubled up. Alex had to rush out of the room. They literally rolled on the floor. And because of their extreme reaction, I doubled up with laughter too. They were obviously not used to expressing emotions like this. It was a totally new concept for them. A completely ridiculous one. An incredibly unbelievably hilarious one. And through that wonderful uninhibited laughter, something cleared in me. I felt light again; even happy. And, without premeditation, I told them all about my hopeless, impossible options and my fear of the tourist racket up the Sepik River. Again they listened, fascinated, intrigued, relapsing from time to time back into a few regurgitated peals of laughter.

Then Herman piped up with surprising confidence. He had the answer. It was simple. In the morning he would take me to see Anton Sakarai. Anton was the Administrative Director of Raun Isi Theatre; he spent most of his time in the government office which accounted for my not having met him. Until recently, Anton had been a council worker in Ambunti; he knew the area like the back of his hand. He would be able to help me arrange my journey to Wagu. With Anton's help, it would be easy. And yes, a few tourists did travel up the Sepik from time to time, but most of them went in organized parties. And yes, they probably paid plenty of money but I wouldn't have to get into any of that. I needn't worry at all. Herman spoke with such confidence, with such easy conviction and the others nodded in such total affirmation of his words that I believed him. There and then I made up my mind. My last try would be at Wagu. And then I remembered my Angel Card – humour. Well, maybe it hadn't been so stupid after all.

The next morning, Herman took me to Anton's home as arranged; and we found ourselves sitting under a tree in his garden close to his small prefab bungalow. Anton was having a music practice with three young guitarists from his church. We sat and listened. He brought me a large plate of fish and ibica and his baby children peered at me from around and under the house. Anton was a family man with a full beard and a round belly. His wife was called Nancy; she was a cousin-sister to Alice, Larry's wife. And yes, of course he would assist me. Everything that Herman had told me had been absolutely correct. Anton would contact his ex-colleague in Ambunti who would arrange a place for me to stay and who would also arrange for a council boat to take me from there up to Wagu. Anton would try to find me transport to Pagwi, the highest road contact point on the Sepik River, and from Pagwi, he would also try to arrange for river transport up to Ambunti. And finally, he would write me a letter of introduction to his ex-colleague and to the school teacher at Wagu.

I'm not sure if I met Anton on Saturday or Sunday and I'm not sure whether I left for Wagu on Monday or Tuesday, but, whichever day it was, he fulfilled all his promises and sorted out my itinerary. Somewhere along the line he also arranged for a vehicle and for Larry to drive me to the beach for a swim: an unheard of respite in the manic sequence of events that had been driving me along. We swam from the beach at the International Sepik Hotel and were even given free beers as a favour to Larry who had recently performed traditional dancing there with the company. It was a long white beach under the fringe of palm trees that I had first trundled past on my way from the airport. The water was almost too warm to refresh, but I enjoyed a languid moment lounging and basking in the relief of being away from the hot streets, my hot room, and the telephone boxes outside the post office.

Sometime around then I also met Mary Sundrouwau and we had a long heart-to-heart sitting outside by the large round Raun Isi water tank. Previously, Mary had held the post of Assistant Secretary at the Department of Culture and Tourism. But she had resigned and now she ran East Sepik's first women's centre. She was having a running battle with the Premier. Repeatedly he had refused to see her. Finally she had pushed her way into his office and they had had a shouting match. He was so threatened by her, so convinced that she was a lefty extremist; but all she was doing was trying to improve the rights of the women of the Province. It was an uphill struggle. Traditionally it was a fiercely male-dominated society, and the local men were reluctant for it to alter. After generations of submissiveness it was extremely difficult for the women to stand up and dare to speak out. But Mary was adamant that things should change. She had commendable strength and commendable determination, though sometimes she felt that the mountain was just too steep, that there was just too much against her. I gave her a lot of acknowledgement. I applauded her efforts and empathized how hard it was to work in a vacuum without support. Mary was a big woman, a warrior woman, but she had a tired heart. It seemed she had never had a response like I gave her, certainly not from a man; and there by the water tank we felt a bond between us. Mary was also going to Ambunti; she had to attend a conference there with several other delegates from Wewak. Anton arranged for me to join the party. And that is how I found myself back on the Maprik highway: this time out in the wind on the back of a government vehicle. And this time, if Nod had been watching me leave, his alarm would have been tinged with approval – my status in PNG was definitely on the up!

❖ ❖ ❖

From Nigel's journal. Sunday 19 June.
Arrived at Rockhampton thirty-five minutes late, 3.55 p.m. and 29 degrees – some good heat but, alas, no Gordon and Mary Tompson. Their daughter, who organized the Melbourne Mastery, had, I hoped, told them I was coming. Waited. Tried to phone them; no phones working – unusually; up to now Australian call boxes had always worked. Found one that did, but no reply. Waited. Then a large, six-foot, six-inch-muscle-bound man, looking not unlike Ronald Reagan, approached: 'Are you Nigel?' They had been waiting at the other gate! Mary resembled a pouched hamster – very friendly and warm. Into their four-wheel-drive land cruiser and off on an hour's drive south. Gordon rules. Nicely. But he controls everything. A self-made man. Shrewd and aware. A man born to the land and who knows how to respect it. With balance. A conservationist – a 'realistic one' – he says. 'If central Australia is overrun with kangaroos there is no harm in shooting some.' He stopped using spray chemicals on his land long ago – it worked; his land flourished. Stopped using sprays on his cattle. It worked; they stayed disease-free.

We drive beside beautiful lush rainforest hills and past plains of tall sugar cane, some in delicate purple flower (like pampas grass), the hot, setting sun behind us. Arrive at 'The Donga', their caravan-type home – portakabins put together, set in deep bush

– just as it gets dark. Plenty of pretty, grey, black-eyed wallabies bounding along in front of us. I see some corpses lying by the side of the road. We turn into the red sand/mud bush track; gum tree-lined and 'tall boy' scattered through the bush. Pull up by the gums, planted palms and flower garden. Huge eagles' nest high up in one of the gums. Bush turkeys gobble around. I suffer from my decision not to declare my vegetarian diet and eat meat like I've not eaten it for years – mince, bacon, pork (roast and boiled), fish, chicken, more bacon and beef – thank god for one cheese and salad lunch on my own one day! It's a prawn farm, so prawns abound.

One morning at 5 a.m., glad to be feeling 100 per cent fit again, I get up and walk to the farm. Huge, oblong, one-acre ponds. Clay-banked sides, some of which have suffered in the recent hurricane. I peer into the murky water and see them – hundreds, thousands of prawns, crawling-swimming in the muddy slime. This is the only black prawn farm in the area – the black ones are particularly popular with the Japanese. Later I am taken on a tour of the property. Wild, surf-pounding, mangrove-edged beachfront which Gordon and Mary are hoping to sell to the Japanese to make into a resort. Millions of dollars if they get the right deal. They show me a book about the Tompson heritage which traces the family back to the first fleet convicts – something that makes them proud – 'Australian Royalty' they call themselves . . . seventh generation.

IV

Just before Maprik the road divides and we turned off down onto the flat swamplands of the Great Sepik Plains. The road here was even worse, deep troughs and pits where it had completely collapsed. Sometimes we had to veer off and plough our way through the bankside mud. And sometimes we had to nosedive into a *barat* (ditch) of water several feet deep where the swamp had taken over and reclaimed the road. All around, the tall Sepik grass ruled supreme, with only small stands of toppling, insecure forest. The porcelain sky was a heavy basin pressing down on our heads; the only relief, a distant line of mountains creeping along the horizon. There was almost no other traffic, just a few, dark-skinned, half-naked and dispirited-looking local people trailing between the sparsely positioned villages that bordered the bleak roadside.

Pagwi, the sub-district centre, on the banks of the Sepik River itself, felt like the back of beyond. An ugly, haphazard assortment of small meagre buildings and one corrugated trade store on narrow metal stilts set back from, but facing, the river. We parked right at the water's edge where the track petered out. The council boat had not yet arrived to pick us up. The muddy river stretched grey and uninviting and the humidity was sickening. A cloud of mosquitoes, that had been waiting especially for me, descended with a vengeance. I hurriedly plastered myself with mosquito cream and went to buy a bottle of pop. The trade storekeeper was an expat Australian; a chirpy, wiry, grey-haired man, keen to chat. He had been there for over twenty years, looking out on that swirling stretch of river. In exile from what, I wondered, and in penance for what? In the old days life had been pleasant enough, but of late things had changed for the worse. The trickle of tourists had tailed off to almost nothing and the local lads were turning into rascals. But, of course, they hadn't burgled him, they hadn't given him any trouble, he added emphatically; he was everyone's friend, they depended upon him. Tinned fish, tinned beef, crackers, salt, sugar, tea, Coca-Cola and Seven-up, cigarettes, matches and batteries. Mr Chirpy pottered and wiped down his counter; and chirpily greeted a vacant-eyed woman who begrudgingly deposited a small heap of toya before him.

At last the council dinghy arrived and I, Mary and the other delegates boarded. It was cooler on the river and the mosquitoes were blown away. Even the humidity seemed to break up a bit. For two hours, or maybe two and a half, the powerful outboard motor pulled against the heavy current as we followed the turnings and meanderings of the great grey expanse. The far-off banks were walls of Sepik grass and, sometimes, overhanging mangrove trees. The line of creeping mountains was getting closer. My image of the tropics was always of vivid colour; in reality, sometimes the reverse is true. It's as if the heat has drained out the pigment, as if the heavy blanket of humidity has dampened and deadened the vibrancy. That's what Ambunti was like. Or was it just my own weariness that drained and blanched and deadened? Whichever, as we pulled in, Ambunti looked almost as bleak and inhospitable as Pagwi. To the right, small scattered houses and an office on the hill, ahead the narrow grass airstrip, and to the left, the mission, the lodge and a few trade stores.

Three students were waiting for me. I was their assignment. They were on a three-week placement, learning administrative skills. I parted ways with Mary and the delegates, and the students took me along the airstrip to the main complex of low, one-storeyed government buildings beyond. There I was introduced to Julius, Anton's ex-colleague. Yes, Anton had informed him that I was coming. Unfortunately, because of the conference, all the accommodation was used up. I would have to sleep with the students on the floor of an empty, unused worker's house. Julius was preoccupied and not particularly friendly; no doubt he had the conference on his mind. The students took me to the empty house and showed me a tap in the long grass of the overgrown garden where I could wash. One of the council workers then informed us that we were to eat with him. He apologized that relations with his wife were not good, so we ate outside in the *haus win*, the shack with only a roof where people relax and siesta in the heat of the day. Supper was basic: rice and the inevitable tinned fish. He apologized again; but we all assured him we were grateful for anything.

While we were shovelling up the grub, another white man appeared: a tall, hyped-up fair-haired Australian. It was the Executive Adviser; the one who hadn't known about the forest on the phone. This time he seemed to know a lot. The pupils of his blue eyes were dilated, there was drink on his breath, his body was taut and excited. He had come up to Ambunti for the conference, but he had come by plane. He was here to put forward a major logging proposal for the area. All the preparatory work had been completed: surveys, feasibility studies and funding applications. His proposal would bring millions of kina to the province. Up at Bisorio, the kauri pine trees stretched forever over a deep rich carpet of moss. He had been there. He had seen them. The Japanese would pay a fortune for that timber. I casually asked about the environmental side. Was there a plan? Were there safeguards? Oh yes, sure, they wouldn't take the trees all at once. Not at first anyway. They would start close by at Wagu. My ears pricked up. It was my turn for my body to go taut. 'Wagu?' I asked innocently. 'Yes, the primary forest stretches all the way from Bisorio down to Wagu.' 'So, the environmentalists would applaud you?' I pushed gently; 'I don't know, they should', he replied, suddenly suspicious. 'That's great then', I retorted lightly.

The sharp question marks of caution that had momentarily crossed his eyes passed away. The bravura returned. He was confident. There were only a couple of guys who might try to

Wagu village, Papua New Guinea.

Waga on Wagu Lake.

Habe *(front)*
and Lucas Ketapi
(behind).

oppose him; only a few hiccups to everything being sewn up. The manic man paced up and down, his pent-up aspirations crazy for a sounding-board. But I carefully didn't show too much interest. After all, I was just that writer chap, the one working with the National Theatre, who had just wanted to see a bit of the wild. Little did he know my pupils were dilating too, taking in and recording every syllable. Little did I know that this was the beginning of another journey, far more challenging, far more demanding than any forest trek.

The Executive Adviser also spoke of his nationalized status. He had married a local woman in the Angoram district and he was now accepted as one of the clan. His efforts to protect his wantoks from exploitation were succeeding. In PNG the local people own the land; it is handed down from generation to generation. But recently they have often been tricked out of their ownership and so he was getting their land registered. It was time for the landowners to get their portion of the pie. But how big was *his* portion going to be, I wondered? In that panther-like pacing I saw the vision of priceless, tumbling kauris filling indeed the coffers of the people and the coffers of the province, but also filling to overbrimming his own coffers too.

I was unnerved by my chance meeting with the Executive Adviser. It took a double session of yoga before there was any hope at all of getting any sleep on the devastatingly hard floor. In India I had seen a panther in a cage. Its ice-blue eyes had startled me. And it was spattered with blood from its vicious attack on the carcass that had been thrown to it. Like a strange kind of *déjà vu*, I felt something of the same danger here, something of the same ruthlessness, the same ice eyes. But at least I had the strongest confirmation yet that I was, at last, really nearing the primary forest.

❖　❖　❖

From Rick's journal. Wagu village. Wednesday 22 June.
'Only two hours' they assure me as we set off in the fibreglass council dinghy from Ambunti; it's ten o'clock now so we should make it to Wagu by twelve. We cross the wide, sluggish Sepik River and head upstream. After a few kilometres we turn off left along a narrow tributary. On each side high water grass gives way to swamp. Giant white egrets flap away. Soon we begin to pass wads of floating grass. These get bigger and bigger until they choke the whole channel. Now we are squeezing our way through, and the

men who came with us for the ride are pushing and pulling with all their might. Eleven o'clock. It's hot now. There are mosquitoes and ants and the swamp trees are full of ragged eagles peering down at us. Hovering. Swooping. Twelve o'clock. It's even hotter. And I am afraid they're going to turn back. The way is completely blocked. It looks hopeless. Then suddenly we come upon five men in a narrow wooden canoe. They are Wagu villagers, almost naked, bearded, with dark aboriginal faces. They have been cutting the grass, trying to clear the choked way. Apparently it is even worse further up, and so I am going to be left here. My heart thumps as I step clumsily into the canoe. The Wagu men turn their faces away. I notice they have holes at the end of their noses. I sit down between the spears and the long knives. Then the oldest man offers his hand and we shake. His name is Solomon, he is a village elder. There is a zealous light in his eyes and I wave goodbye to the council boat, knowing I am safe.

The men work in silence. Cutting, hacking through the tangled grass. Sometimes they climb out, chest-deep in the thick muddy water. Or, where the water is deeper, they are left hanging to a clump of weeds as they tear and push and split the grass. One o'clock and it's still getting hotter. I have to soak my hat and keep pouring water over my shoulders. Two o'clock; frightened waterhens scurry for cover. Now the men force the canoe through the grass and up onto a mudbank at the edge of the swamp; they leave me in the canoe and disappear into the thicket. It is still getting hotter and my water bottle is empty. I am beginning to feel the edge of panic. But then they return with coconuts and handfuls of a small red fruit, something like sweet baby peppers. They split the coconut open for me and my sweat-depleted body gulps down the elixir-like milk. Solomon unpacks a bundle of strong-smelling, black, smoked fish and baked sago. He shares it with me. 'Number one', he says. 'Number one' is the only English expression he knows, so soon lots of things become number one. All afternoon they go on working. And I sit on the hard little stump of wood, the only seat in the canoe. A test of patience. A test of trust. The lowering sun goes hazy. Ducks fly overhead. The vast expanse of sky begins to turn a dull pink. And finally, finally, I understand that it is time to turn homeward bound. The light falls fast and just as a big moon begins to rise, we reach the edge of the huge glassy lake.

The youngest man starts speaking English for the first time: 'Lake full of crocodiles' he says. Then he points to the distant high mountains. 'Beautiful', I say. 'Yes'; his eyes are shining with pride.

The men are all standing now, dark silhouettes, paddling in silence across the lake. All around, the hills are turning from purple to blue to black. Empty forested hills, home of the legendary cassowary and the sacred birds of paradise. It is night by the time we approach the shore and a few little lights begin to appear. We pull up on the mud outside a large house on high stilts. The man with shining eyes says, 'My name is Lucas, you stay with Lucas'. Someone calls up to the house and suddenly there is a wild explosion of excitement. Women and children tumble down the steep ladder shrieking with laughter and yelling 'White man, white man!' My bag is bundled into the house and Lucas takes me along a narrow path in the dark. We arrive at a creek in a grove of sago palms; we strip and jump into the shallow cool water. Moonlight splashes through the palm fronds. The undergrowth around us is alive.

Back in the house, I am introduced to Lucas's children – Jerome, Keith, Ringo, Barbara and baby Emanuel hanging from his mummy's breast. Barbara and Emanuel scream with terror and continue screaming every time I look at them, while Maria, Lucas's big laughing wife, brings us supper of rice and fish and saksak. Lucas's house is partitioned into several sections. The main one in which we are squatting is furnitureless, except for a couple of carved stools and a narrow, roughly hewn table standing against the inner wall. From it, doorless gaps lead to Maria's kitchen with an open fire on a hearth of stones, the area where the family sleeps, and the small space that is to be my 'room'. As we eat, the neighbours begin to pile in. Some of the women are naked to the waist. All squat low on the ground in the lamplight, laughing gently, looking away. The air is still thick and the windows are holes, open to the night. When you go to the Sepik, I had been told, you will see everyone is dancing. Now I understand what they mean. Everyone in the room is in continual motion, swatting, slapping, warding off the circling cloud of mosquitoes; but the movements are easy, second nature, lackadaisical. Mosquitoes are the enemy of the Sepik, Lucas says, and so the Sepik people have to spend their whole life dancing. Later, after the neighbours have left and the children have fallen asleep, Lucas shows me to my bed: a thin, slightly melted strip of foam under a yellowing mosquito net, especially rigged up in my honour. As I climb under the net, he says through the bamboo partition: 'You not worry, you safe now, you in Lucas house.' The quality of his voice is tender, full of love and pride. Outside, the moon has turned the lake silver. A hollow bird calls overhead. Inside the air is still hot and thick.

Still heavy. Still full of mosquitoes. My heart wells over. At last, have I truly arrived?

❖ ❖ ❖

That first night Lucas also took me to meet the schoolteacher. Along a thin, low path, between tall, dark pulsating trees, the schoolteacher lives in a small house also on stilts. He was dumbfounded when Lucas called up and told him that there was a white man to see him. I handed over the letter and he scrutinized it in astonishment with light from an oil lamp that his wife brought out and held close for him. 'Very good, very good, we will have to arrange everything that you request. We will arrange some interviews, we will arrange for you to interview the people.' 'Oh, no, no', I said, alarmed: 'Please, I just want to be easy, I don't want anything formal.' At one end of the house there was a separate room where the young assistant teacher lived. She came out onto the narrow strip of balcony as well. She was equally amazed and, doing the Sepik dance of swatting and slapping off the mosquitoes, she offered her help as well. Anything I needed, I just had to come and ask. The humble schoolhouse stood silent on the hill in the warm moonlight. The Wagu community school was only four years old; it was still a great novelty and a great treasure to the local people of the village. Previously, there had been no education at all and most of the villagers were still completely illiterate. And, although funds from the education department were very minimal, the friendly headmaster and his dancing assistant were optimistic and pleased.

'Where will you stay?' 'With Lucas; he has invited me to sleep in his house.' 'Oh, that is good; you would be welcome here, but this house is so small.' I was happy walking back through the dark trees. The teachers were outsiders, charming and friendly enough, but it was far more exciting to be up in Lucas's sprawling jungle palace. Spongy, shifting, slatted floor; glassless, meshless windows like big mouths gaping into the black steaming night. Hushed, peering villagers crouching in the hot shadows; mysterious eyes and hunched limbs eerily lit by the hissing yellow hurricane lamp and skinny naked children carelessly wound around knees and laps, softly, safely, perfectly asleep, confident of, but oblivious to, the big black rhythmical hands fanning away the ever-insistent mosquitoes. I felt confident too. Safe too. Cradled in the very lap of rhythmical Papua New Guinea, rocked in the very bosom of the throbbing tropics. The mighty blanket of the forest, tucked up close around me.

On my first morning in Wagu I played with Jerome and Keith and Ringo but alas, not Barbara. Every time she saw the awful white giant she screamed in terror and clung to her mummy's skirt. Then, with the boys leading me by the hand, we went wokabaut to the village. Lucas's house was set apart and to reach the village we had to follow the path that led to the men's creek where we had washed, past the women's creek and up a steep bank. On a gentle slope, two long rows of marvellous bush houses faced each other. Between them, a wide space served as the village thoroughfare; this led up to the aid post, the medical centre run by Lucas, and down to the lapping water's edge below. These houses were all on stilts like Lucas's; strong whole tree trunks as the main uprights and a thick woven thatch of sago palm fronds for the generously proportioned roofs. Children and dogs played along the brown earth thoroughfare and smoke drifted up from the houses.

At the bottom end, the end near the lake, we first came to the mission. It and the aid post were the only two buildings in Wagu with a metal roof. The missionary, an American who had come to translate the Bible into their tokples, and who had stayed for twenty years, seemed to have departed for an over-due sabbatical, though the villagers were vague about where he was. He and his wife had brought up two daughters in the village. Sooner or later he would be coming back. No one seemed very concerned. He was against their traditions and their ceremonies so they had let their spirit house fall into disrepair and it had collapsed just a few years before. The missionary belonged to the Assembly of God; now most of the villagers also belonged to it and most of them went to church. The church itself was a low shack with open walls and simple narrow benches for pews. While the missionary was away, a Wagu man, whom he had trained as pastor, took the Sunday service. But not so many people bothered to show up; mysteriously they were finding other things to do.

Halfway up the thoroughfare we stopped to rest in the Men's House; this was another open shack. A fringe of dry grass hung from the roof and billowed out in the erratic gusts of hot breeze. At one end, there was a high shelf on which the men sat, or against which they leaned, and around the baked floor several beautifully carved stools were scattered. In the centre, a small fire smoked, and, around it, scruffy-coated hunting dogs snoozed. Women were forbidden to enter the Men's House, though they good-humouredly shouted their comments as they passed by. Lucas told me to sit on one of the stools while he went up to perform his duties at the aid post. I should stay and talk to the men. The circle of serious faces looked down at me. Dark, rugged, bearded, aboriginal. Steady eyes, steady breath, muscular bodies. Arrows and spears, flies and smoke. What were we going to talk about, I wondered? My Pidgin was monosyllabic and Solomon wasn't even there to say 'number one'. So I breathed steadily too and in silence tried to absorb this extraordinary moment.

William had talked about the bridging of thousands of years. Here we had to build a bridge too: a bridge across a timeless age of forest knowledge. And though marred, yes, and tampered with, yes, by missionary and colonial, a knowledge still deep-rooted and clearly very much alive. In that gulf between us there was a great silence. An unvoiced questioning. A heavy curtain. I could feel my breath stirring the thick air, I could feel the smoke anaesthetizing my senses as the gulf between us yawned and gaped wide open. For a moment I wanted to go, I couldn't manage this. These other eyes looking into me, these other souls unveiling me. But then it was all right. We smiled. We even laughed. I've no idea about what. But among human beings isn't there always plenty to laugh at? Aren't there always lots of Number Ones? Distant serious faces cracked into twinkling big-jawed recognition. The curtain opened and the gulf slammed closed, just like a crocodile clamping shut its huge and terrible mouth. I had passed some kind of test and I was accepted in Wagu.

Up in the aid post, Lucas was administering to snuffling children with ringworm and pot bellies. Many of the adults had ringworm too. The staple diet was saksak and meat or fish. These people by tradition were not gardeners and didn't eat vegetables or fruit. The shelf of medicines was almost empty. A few unwashed plastic beakers and used syringes lay on a small table. Quietly, patiently, Lucas was doing his best. There was something in his calm unobtrusive manner that reminded me of Jau, but here the conditions were even harder.

By evening, after much discussion and debate, Lucas had organized my bikpela wokabaut. The following morning Joseph, Waga and Solomon would paddle me across the lake and take me into the bikpela bus. And so, once again, I settled down to try to sleep on the eve of fulfilling my dream; this time under Lucas's fragile mosquito net which I had tried to mend where the threads were pulling loose. As at Ilahita, I have no recollection of how I was feeling; I had probably blanked myself off again. I think by now I had built a steel shield around me, a shield on which was written in large fat capitals: FORTIFIED PROTECTION AGAINST THE DISAPPOINTMENT OF NOT REACHING THE PRIMARY FOREST. And I don't think I even took it off at night. Maybe that's why I slept so badly, creaking and clanking through the early hours. And so in the morning I just got up, put on my boots, slung my water bottle over my shoulder and climbed into the dugout canoe. At the narrow prow which tapered almost to a point, the head of a crocodile was carved. All the Wagu canoes had a carving, each one different, to identify its owner. My alarm bells started to ring when Joseph insisted on bringing two of his children. But who was I to say what they could or could not manage, he was well confident that they were up to a wokabaut.

We pulled up on a muddy bank where some other villagers were also landing. A few yards beyond, the luscious singing Sepik grass gave way to the towering edge of the forest. The men and women gathered up their bundles, their bilums and their machetes for another day's work in the bush. We soon came upon three women already hard at it on the soggy ground; they were working the saksak, preparing wild sago. The sago that they eat is actually the pith of the big sago palm. The tree is felled, the bark is ripped off and the pith is beaten and pummelled with a small metal tool. It is back-breaking work and the two younger women never stopped as we approached, but continued, steadily, rhythmically beating and pounding, pounding and pummelling, the sweat dripping down their faces, down their chests and off their naked breasts. Their little children sat around them on the mud, solemnly watching the slow, arduous operation. The older woman, eyes almost lost in the folds of her crumpled face, worked by a small stream. In a large, sieve-like contraption with a long bamboo chute, she was scooping up water and washing the beaten pith. Then she was laying it out to dry in the sun; as a coarse cake of flour, it would then be ready to bake and eat. A little further along we came to a man who was cutting poles for his house. And as we started to ascend a slope, we heard the shrill and piercing cry of a bird of paradise. I caught another glimpse of that foaming golden tail. Another huge, turquoise bird, with a chaotic spectacular crest, thundered away through the trees. In the distance there were more birds of paradise calling.

Our way descended again, and we were a merry band marching along the wide, winding path, pressed hard with villagers' footprints, and shady dark beneath the forest canopy. Waga, who had the brightest of all the bright eyes I had seen, walked with a celebratory swagger. Joseph, strongly set and glowingly vigorous, led his children by the hand with easy care. And Solomon, puffing slightly and murmuring 'Number one', magnanimously took up the rear. God, I must have been a pain in the neck: 'Where are the big trees? Where are the big trees?' I kept asking; 'This forest is half cultivated, this is where the people work. Where are the big trees, where is the bikpela bus?' Joseph kept reassuring me but I kept asking again and again. I had learned enough Pidgin to nag.

Along the side of the path at this point there was a wooden construction, almost like a narrow railway line. This was how they dragged their newly-carved canoes out of the forest, they explained. They dragged them along on rollers. We marched on, and soon the little children wanted to be dragged on rollers too. I was not sympathetic. 'Where are the big trees, where are the big trees, where are the big trees?' Now the path was narrow. We were walking up a steep hill. The trunks of the trees were slim and sleek and Solomon, puffing and murmuring, was left far behind. 'He is on the edge of being an old man', Joseph explained in Pidgin. But I didn't want to slow down for him, I was going mad. 'Where is the bikpela bus? When will we reach it?' Suddenly we came out into a small clearing. Below, the blue lake stretched away. We had walked in a big loop, we were almost back at our starting point. I seized up.

In the clearing a man and two boys were building a canoe. They had felled a tree which had smashed and split open the undergrowth, and with simple axes they were cutting and gouging and hollowing out the long straight trunk. For a while my nagging ceased. I sat on a stump and looked at the lake. It didn't even turn grey. 'What is the matter?' said a timid voice. One of the boys had been to school in Ambunti and spoke a little English; his name was Frank. I explained and he translated my words into Pidgin. Oh, they had thought I'd just wanted to go for a nice walk. They had not understood that I wanted to see the big forest. They just thought I wanted a spin; to see the life of Wagu and hear the birds. Silly ridiculous Ricky held up his shield for fear of going completely demented and hissed back his exasperation. Oh why, oh why, oh why, didn't he just want to hear the birds sing? And oh why, oh why, oh why, couldn't a nice spin satisfy? The shining eyes of Waga and the glowing eyes of Joseph were upon me. They were just waiting, waiting to see what would happen next. 'You talk with Lucas', Frank whispered ruefully. 'Tell Lucas about it.' 'Yes, I'll have to', I blurted back, 'I will have to explain it all again. I will have to make it even clearer. I'm in a hurry now, my time is running out.'

Having disgraced myself by allowing an angry rasp to creep into my voice, and discredited my guides, whose only wish was to please me, I tried to make up for it by taking a photo of the canoe and showing my admiration for their highly-skilled craftsmanship. We all looked down at the half-finished dugout. An incredible amount of patient work was still required; but, unlike me, the three canoe-builders were not in a hurry. Dominic, the second boy, wore a necklace of blanched snake's vertebrae and he was the youngest one in the village to have the holes in the end of his nose. The master builder was massively muscular and seemed to know neither English nor Pidgin. All three were pleased that I liked the canoe and all five were pleased that I was smiling again.

It was already evening as the canoe slipped out onto the lake again. Waga stood firm and perfectly balanced, pulling on the long oar. And, as the forested hills mellowed in the watery melting light, his eyes were still the brightest and there was still a swaggering lilt in the almost musical motion of his rowing. Back at the house, Lucas lit the hurricane lamp in his slow, steady, methodical way. He summoned Frank, and another long debate and discussion ensued. Waga and Habe, Lucas's neighbour, were chosen to take me to the big forest, to the far forest; Frank would come too as interpreter. We would spend three days in the bush. We would start tomorrow at the crack of dawn.

We did. And this time Lucas drove us with his outboard motor around the bulge of land on which Wagu was situated to the very bottom tip of the lake. We waved goodbye and set off on our journey for the *bikpela diwais* (the big trees). We walked for several hours, mostly uphill. My lips had swollen and erupted again as a result of the long day in the canoe. I was afraid that they would go septic in the heat, and so I kept them coated in Savlon. But my streaming sweat diluted it and the gungy mixture trickled and dripped off my chin. At the height of midday we stopped on a white pebbled beach beside a fast-flowing river. We swam. We ate. And the coconut milk, with which they had filled my water bottle, was my saviour. There were giant, electric-blue butterflies; a profuse crimson flower called the flame of the forest waterfalled down the trees on the river bank. We crossed the river and we cut a hole in the forest wall. We crawled through it into the echoing, green cathedral and walked on. The afternoon began to dull and the colours began to deepen. It was time to set up camp. Waga and Habe began to search for a suitable site.

We were close to the river. The ground was very wet and treacherous. We were cutting our way. I must have asked Frank something; maybe I asked him how many hours tomorrow it would take to reach the big trees. Frank didn't answer at first; he had a rueful way about him anyway. I don't think I pushed him. But then he said something like we were already there. I think I must have flayed my arms about a bit, I might even have shouted, because Waga and Habe came hurrying back. And all three stared with open mouths. The idiot was raving again. I lost my balance and fell into knee-deep black mud, grazing my arm against a frond of jagged spines. Wasn't it kind of them not to laugh? I'm sure I would have.

What happened next I remember very clearly. An invisible somebody got hold of my shoulders and shook them. The same invisible somebody said with great deliberation: 'Ricky, for god's sake, slow down. Take stock. Or you really are going to come a cropper.' I pulled myself out of the mud and we all sat down. Long pause. Only the merciless river continuing by. And the tall thin trees dead still. A longer pause. Then Frank asked ruefully, 'What you like?' 'I don't know', I answered quietly; 'I don't know.'

'You not happy?'

'No, me not happy.'

'Me sorry.'

'Me sorry too.' Waga and Habe shook their heads slowly. Pause.

'So, is there really no bigger forest,' I asked even more quietly, 'no bigger trees?'

'Oh yes, but it is far away. Too far away.'

'So, we go there tomorrow, OK?'

Waga and Habe shook their heads again. 'Too far.'

'Why? I want to go. That's what I came for. Surely if we get up and walk all day we can get there?'

'You have to go all the way to Gahom.'

'What's Gahom?' I asked.

'The village of our wantoks. It is three days' long walking through the big forest.'

'So? Let's go. Let's go there, I don't mind how long it takes.'

'Next time. Next time. Now it is too far.'

Long pause. I was trying to obey the invisible voice.

'We make camp now. We must hurry. You hungry? We make *kaikai*. Tomorrow we show you special trees, the special trees worth plenty toya.'

As Frank and Habe began to cut a clearing for the camp, Waga set off along a fallen tree trunk that bridged the river. His eyes were as keen as they were bright and within no time at all he returned with several, large, dangling, kicking fish which he had speared. I sat down on a jutting-out root beside the river. If this was it, I had better start enjoying it. But the rainforest is no place for reverie or whimsical reflection: two giant black wasps descended upon me immediately and refused to leave me alone. I returned to the camp, they followed me. I sat by the now smoking fire trying to ward them off but they had no intention of going; I wouldn't have minded too much but their sting was quite nasty. This dance requires bigger movements than the mosquito dance. Waga came up and asked me what I was doing. With one fell swoop he matter-of-factly killed them both. This white man really was a bit of a twit! The fresh fish was delicious. Earlier, Waga had put his hands into a large mound of earth and pulled out two enormous eggs: wild fowl, Frank had explained. Now they cooked them for me. They were almost all yolk; strong orange in colour, strong orange in taste. But it was all good protein.

With sure, fast hands the night quickly engulfed the forest around us. The little lamp that Habe had carried glowed encouragingly, and, together with the smouldering fire, formed a tiny arc of safety and comfort around us. My three caretakers sat up and chatted quietly. Habe's lined face and secret eyes showed full contentment as he puffed on his *brus*, his home-made bush cigarette. I lay back, curled up on my groundsheet and, as I did so, their voices were half drowned out by the inpouring sounds of the jungle; it rolled in on us like a great tide. A mainswell of belching frogs and crackling, clicking, whirring cicadas. A foam of whispered hissings and purrings. And occasional distant breakers of low vibrating booms or the occasional muffled scream. Suddenly there was a big plop in the river close by. 'Bikpela pukpuk' (crocodile), said Frank with yawning disinterest. My groundsheet lay on the outside, nearest the river. I asked Frank to change places with me.

In the morning we climbed the steep hill under which we had camped and they showed me some fine specimens of the kauri pine. These were the trees that the Executive Adviser had told me about. Incredibly tall and incredibly straight, they thrust up through the clouds into the sky. Yes, the government people had been here to look for them. They had also camped here. The government were going to come and cut them down. But the trees were few and far between and the slopes were steep; the damage caused in extracting them, would surely be enormous.

Frank was looking at me anxiously. 'You happy now? You like the big trees?' I tried to be, and I tried to say yes. And they tried to be pleased. But if this was it I saw no point in staying another night in the forest. The clawing humidity, the hungry insects and my flagging strength did not bode well for another night around the camp fire. Not just for the fun of it. So we began to retrace our steps. It was a long way. We passed kicked up earth where wild pigs had been rooting for food. Suddenly Waga froze. There were two of them, just over there. He raised his spear. He took off on light feet, running like the wind. He hurled the spear and missed. Frank pointed out a huge lizard-like creature, clinging to an upright branch. It was so still, it appeared turned to stone. '*Gutpela kaikai*' (good food) Frank said, licking his lips. 'No, please don't kill it.' 'No, me no kill it', he said ruefully. We crossed the river and passed the white beach. We left the electric blue butterflies behind and the crimson flame of the forest. We trudged uphill and for hours I don't think I saw anything at all. I was fighting that sober stern voice; kicking against blank walls. Trying to ignore the terrible tug of those forever out of reach *really* big trees.

I hardly noticed when Waga froze again. I had to be cautioned to stop a second time. What was it? Waga was beckoning me to tiptoe to him and look up. There were birds of paradise in the canopy directly above us. Several of them, and they seemed oblivious of our presence. My previous sightings had been fleeting only, but now here they were in their full breathtaking beauty. William had said of the birds of paradise that they are higher beings than us. Now I understood what he meant and why they above all are the figurehead and the inspiration of the Melanesian spirit. Pure heaven somersaulting over my head. Yellow and white and gold in frothing feathers. Creamy foamings of cascading tails. They were cavorting, pirouetting, hanging precariously upside down. And then, on a whim, with a flash of auburn wings and a careless toss of the whole caboodle of golden and snowy lace, they danced off to perch ecstatically somewhere else; grazing the sky with another delicious swish of buttercups, sunshine, snow crystals and spangled stars. There were four or five of them trying to outdo each other. Sleek yellow heads with deep green bibs, spiralling amongst the leaves; their piercing cry of haughty omnipotence splitting the currents of air down which they gloriously skidded. Frank whispered in explanation: this was the place that they always came to; these were the trees on which they fed. Now they were moving off. And their calls, like cut diamond, like tangy nectar, like a divine proclamation, resounded and rebounded over the quivering forest basin below us.

I looked up again at the trees. Their trunks were slim and whitish. Their boughs were high and bouncing. The leaves themselves were delicate and small. Birds of paradise. Trees of paradise. I was completely happy and completely satisfied at last. I had been clinging on to too fixed a dream. Why had I got such a one-and-only image of the forest? I was in Papua New Guinea, not in the Amazon. There were many, many different kinds of primary forest. I was in one of them; there was no doubt about that. Big trees, small trees, fat trees, thin trees, the primary forest is the forest that has never been cut, has grown and multiplied of itself through millennia of time. And, but for a few canoes and a few main posts for a few bush houses, this forest I was in remained undisturbed as it always had been. I had been supremely privileged with a close-up glimpse of heaven. And under the trees of paradise I had, thank God, come to my senses at last.

We strolled on, and I basked in the fullness of the magic afternoon. The light was mellowing and the canopy above our heads was shimmering. Birdsong poured out of the boughs and cricket chatterings were already beginning to crescendo in the emerald undergrowth. Waga froze once more, there was something else up in the high branches. It was a *cuscus*, a furry primate. It was dashing, nimble-footed, to hide in the top of a large hollow tree trunk. Habe and Frank lit a fire in the trunk; the plan was to smoke it out. But though their smoke billowed up, we never saw it again. Hopefully it survived the smoke and did its coughing after we left.

Down at the lakeside there was no canoe. We were a day early. How were we going to get back to Wagu? There was only one way: to walk it. It took a good two hours more. Two hours on top of what I had thought was the last step I could manage. Cockatoos shrieked their warnings as night fell and, as we finally neared the village, the big village drums started beating in welcome. As I staggered out of the trees and tottered into the space between the Wagu houses, Maria and children were already there to meet me. 'Oh Richard, oh Richard!' They were so relieved and so happy to see me safely home. In the delight of the moment, my exhaustion totally left me and I sat on the steps of one of the houses for a while, entertaining the villagers. Then for a dip in the creek, and two whole pineapples to myself which I guzzled in greediness; my sugar-drained body absolutely gulping up the sweetness. That night, a totally knackered but happy fellow lay down under the mosquito net, and those gorgeous wings and frothing feathers transported him to a peaceful sleep. I also had a new dream. I had to go to Gahom, of that there was no doubt. But not tomorrow; for the present I was content.

On my last day in Wagu, I made a final attempt to make friends with Barbara. She still yelled the place down whenever the horror of my looming figure came anywhere near her, much, I'm afraid, to the wicked delight of Jerome, Ringo and Keith, her sadistic brothers. And so, on the steep ladder outside the house, I reached over for her. If I actually held her, I thought, if I played with her and sang with her on my knee, surely, surely I would be able to bring her round. I was wrong. The scream of terror tripled and she peed all down my trousers. The wicked brothers hooted as, defeated, I returned her to her mummy. Oh, dear little Barbara, I'm so sorry, please forgive me. The depth and power of her fear was extraordinary. I found myself wondering if it had sprung from something further back; a deeper memory, even a karmic one. Or somehow a distillation of the collective memory of her people, a memory of horrible abuse and horrible mistreatment by the early bludgeoning whites.

I also went to see the headmaster again. He told me bitterly that Wagu had been forgotten, passed over and left out of the government's plans. Where were the loggers, where was the development that they so desperately needed? There had been talk and more talk but never any action. I felt my own heat rising. I had to say something in answer. I couldn't just leave it be. I told him forcefully about the destruction that I had witnessed. Logging and quick money was one thing, but the long-term devastation of a beautiful forest was another. Before he welcomed the loggers perhaps he should have a real think about the consequences. In other parts of PNG, in the Gogol Valley that had been much publicized, the lives of the local people had already been ruined. Of course development was important to him, of course I could understand that, but wouldn't it be better to find an alternative development in which the forest was preserved? The schoolmaster's ears pricked up and he back-pedalled fast. 'Yes, yes, of course. What you say is true. Perhaps we should call a meeting for the men of the village so you can speak with them about this.'

He didn't; but, at my request, Lucas did. And so I held a meeting in the Men's House and warned the villagers of the dangers ahead: exploitation, overlogging, the problems around reforestation, the threat to wildlife and the effects development could have on their community. They listened with rapt attention as I held Solomon's hand and addressed my words to him, interpreted by the village government representative. I also promised to send them some back-up information and encouraged them to form a watchdog committee.

The elder, Solomon, absorbed my words with an air of great

profundity. The government representative was Andrew, a tall man whose handsomeness and sensitivity was blurred by a troubled cloud that hung around his stooping shoulders. Andrew lived in the biggest house in Wagu, opposite the mission. I was keen that he should do the translating. I was keen for him to be included; I didn't want any suspicions that I was agit-propping. I was only giving a warning, only offering my own experience of what I had seen with my own eyes. I tried to keep it simple, short and unemotional. But looking into the deep inquiring Wagu eyes around me I knew how vulnerable and gullible these people were. And in those long, strong moments, the gulf now bridged, I saw how fragile and how threatened was their forest and their life.

Lucas took me down to Ambunti at the crack of the following dawn. I had cut things pretty fine. My plane left from Wewak that evening and my jet for Sydney the following afternoon. But I had anticipated that this might happen and I had brought enough cash for a plane ticket from Ambunti to Wewak; the flight, by TelAir, the local airline, was only forty minutes. However, soon we learned that Monday was the only day on which there was no flight. So Lucas took me to one of the churches to meet the man that booked passengers onto the mission planes. The only mission plane had already left and no more were expected for a day or two. We tried to find out if anyone was going downriver by boat. They weren't. And even if they had been I would have been too late; the PMVs from Pagwi left very early in the morning. So that was that, I was stuck.

At the office of the Pacific Island Ministries, I telephoned Mark in Port Moresby. 'Ah, Richard, I thought you'd been eaten by headhunters', he chuckled, and I imagined him preening his smart Afro haircut. 'No problem. I will change your Wewak flight to Wednesday morning and I will change your Sydney ticket to Friday. Friday is the next flight out of Moresby to Sydney.'

'Thank you, Mark, I don't know what I'd do without you.'

'Stay in Wewak forever probably. Turn into a Sepik warrior.'

I didn't fancy traipsing back up the airstrip for more of Julius's reluctant hospitality. Lucas suggested I might be able to stay with his cousin-sister, but I just needed to crash out by myself and so I decided to settle for the ill-famed Ambunti Lodge. Ill-famed only because it charged such exorbitant prices, out of all proportion with what it offered. I booked myself in; they unlocked the shower. I explained to Lucas that I needed to rest and I lay down in the little square room under a rattling fan.

I half dozed peacefully for about an hour. Then I began to be plagued by the madness of what I had done. Julius hadn't really been unfriendly, just preoccupied. After all, he had a whole conference to organize; I had probably been the last straw. The students had been very friendly; they would be looking forward to seeing me again. The empty house had been perfectly OK for the odd night, and the meal outside the council worker's house had been fine. So what was I doing in this lodge? Paying through the teeth for nothing. Supporting a racket that wasn't even supporting itself. Where were the visitors? Where were the tourists? I was the only guest in sight. I got up quickly and repacked. There was nobody in the bar so I wrote a note. I explained that I had changed my mind and gone to stay with my wantoks. I would come back in the evening to pay for my cup of tea. And I left.

As predicted, the students were delighted to see me and even Julius managed a smile. After supper we sat in the large courthouse. They had homework to do and I thought I'd take the chance to catch up on some notes. I opened my neglected journal and wrote one sentence: 'Sitting in the council chambers of Ambunti, remote district centre up the Sepik River, first electric lights I have seen for two weeks and whirling fans trying to keep out the mosquitoes. I am the guest of the district officer . . .' But I was more tired than I had realized. Dog tired. Ready even for the hardest of floors.

On Tuesday morning the TelAir flight was unsure; it had rained a lot, maybe too much for the aeroplane to land on the narrow grass runway. I tried to phone Nod, back in Sydney now, to tell him that I wouldn't be coming today. I couldn't get through. I went back and sat on the edge of the airstrip waiting. Flummoxed. I tried to phone Nod again and finally, just before midday, I got through. His voice was surprisingly clear and close. I told him the time of my Friday flight. And even as I put the phone down I heard the distant droning of an aircraft. Excitedly I ran back up the side of the runway as the small plane swooped out of the sky and landed. Waga appeared from nowhere to say goodbye, and Petrus, another Wagu man, with him. Andrew, the government representative, appeared as well; he was flying to Wewak too. There was a third passenger and a young Australian pilot; between us we managed to fill the six-seater plane pretty well. We took off almost immediately and juddered along with the winding Sepik River beneath us.

At Raun Isi I was welcomed like the prodigal son. Most of the company were back now and they piled out of the kitchen to greet me. In the evening, as Alice and Larry were preparing my farewell supper, Anton arrived by truck with his wife Nancy and several members of her family. He had other ideas. I was instructed to jump on the back of the truck and off we bumped, turning left past Sunset Market and out of Wewak into the lush countryside. This was the coast road, it went north all the way to the border with Irian Jaya. This was the last thing I felt like, another journey; but the wind and the flying evening colours were refreshing, I had to admit. About forty minutes later we turned off down a narrow track towards the sea and stopped at Nancy's village right on the beach. Two of her cousins walked with me on the perfect curve of the white sandy bay. The sky was as red as the flame of the forest and its flowers were scattered over the sea. Across the water the silhouette of a large island loomed and at our feet the white sand turned pink. I stripped off and ran into the red sea. The cousins laughed, it was just another night in the back garden to them. When I came out, both water and sky had turned magenta and the sickle moon was already gleaming over the ashen island. The feast was laid outside on the sand and Nancy's mother presented me with a little billum that she had woven herself.

When we finally lurched back to the Raun Isi campus I had to sit down for a second feast. Larry and Alice had everything waiting; I couldn't disappoint them. The actors whose room I had slept in had now returned and so I spent the last night on the floor of the little office. Anton and Nancy came back at 5 a.m. to take me to the airport, with Nancy's father driving. They gave me a wonderful farewell and, uncharacteristically, the plane took off on time. Mark was waiting for me at Port Moresby. 'Richard, goodness, whatever's happened to you? No wonder the cannibals didn't put you in their stew.' He had borrowed his boss's car and he drove me, a bearded, hollow-cheeked wreck, to Air Niugini Hill. Campbell was out and the first thing that he noticed on his return were my boots lying by the door. He didn't recognize them as mine and he got a shock when the white spectre appeared. He had to hurry back to work and I asked him to get a message to William at the National Theatre.

That evening we sat out on the balmy balcony together. Campbell was of course dismayed about my wokabaut in Ilahita. The river we had come to was only the beginning. They were supposed to have taken me much further. We hadn't even reached the place where the big forest began. But never mind, I kept telling him: 'I saw the bird of paradise and I had a wonderful time with your family. They are wonderful people and they want you to go and visit them soon.' Campbell's face clouded over; the situation was more complicated than I had understood. Shortly before his father died just a few years ago, he had come to Port Moresby to persuade Campbell to marry. To honour his father's request, Campbell had reluctantly conceded. He had married a young Christian woman and they had adopted a son. But Campbell's ways had changed; after all, he had never spent much time in his village. Those childhood years in Melbourne had taken their toll. The night when his white foster dad had died, the young Campbell had wandered the streets, feeling that a part of his own spirit had died as well. Perhaps it had.

Campbell's life had been troubled ever since. The marriage had been a disaster. He had found his wife's rigorous Christianity intolerable. He had found the prying eyes of his family even worse. They didn't understand him, they couldn't understand him, and they just made him feel guilty, ashamed for not fulfilling the role that had been carved for him. Now all he wanted was a divorce. He was planning to resign from Air Niugini and move across to Australia. He had saved up enough money to buy a property. He would live with his white brother. They were very close. His white brother was the only one who understood him. But I could see it also wasn't that easy. He was still a member of the Cassowary Clan. He still had the forest in his blood. When the mission had bought a sawmill and had started to cut down the trees on his land, he had written them a warning letter. He was ready to go and threaten them at gunpoint. I remembered his story of pinning the passengers against the wall. Yes, he confided, when he got mad, he got out of control. Someone else took over; he didn't know what he was doing. Yes, he might well go to Australia, but I could see that half his soul would always be in Ilahita. 'I drink too much. Always drinking, always getting drunk. I must kick the habit, it's doing me no good.' The starry wind played around us. But Campbell needed more than a starry wind to soothe and heal his torn heart.

On Thursday, I waited for William all day and wrote my letter to Mother, Father and all. Campbell had passed on my message so I was sure that sooner or later he would arrive. But he didn't. Maybe the message had never got through. In the evening, Campbell got me a taxi and I went over to William's house to find him. He and Puele were just finishing their supper; the message hadn't got through. 'We thought you had already gone back to Australia. We thought you had forgotten us.' William was a sorry sight. He had a bad eye infection; he could hardly see. And his spirit was down too, he was having a battle with his actors. A visit to Townsville in Queensland had been on the cards, but he had decided to cancel it. He had felt that the company wasn't ready. The actors were angry; they had been looking forward to their sojourn in the west. There had been a mutiny and now he didn't know what was happening.

We had pencilled in our Mastery for the following month. I had planned to come back with Nigel on a flying visit just before we finally left for home. I had said that if he could get funding it would be great, but even if he couldn't, it didn't matter, we would come somehow. But now he said sadly that the Mastery was off. Not because of the funding, but because he couldn't guarantee that his actors would show up. William was very, very sorry and I was very disappointed. It would have been such a marvellous way to have ended our trip, doing a Mastery with the National Theatre of PNG. Next time, we both agreed. Next time we would certainly make it work. And so I left a sad William and a worried Puele. And the only actor who had not mutinied drove me back in the theatre truck.

In Sydney, I walked straight off the plane into a Mastery workshop with a fully-recovered Nod. A few days later Campbell came to visit us on a stopover before flying back to Port Moresby. Here he seemed even smaller and even shyer. But it strengthened the bond of friendship between us and widened it to include Nigel. During the following week in Melbourne, just after our very final Mastery, William rang out of the blue. Things had changed for the better and the Mastery could go ahead after all. But it was too late. Nod had just had a malarial relapse and we needed a final relaxing week by the sea before we faced the homeward journey and the picking up of our old lives.

And so we did get our quiet week by the sea together, finally, after nine months, at Forest Beach in Queensland: a downbeat, undeveloped corner, without resorts or holiday parks, that Nod had spotted earlier. It was all and more than we had hoped for. But my head was still ringing with PNG and my wonderful Melanesian friends. I tantalized Nod with my stories and soon he was aching to go himself. So there on Forest Beach we resolved to return, come what may. And we resolved to make that trek, three days through the forest and three days back, to the remotest of all remote villages – Gahom. But could we just go home and wait for our next trip, while Lucas and his friends were being tricked out of all that was precious to them? On my last night in Wagu, when I had looked into their gullible eyes, I had made another resolution: somehow, *somehow*, we would help these people help themselves to save their forest.

PART THREE

BIKPELA WOKABAUT
LONG GAHOM

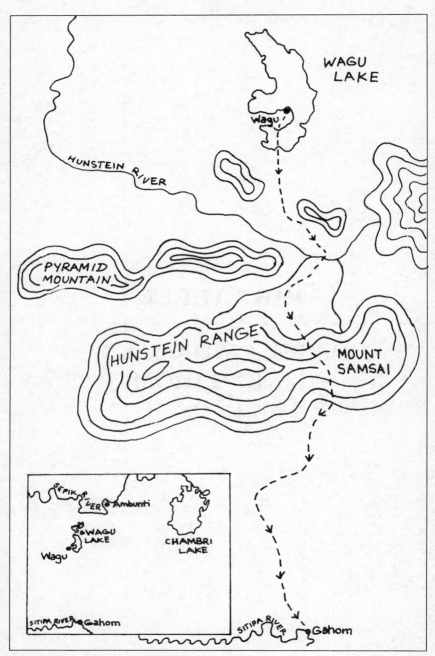

Wagu Aid Post, P.O. Box 52, Ambunti, Wewak, ESP, P.N.G.
18.10.88

Dear my brother Edmunds,

I have received your letter already, with three photos in it. I was very happy when I got your letter. I was very happy when I see our picture plus your picture about the journey to the bush and Waga was standing in front of the canoe and paddling out towards the lake.

Here in the Sepik it's time for rain and a big flood everywhere in the Sepik River and the lakes. It's time for high tide now. You came here in the time for dry season, now it's time for wet season. Yes you have asked about development. So brother if you have any information about any development please be hurry. Otherwise there will be some companies come and take the place. If you have been to London, you have to send us information quickly. I have heard that the Provincial Government will send their Mobile Show to Wagu to cut timbers. That's why I'm telling you, that you have to be hurry.

Yes Richard here in Wagu village we are all o.k., no problem, we live happily and friendly. Oh I forget to tell you one thing. Last week on Monday 3rd October they have shot or killed one big crocodile. They have hunt the crocodiles in the night and shot one big one. We all have eaten the meat of that crocodile. It taste nice. Good meat from the crocodile.

Yes Richard, Barbara was very happy when you left us. She said now I'm by my self Richard is away. She said Richard has gone for ever and he will not come back again. I hope you have harvest your wheat already. Perhaps I might visit England sometime if I have good friends in England. Yes Richard when you and your friend wants to come please just find one camera only for me. Here in Papua New Guinea is very expensive. That's my request to you and your friend Nigel. He didn't see us maybe he will see us when you take him with you. So Richard if you have some information to develop Wagu village you have to hurry and send some information to Solomon and Andrew.

So that's all I have to tell you, and I will be waiting to hear from you. My family would like to say hello to your family and have a nice time in England and thank you for sending us the pictures with the letter. Hello from Solomon, Keith, Ringo, Barbara and Emanuel to you and your family. And that's all of our stories, I think I have to end up here, nothing else for us to talk about it. We are just waiting to hear from you my brother. Lukim yu bihain.

Yours truly friend, Lucas K

I

When Lucas's letter landed on the stone floor of the Suffolk cottage, I was as excited as a little boy receiving his best Christmas present. It had been hard settling back into a cold and depressed UK, and this was the reassurance I needed; the proof that my exotic adventures were as real as the collapsing NHS and the escalating homelessness. And better still, that there was a tangible link between Wagu village and Lawshall Green, a direct line, an open bridge, a miracle in itself. I showed the letter to Nod. I read it to my neighbours. We all delighted in its contents.

Both Nod and I had been deeply shaken up by our travels and we had been obliged to take a long discerning look at our lives. On the homeward flight we had been reluctant passengers and we had written down all the reasons why we dreaded coming home. We were so full of rich experience and vibrant energy, we were terrified that it would all be whittled away. How to avoid falling back into old ruts? Those brick walls, thwarted endeavours and frustrated creativity. The lot of the writer and the actor can so easily become a passive one, dependent on other people's decisions; so easily we can become the victim of circumstances beyond our control. This needed to be remedied. We needed to take charge of things and forge our own paths forward. To counteract the victim syndrome, Nod's major initiative would be to move from acting to directing; mine would be to stop sending out unsolicited scripts. I had been doing it for twelve years. The mountain of rejection slips was high enough.

Our response to all this was to start our own production company. Enough hanging around at red lights. We called it Green Light Productions: green for go and green for our love of the natural world. It would be our tribute to the people we had met and their endangered surroundings. Our aim and our dream was to find a way to link art and nature; to show that art, people and the environment are inextricably woven together. What's culture without green trees, fresh water and clean air?

The first step was to gather a board of professional advisers around us. The second step was to find a venue for our first production. We almost came unstuck. The London Fringe theatre is a law unto itself and we edged perilously close to feeling powerless again. Initially we had planned to mount the play that we had read in Sydney, but Sonia Saunders of the New End Theatre in Hampstead read my other comedy, *Rissoles*, which is set in a vegetarian restaurant in our local Bury St. Edmunds, and she said, 'Yes please'. Breathing a deep sigh of relief, we said: 'Yes thank you'. Barely a week after our arrival home, and coming quite out of the blue, Nigel had been offered the post of Assistant Director on a new Iranian play at the Young Vic. He could not have hoped for a better apprenticeship towards his own departure into directing. Meanwhile, I worked as a painter and decorator, cycling through the London drizzle with my overalls and brushes. A less high-profile apprenticeship. Nonetheless, it provided bread and butter for my liberation as a playwright: the first full theatre production of one of my plays. For more bread and butter, Nod also continued to lead his workshops at the Actors' Institute, and I did my first Daring to Write there too.

But beneath all this activity, Lucas's threatened rainforest weighed heavily upon me. On parting, he had presented me with the highly-prized gift of a stuffed bird of paradise. I had wriggled out of accepting it by explaining that it would be illegal to take it through customs. So, instead, he had given me a carved version, perched on a drum and spears. I had hung it up to help inspire me, and to stop me closing down and opting out of my resolution to assist him. Though I had not fully realized it at the time, part of my original purpose in travelling had been to find motivation – motivation to become an active player in fighting the fire of environmental destruction. But now my helplessness felt worse than before, not less; for now it was spiced with guilt. Personal guilt. I had sworn my allegiance to Lucas and his people; but what was I doing about it? What could I do? What could I do for Wagu, and what could I do for the forest? I wished I'd been born in another age when adventure was adventure; when one could explore the wonders of the world without having to be plagued by the knowledge of their imminent destruction. But wishing wasn't going to do much good for anyone – certainly not my cascading birds of paradise. So, against an insidious wall of inertia and a rising longing not to vault over it, I finally brought myself to telephone the Tropical Rainforest Department of Friends of the Earth. I spoke to Simon Counsell, the Campaign Director. He asked me to write down everything I knew and send it to him. So I did.

I summarized all I had learned about Wagu, its forest and the proposed logging operation; then concluded with the main questions that had been asked me in the Men's House. What was the minimum area that would need to be left unlogged to ensure the preservation of the wildlife? What was the maximum area that could be logged and successfully replanted? What area should be left untouched around the village to allow for the continued practices of hunting, sago-cropping and canoe building? Anxious as to what I might be getting myself into, I also added: 'If FOE want to investigate the logging plan and try to intervene, I support you – but please dissociate my name from the operation. I plan to return to East Sepik next year and do not want to be taken for a spy or refused a permit.'

Simon Counsell put me in touch with a post-graduate from Plymouth Polytechnic who had done a special thesis on logging operations in Papua New Guinea. Patrick Stephenson came to dinner and I was thrown into the deep end: the disastrous logging malpractices of both the past and the present, the appalling exploitation by foreign logging companies, the total disregard for local people's environment and culture, and the staggering corruption of the Papua New Guinea Government. This had all been tabled in the revelatory *Barnett Report;* and, having completed it, Justice Barnett himself had had to escape back to Australia after being stabbed with a knife in his back. What *was* I getting myself into? Patrick spoke on, incessantly, baffling and bamboozling me. But one thing was clear. Before we could do anything, we needed some concrete information on the forest, on its ecology, and on the prospective logging operation. Patrick had contacts. I had contacts. Letter-writing was the first priority. But I was dragging my heels. The first letter was already long overdue: my letter to the people of Wagu answering their questions. I had already received a reply from Simon. It had not been as specific as I had hoped, but it did make me realize what an unknown quantity Papua New Guinea still is. From it, I constructed my letter as best I could and I sent two copies, one addressed to Solomon Makafa, the 'number one' elder, and the other to Andrew Wamnai, the local Government Representative.

Simon had pointed out that the villagers themselves would be the best judges of some of the topics raised, and so I threw several of the questions back to them: 'How big an area does the cassowary or the wild pig need to run in? How far apart are the trees that the birds of paradise use to perch in? Where are the best trees for building your canoes?' I then expounded a simplified theory of reforestation and highlighted the major dangers of logging. I also warned: 'Remember that your forest has taken hundreds of years to develop. When it is cut down, even if the reforestation programme is carried out with great care, it will never grow the same again . . . Solomon and Andrew, remember at all times that your people are the landowners of the forest, and the logging companies have no right to cut without your permission.' When I had left university, disenchanted with Biology, I had never imagined that my scientific sloggings would ever come in useful; in fact I had often regretted the cramming I'd had to do for my finals. But now there was a link. And though I'd forgotten every single fact, and my text books had been collecting dust for over twenty years, that old technical training was suddenly proving useful. It was helping me to order, categorize and summarize points and ideas, and would become even more valuable as time went on.

I hoped my letter to Andrew and Solomon was simple enough. I didn't expect an answer. I didn't get one. But, one night, about 3 a.m., there was a phone call. It was our jokey Air Niugini friend Mark calling from his reservation office in Port Moresby. He was coming to Europe for an international conference; he was passing through London and would like to see us. Mark stayed a couple of nights at the Notting Hill flat. We took him to see Big Ben and Buckingham Palace. We took him to see them again. He couldn't get enough. His visit also coincided with bonfire night and he enjoyed an excellent bonfire party in a garden off Kensington Park Road. It was lovely having him padding around the flat in his bright pink *laplap* (a multi-purpose piece of material that can be worn as a garment or used as a bed cover); another confirmation, another reassurance that the Papua New Guinea journey wasn't over – it had only just begun.

Over Christmas and the New Year I went on my annual meditation retreat; this time to unromantic Birmingham. Before the course began, I wrote in my notebook: *How to meet the challenge of the rainforest and Papua New Guinea full on?* It still all felt impossible; like trying to wade against a great flood-tide that would eventually wipe out my puny little efforts anyway. 'So why bother at all?' yapped the ugly voice of negativity. Why indeed? After the course, to keep the negative voice at bay, I wrote down: *Rainforest Action*, and followed it with a list of all the things that still needed doing. I realized that I would have to commit myself to one rainforest evening a week: surely, knowing what was at stake, I could make space for that? But at the same time, the Green Lights were beginning to flash and the *Rissoles* were beginning to sizzle. I had a major script revision on my hands and Nod had a sponsorship appeal to launch. We had schedules, publicity, casting, rehearsals, stage management and budgets to sort out – and so it went on. Nod also made a lightning workshop return to the Antipodes to keep our contacts alive. And back in Suffolk, trying to focus on an in-depth reappraisal of my comedy characters, the weekly rainforest night got repeatedly postponed.

On a bleak and vengeful 11 February, when my guilt and the yapping voice were both at each other's throats and I could concentrate on my comedy no longer, I slammed my script shut and gave myself over to an entire and unprecedented *Rainforest Day*. I ordered some publications. I wrote a stack of letters. I tried to clarify my objectives: what, oh what was the way forward? We needed to prove the ecological specialness of the forest. We needed to know the specifics of the logging operation and its timescale. We needed to find a way to help raise the local people's awareness of the dangers. That night I realized that my chief obstacle was none other than my old mate, fear. Such a devious and cunning fellow! When the five oarsmen had first paddled me across Wagu lake, my awareness of the fragility of the virgin forested hills had been too painful to acknowledge. And now my terror that they might already be under the chain-saw's beleaguerment was so great I literally couldn't bear it. So I had kept on trying to do an ostrich job, hiding in the sand of my other activities; and every positive move was followed by a relapse into the trough of procrastination. How to take myself in hand? How to face the situation squarely? How to stop the sabotage of fear and negativity from undermining me? I expressed some of these feelings to Patrick.

He wrote back in his large, flowing hand on the headed paper of his window cleaning business:

> There are three things against you when trying to stop tropical rainforest destruction –
> 1) feeling totally depressed with the whole situation and not knowing how you can help
> 2) feeling frustrated from lack of support from pressure groups like Friends of the Earth
> 3) not wanting to totally commit yourself to something you don't think you can solve.
>
> If you let these three factors win then you let the thing you love the most be destroyed, i.e. the rainforest. The thing is, feeling depressed or great despair is not going to solve the problem. It isn't going to stop ecological and cultural decimation, is it? So what I do is just put these things out of my mind totally and do everything in spite of the forces against me.

My letters to Campbell, William, Anton, Malcolm (the expat engineer) and the PNG Friends of the Earth had received no replies. Heeding Patrick's words, I sent a second round. I also tried a new tack. The need for concrete evidence of the uniqueness of the forest was paramount, but I still didn't know how careful I had to be. Could my investigations really get me into trouble? Could they jeopardize my chances of returning? Or was it just paranoia? Because no one could tell me, I wrote my letters to Government departments under a pseudonym. I posed as a British botanist called Joe Diamond who was planning a visit to PNG and was requesting information on the Kauri forests of the East Sepik. But Joe only got one reply. It was from the Acting Assistant Secretary of the Department of the Environment and Conservation and it just informed Joe that his letter had been passed on to the Department of Forests; the Acting Assistant Secretary's note to that department was also enclosed. But neither it nor Joe's further appeals bore any fruit. So much for Joe. I buried him in the garden and the illustrious botanist was never heard of again. I also contacted a real botanist, a student friend at Durham University. I asked her to write to the Botany Department of the University of PNG. This time the plot ran as follows: Sasha was planning to do a Doctorate on tropical rainforests; she had heard from a friend about the Kauri forest at Bisorio in the Sepik; she wanted to make a research trip there and needed detailed information on the area. The Head of Biology wrote back. But somewhere along the line communications had turned into a game of Chinese whispers. He had not heard of the term 'Kowhai' forest and he had not been able to locate 'Bisono'. Another detective story bit the dust. I was getting absolutely nowhere.

However, the plot did continue to thicken. Another letter arrived from Lucas. Relief. Nothing had happened yet. But he did speak with concern about a big company, the Billimer company, that was coming to cut the timbers. Patrick tried unsuccessfully to track down this Billimer company. Perhaps it was a subsidiary of a bigger company; the major Japanese, Malaysian and Indonesian companies were renowned for camouflaging themselves behind apparently innocuous local operators. But then again, maybe Lucas just meant billionaire. Maybe Billimer was a local Pidgin term for rich or big? What could have been a vital clue remained another gloating question mark.

And then, woosh – it was April and I was legitimately swamped by Green Light Productions. The auditions were set, the publicity was out, there was only one thing missing – the completed script. When Nigel could wait for it no longer, he chained me to my study desk and sat in the cottage kitchen waiting through the early hours until it was finally complete. We opened on 9 June and broke box office records at the beautiful little New End Theatre. We played for four weeks and, by closing night, had well and truly stretched ourselves beyond our limits. The amount of organization, the workload and the weight of carrying a show proved far more than we had ever envisaged. On the day after closing we found ourselves lost in the wastelands of Enfield (North London) in a hired van. We were returning scaffolding that had come from Southall (West London): work that one out! We were well and truly knackered. But there was still lots of winding up to do, lots of tying up of loose ends. And the momentum we had created called for further work and a further plan of action. To give our heads a rest, we went to see the American film, *Do the Right Thing*. I hardly saw any of it. I had suddenly realized *we* had got to do the right thing: we had got to have a break; otherwise we'd end up burning ourselves out like so many other people who have grappled with artistic endeavours. And so we went down to Sussex to stay with my family, and walked the white chalk cliffs of the rolling Seven Sisters. Oh the blessed salt wind! It at least partially brought us back to our senses. A week or so later I led my first writers' weekend retreat in Suffolk, and a couple of days after that I had a powerful dream. I wrote it down on 8 August along with a complex outline of notes which debated our travel options. Should we make our next trip between October and February, or should we wait until December and come back in April? There were pros and cons to both options, but the dream omened that the decision would soon be taken out of our hands.

In my dream I am in the grounds of my old school and notice horrible blotches on my calf – white ulcers and big blood clots. Next, I have AIDS. I'm in Scotland in a sort of guest house. It is breakfast time. I am in deep anxiety and panic about what to eat. I know I must choose something nutritious. I order eggs and tomatoes. Then someone looks at my leg. The small open sore above my ankle is a terrible sign. It means that the disease has already gone quite far. The woman who is looking at it points to the rest of my leg. I see, with horror, that lesions have developed. They are running with pus. I tell her, in rage and terror, that I don't want to look at it yet. I run out into the hall to the call-box. I must telephone Nod and my parents too. But I only have four ten pence pieces. They aren't enough. I hesitate. I am still in a state about my breakfast and I run back to order the tomatoes. But I must get through to Nod. I am desperate. Distracted. Overwhelmed by the life-threatening reality of this illness.

As I surfaced slowly out of sleep and realized it was a dream, the relief was enormous. But my neck felt tight and my head was slightly feverish. Two days later, I was rushed to hospital in Bury St Edmunds with what turned out to be malaria. I was only kept in hospital for a week but the convalescing period was slow. I remember the triumph when I managed to walk around the small field at the back of the cottage for the first time, and when I first drove the car up to the village Post Office. However, it wasn't only my physical strength; I experienced a weakening of my mental capacity too. For a while, I had to drop everything. I went into a sweat just picking up the phone; and my lurking antagonists, anger and fear, began to have a field day. To stop them overwhelming me, I made up my own recuperation programme which I called 'walking your way to health'. Each afternoon I took gradually longer and longer walks through the blackberry and rosehip autumn countryside. When I managed to walk all the way to the well-known village of Lavenham, I gave myself a medal. But it was only a couple of steps compared with my longed-for trek to Gahom. Would I be anywhere near fit enough for that? Was I crazy to be even still contemplating it at all?

Nigel was directing two plays at Rose Bruford College of Speech and Drama: a little-known Brecht and an obscure Restoration comedy called *The Emperor Of The Moon*. His time was chock-a-block; and so I had to organize Green Light's first Rainforest Benefit myself. We had already booked the New End Theatre for an evening of new writing; it was too late to cancel. We also had to secure a date and venue for our next production. And, as I got stronger, I was also determined to do at least a little writing. But after only a couple of mornings, I had to face the bitter realization that, although my idea for a rainforest radio play was coming alive, my mental strength just couldn't contain it. I had to close my manuscript, and put it away; for a writer that's about the hardest thing to do.

We had planned to leave at the beginning of December. Masteries and writing courses in Australia and New Zealand would cover our fares and bring in some income. Workshops in Papua New Guinea with the National Theatre and Raun Isi, and in Indonesia with Max Arafin's company that had presented *Princess Mandalika*, would break new ground. Nigel had also been invited to lead a workshop in Singapore. But we had left our bookings too late. Trying to sort out our itinerary was even harder than the first time round. Meanwhile, Nod was struggling with the huge cast of *The Emperor Of The Moon* – the play ended with the entire zodiac appearing on stage, 32 actors, chariots, choral singing, dry ice, the lot! And I was battling with indecision, and a growing longing to give up. My confidence was at zero; no state to be speeding round the world. Besides, we didn't have the money anyway. We would have to play a complicated and alarmingly creative game with credit cards. We seriously considered forfeiting our credibility and cancelling everything.

Then, within about a week, four letters arrived: one from Max on Lombok, one from William in Port Moresby and one each from Larry and Anton in Wewak. We had sent them our proposed itinerary with a list of workshop options they could choose from. They had all made their choices. Then a letter from Lucas also arrived. Waga and Habe were just waiting for us. They were just waiting to take us on the *bikpela wokabaut long Gahom* (the trek to Gahom). Indecision was suddenly a thing of the past. My spirit rose with a great whoop, like the phoenix out of the ashes. Whilst juggling a last-minute deluge of Green Light business and forward planning towards our next production, we paid the balance on our air fares, went for our hepatitis jabs, polished our rainforest boots and refilled our medical kits. To date, my chequered rainforest efforts had got almost nowhere. My few answered letters had contained no elucidating information whatsoever and I knew little more than I had on my arrival home eighteen months before. So, in addition to our workshop programme and our wokabaut, we had another urgent quest: to find out the facts about the forest and the logging company. This was essential if the trees of paradise were to have any chance of being saved. But how? And were we already too late?

II

Our first port of call was Singapore. Nod had an elegant lunch with the doctor who was interested in his Mastery workshop and they planned one to be held on our April return. Although the tourist map boasted a virgin rainforest close to the centre of town, Singapore, Nod and Rick were not sorry to part ways. Surely, this was the ultimate antithesis of our final destination.

From Rick's journal. Monday, 4 December 1989.
Singapore is my nightmare. One giant concrete high-rise shopping centre. A paradise to some: a hell to me. Catch a blade of grass if

you can. Under Scotts five-storey super department store there is a 'picnic court'. The central area of the basement is laid out with plastic tables and chairs; each has a gaudy, jauntily-angled sun umbrella. The sun is fierce neon lighting. In a large circle around the picnic court are a host of fast food counters of all descriptions. Everywhere is spotless, sterilized and scrubbed: every counter, every table, every floor is shining, dancing, reflecting sparkles of the jolly neon sunshine. The picnic court is packed with families: munching, chewing. Smiles as white as the polished floors, eyes as sparkly as the spotless counters. Babies and mums, grannies and dads. Why eat at home any more? Make every night a fast food picnic. Granny has never had such fun, her youth of toil on the real Mother Earth a distant fog of the past. No one drops a single crumb. In fact, to drop litter is a criminal offence. Yet, every single shake, steak, biriany and chop suey is served in throwaway plastic foam; so that, at the end of each night, there is a veritable chlorofluorocarbon mountain. And, as the invisible CFC monster rips the wrapping paper of the world apart, a man is jailed for dropping an empty cigarette packet, and the *real* rainforest (not the one on the tourist map) is shredded into toothpicks.

In Perth, our travelling show commenced with the first Western Australia Mastery. After it, we spent a few days on the wild coast and visited an Australian version of a kauri forest. Though sadly shrunken almost to extinction, it did give an indication of how magnificent the forests of the past must have been. And there, between the wide straight trunks that towered upwards into the sky, our biggest kangaroo to date came lolloping to meet us. We also caught a glimpse of Western Australia's munificent wild flowers, in yellows and mauves and pinks; we saw them just in time as the summer sun was already beginning to shrivel them up. Then, via Sydney, it was off to Cairns to await our Port Moresby flight. We found a traditional wooden Queensland Hotel, suitably run down to make it cheap. Its wide encircling balcony yawned open into the December heat and its large, high-roofed dining room with only two tables set for breakfast had clearly seen more opulent days. There, in our narrow dark blue room, I found some time to reflect on my father's recent death. He had died suddenly in the middle of our autumn rush; as the inspirer and feeder of my travelling spirit, his loss was great. I also looked forward to introducing Nod to my Melanesian friends, and to observing his reaction to the multitudinously coloured world of PNG.

At last here I am in Papua New Guinea and it feels quite normal
– I mean I feel comfortable, welcome, at ease. After so much
preparation and anxious anticipation, here I am – and funnily
enough, I'm OK!

We left Cairns this morning at 9.30. It looked like we weren't
going to fly Air Niugini when we checked in, and I sat in the
departure lounge angry and disappointed; I had been so looking
forward to the special atmosphere that Rick had described. But
then the Air Niugini cabin crew, dressed in their brightly coloured
dresses and shirts, invited us to board the Fokker 28 plane. About
a seventy-seater, it had 42 passengers, including a group of eleven
PNG Nationals. They sat at the back, smoking and drinking. It
appeared they had been on a religious convention; they wore red
badges bearing the name of a Christian society and were bade
farewell by a couple of evangelist brothers. Small, slightly dwarf-
like bodies, bearded, big noses and round eyes. I was captivated
and fascinated by their playful spirits. My heart immediately
popped open. Behind us sat a white nun, travelling alone, in her
grey, calf-length habit with a large metal cross round her neck and
tight wimple. She told me it was her first visit too and this made
me think of all the other missionaries who have gone to 'save the
needy souls'. Yes, the smiles of the cabin crew were genuine and
made me watch the safety demonstration that I usually ignore.
The painting on the class-divider screen was of a lake with canoes
and paddles in pale lilac and pink. *Paradise*, the in-flight magazine, contained beautiful pictures and well-written articles. I also
noticed it had been awarded best in-flight magazine several years
running. Sadly though, no invitation from a flight steward to stay.
But then, unlike Rick's first visit, we had already been invited to
stay with William and Puele.

Flew into Port Moresby; only a one-and-half-hour flight. First
sight was of a small, white sand beach and sparsely-clad hills;
blue mountains in the distance; a road with little traffic. We
disembarked into dense humidity, even at 10 a.m.; down the steps
onto the hot tarmac and along into the Immigration hangar. Fans
whirred overhead; long, slow-moving queue at passport control
and customs. A thorough check through my bag, and my heart
thumped, scared they might find fault with my visa. Then there he

was: unmistakably William. Big. *Black*. Curly black hair. Brown and white blood-shot eyes. Smooth deep warm voice that I recognized from our telephone conversations. He wore a beautiful, green, red and white patterned shirt. Big, wide, flattened feet with pink toe-nails. Warm strong handshake. I felt shy. Mark, too, was there to meet us. His visit to London came tumbling back to me. His hair still immaculately cut, oiled and shaped into a perfect 'afro' style. He hugged us and shook hands and giggled.

Out of the hall we went. First I noticed red betel nut stains on the ground. People: strolling, sitting, leaning, sprawling on bags. Mothers clutching babies tightly to them. Women with intricate tattoos on their faces and arms. It reminded me of a scene at an Indian bus station. Straight away we changed money and bought our tickets for Wewak. Even though Mark had arranged a good discount, the price bit severely into our funds, and I got scared and wondered if we had brought enough. Then we walked to an open-backed truck. Eddy, the National Theatre Company driver, a man over six feet tall and well-built, insisted on carrying my bag. We jumped onto the back of the truck, but William suggested we ride inside the cabin; we were already streaming with sweat. We drove slowly through Port Moresby, past thronging markets. Lots of heavy-fuming diesel exhausts of trucks and buses. Even though the town is heavily urbanized, there is still a sense that the jungle could reclaim it very quickly. Signs in Pidgin; Coca-Cola, Pepsi, Toyota, Hyundai, Fuji-colour. Mostly Japanese cars, trucks and utes (utility vehicles). We turned into Waigani district, passed the police station and 'Cut-Price Supermarket' that William calls 'Cut Throat'. Then another big open market jammed with people, fruit, vegetables, children, women in bold primary-coloured smocks and skirts, men in jeans and T shirts, highly Westernized. Dogs roaming free, skinny, uncared-for. Litter everywhere, betel-nut-stained roads and pavements.

We drew up to William's house. Two-storied, concrete, tin-roofed with louvered glass windows and a tall chain fence around it 'to keep out the rascals'. Opposite, The Brotherhood of Christ Mission: a large, open-sided, tin-roofed building with about seventy rows of wooden benches; a platform at one end with a plain cross-shaped lectern serving as a pulpit. They assemble and sing loudly every night except Monday, William warned us. I was introduced to Puele, round faced with honey-glow skin, graceful and shy; and to Ani, their four- year-old daughter, who has the remnants of bronchitis and frequently coughs until she is sick. Ani silently and bravely showed us to a big upstairs room with fan and built-in wardrobe. Two beds are made, one with a pink candlewick bedspread and pink and red sheets, the other, yellow spread and green and red-flowered sheets.

This afternoon we walked up to Mark's house – three minutes away. He is caretaking a VSO co-ordinator's house; a single-storey bungalow on high stilts with a large balcony covered in potted plants. Tuppence, an old smelly black Labrador, comes with the house, she has had four 'masters' already. Mark welcomed us and pointed to the iced water in the fridge – it is safe to drink tap water here. We sat on the balcony and he showed us the photographs of his London trip; especially proud of the one I took of him with 'Benny Hill' at Madame Tussauds. He also likes the one of him in front of Big Ben.

Tonight, William, Rick and I meditated together, the Mission singing in full swing. Then we talked business. The National Theatre have to go to perform at the Commonwealth Games in New Zealand on 15 January. Shit! They will miss the workshop. But William has contacted the Moresby expatriate theatre company and he has been in touch with the outlying community theatre groups. Rodney, his administrator and he are both eager to participate. Good. He has already arranged some radio interviews. Very good. For supper, Puele prepared delicious yams, pumpkin, cabbage soup and salad; they also prefer to be vegetarian. Puele and I are shy of each other. Although she mostly speaks in Pidgin, I know she understands English well. But it means I will have to work hard at my Pidgin.

From Nigel's journal. Tuesday 26 December.
Christmas in Papua New Guinea is certainly different from England or the Indian Christmas we spent at Dwarka on the first trip. William and Puele made us a traditional dish from his island home of Bougainville; it is called *tamatama*. He lit a fire outside and boiled tapioca roots: they are bright golden yellow. These were then put into a hollowed-out tree stem and pummelled with a long wooden pestle to a creamy mush. Puele scraped it off the pestle with some string and rolled it into small balls. She scraped coconuts and extracted the cream by sieving the coconut through a piece of sackcloth, then boiled the cream vigorously on the fire. William told us that in his village at home they give the coconut-cream boiling job to a blind person – they can hear when it starts cracking, the indicator that the rich smooth substance is ready. He then dropped the balls into the boiling liquid for a while, then served. Mmmm . . . scrummy! Not at all like tapioca pudding at

school. Puele's family joined us: her mother, sisters and their husbands and her brother. We all ate too much and they crashed out in front of the telly. Ani shared her chocolates with us but kept her miniature Christmas pudding all to herself. We played cards – the turn over and match the pairs game – Ani calls it 'Richard and Nigel'. I also read her the story of Rapunzel that we gave her; she sat still, taking it all in.

Today we drove up into the National Park to see a big waterfall and the remaining forest near Moresby. We stood on the edge of a high cliff overlooking a deep valley thickly forested. High-pitched screeches rose up – 'Birds of paradise' said William. Eagerly I scanned the view, but alas, no sighting; I'll have to wait till we get to East Sepik. On the way home we stopped at Puele's mother's house in a ramshackle settlement on the edge of Moresby; hastily-erected single-storey buildings made of block-board partitions and tin roofs. Hers was set among coconut palms and mango trees. William picked plenty of deliciously ripe mangoes and, after eating them, told me to rub in the juice that had spilt on my hands. 'You lot always run for a tap when you've eaten fruit to wash all the goodness away; rub it into your skin, it is good, the oils are rich.' Then, up a tall coconut palm he shimmied; something he hadn't done for a while. He tied his trouser belt around his ankles, removed his T shirt and up he went. At the top, he dislodged a couple of coconuts and they hurtled down to the ground leaving big indentations. 'I must remember not to fall asleep under a coconut palm' I said. I drank the sweet pure milk, the first time since Indonesia. Mmm, I could drink that all day. We sat on the *haus win* – a raised platform beside the house that catches the cool afternoon breeze. Whack! Kiri, Puele's sister hit me hard on the leg. 'Hey' I said. *'Nat nat'*, she laughed gleefully and showed me a squashy bloody mess of dead mosquito on my leg.

On 27 December we flew to Wewak. For Nod it was one hop further into the unknown. Anton welcomed us at the airport like long-lost brothers. A well-trained bureaucrat, he proudly presented us with a detailed itinerary. He also gave us a copy of the following notice:

EAST SEPIK
DIVISION OF CULTURE AND TOURISM
PUBLIC NOTICE

Raun Isi Theatre wishes to inform the general public that there will be a workshop titled 'The Mastery' to be hosted at Raun Isi main campus (Kaindi) from 9 a.m. to 5 p.m. from the 9th to the 15th January 1990.

The workshop will be conducted in two (2) parts:
Part I: Course Title: Theatre and Acting
is for Raun Isi Theatre personnel only and will run for three days (9th, 10th and 11th January)
Part II: Course Title: Daring To Write
is open to any interested individual (i.e. students, g/roots and public servants) who has wanted to write a book or a play but doesn't have the know-how. Perhaps this may be your opportunity to get into the heart of writing. Enrol now and explore to master the art. This course will run for 4/5 days (12th, 13th, 14th and 15th January).

P.S. Due to limited space, we will accept only 25 applicants with a registration fee of K5.00 per head. For more information call into Provincial Assembly Block and see the Director or phone 86 2333 and ask for Mr Sakarai Anton. (Wishing you all a merry Christmas and a happy New Year 1990.)

At the Raun Isi campus, Larry, Alice and the actors were waiting to greet us. At first they were overcome with shyness. Shyness at meeting Nigel, a *real* English actor. But also a kind of astonishment. It was as if they couldn't quite believe that I had really, really returned to see them again. But soon we were laughing around the old kitchen table and it was hard to believe that I had been away for eighteen months.

On 28 December we finalized the workshop plans and bought provisions for the trip upriver. A *toksave* (message) was also sent on the radio to tell Lucas we were on our way. On the 29th, Anton arrived in the early morning with a government vehicle and Raymond, the shrewd old goblin of a driver, who conjured us with dare-devil speed over the forested mountains and across the swamps to Pagwi. This time round we were travelling by courtesy of the DPI (the Department of Primary Industry). Their topsy-turvy headquarters stood by the water's edge down a muddy track away from the trade store. When Raymond halted with a flourish of screeching brakes and pointed triumphantly at his watch, having broken his own time record by several seconds, the DPI officers were only just waking up. And amidst yawning limbs and naked torsos, there was much debate as to who was supposed to be picking us up. But at last, out of the morning mist a swarthy and taciturn boatman called Samson appeared and without more ado he headed us up against the current towards Ambunti.

The atmosphere of the outpost was as strangely lugubrious as ever. And there was no Lucas to meet us. We had brought a drum of petrol for our return trip to Pagwi and in the awful, draining, midday heat we dragged it up the hill to the DOIC's office (District Officer in Charge). The office was open but empty. Piles of dusty files in the cramped hallway and a walkie-talkie spitting on the officer's small desk. We waited. No one came. We tried to replenish ourselves by sucking the juice from the fallen fruit of the star tree outside the entrance; but the juice was sour. Finally, we hauled the diesel drum into the hallway, wrote a message on it, and wound our way down to the lodge where they gave us lukewarm tea and stale tinned-meat sandwiches. A group of overweight local Government Representatives were sitting round drinking beer; one of them was Andrew Wamnai. He shook our hands in awkward and self-conscious welcome. He hadn't known we were coming. He didn't know where Lucas was and he didn't mention my letter. Zapped and disheartened, we asked to lie down in the passage while we waited. Announcing he was Lucas's wantok, the Acting Manager, whom I had not met before, unlocked one of the bedroom doors and let us lie on the bed. It was the room next to the one from which I had previously absconded.

Trudging about in the heat had exacerbated a headache. Now the sick throbbing brought back the terror of malaria, and with it, all the tirading old rubbish. Why was I back in this god-forsaken place? Why did I never listen to reason? Neither the rest, nor another cup of lukewarm tea did anything for my head or my mood. And back in the main reception area in the decreasing light (the generator did not go on until seven o'clock), the dusty wicker chairs and the masks and other carved artefacts that hung on the slatted walls looked more half-hearted and forlorn than ever. Just as I was beginning to beg the ground to swallow me up, a Wagu boy tapped on the mosquito-meshed window: 'We go now – you come?' The man who was heading his canoe homeward-bound shall remain nameless; every story has its dark horse and he was the dark horse of Wagu. I had recognized him as such on my first visit; but just as I had initially blanked out those ominous logging stations along the Mahakam, so I had chosen to ignore his reputed ignobility. Now, in the spooky twilight, he was offering us a lift. Well, Lucas was certainly not intending to show up, so it felt like we had no choice.

Soon we were crouching on the wet floor of the long canoe as he cut at right angles across the force of the river. He shouted jovially to the men waving from the top of the steep muddy bank. But his joviality was hollow. He was tall, handsome and bearded, but there was a limpness in his big frame and a derelict glaze in his bloodshot eyes. We were heading for Malu, the village on the opposite side, and now he shouted jovially to the men standing at the top of the other muddy bank. Under the glowering sky, he mimed swigging down a can of beer to me; when I shook my head, he turned away with a sneer. He wasn't jovial: he was drunk. As we pulled in and moored against another canoe, he lost his balance and we almost capsized. He apologized to us, but hissed a scalding oath into the ear of the boy beside me. Then, staggering up the bank, he declared that he was fetching more beer and yelled orders at the men. His voice had become lethal. There was shouting and disagreement. In the darkening shadows from the overhanging trees, I just caught a glimpse of the fear in the eyes of the boys crouching with us. We were all at the mercy of this madman. Could we trust him to get us to Wagu? And at night, through the crocodile dark? Things were going from bad to worse fast.

Suddenly, another canoe was approaching and one of the boys cried 'Lucas, Lucas!'. I took up the call. Lucas, our salvation! This time the shouting was felicitous and his boat sped towards us out of the mottled gloom. Lucas had been to Pagwi and all the way to the Maprik market. They had left at four o'clock in the morning. No, they had not heard the toksave on the radio; they had not known when we were coming. Lucas reached over and shook my hand and just for a split moment allowed his secret shining eyes to meet mine. But his boat was full to overflowing and the dark horse was shouting down harshly. Lucas remained calm: 'You come to Wagu with us, no problem'. And as the boys jumped in and out helping him to reorganize the canoes, the younger woman with Lucas, whom I now recognized as his wife, called out for batteries and then came forward and took my hand. 'Richard,' she whispered, 'God bless you'. I introduced Nod. 'Are you Maria?' he asked. 'Yes, God bless you'. Her eyes were translucent flowers and her voice was a perfect weaving of welcome.

Night falls fast on the mighty Sepik River. There is only a dull sheen now on the vast expanse of swirling water and, overhead, the huge black clouds are piling up portending thunder. As we turn off into the narrow tributary, the whitish corners of the sky turn green and all is bathed in an uncanny green light. Lucas's canoe is overladen. Its rim is only an inch above the warm, oily water and its small outboard motor is straining. In the prow of the canoe, two boys crouch, buried in bilums and bursting sacks from the market. Behind us, a wrinkled old woman is curled up asleep. Behind her, Maria sits, cradling her little Emanuel. And behind her, Lucas stands at the helm, steering us into the dark. My first journey to Wagu was by burning day; Nigel's is by dangerous night. Nothing here is ever as expected. Isn't it time for me to learn this and stop losing faith?

Suddenly there is an almighty thud as we smash into a floating log. Maria screams out, the canoe judders and spins and, for a long split moment, we are going to capsize . . . Then Lucas lifts the engine out of the water and the boat steadies. As the motor sputters to silence, we are engulfed by the great Sepik chorus: a thousand frogs, a million crickets, croaking and soaking, cracking and snapping. The grass itself is alive, pulling out of the crocodile mud, hissing into the hot rising wind. And startled waterfowl skid away, screeching down low covert corridors into the swamp, while a last giant egret swoops and glistens above us and then dissolves with a doomful cry.

Lucas starts up the engine. One of the boys holds out a torch and flashes it from side to side. Now we understand why Maria called out anxiously for batteries; the light is feeble and the high, eerie walls leap up in front of us, barely in time for Lucas to adjust our course. Nobody speaks. Lucas's concentration grips us all: it is as sharp as an arrow and its bow is his clean will, bent to the job at hand – the delicate, dangerous job of bringing his human cargo through the night. We hit another log. And another. Each time, Maria cries out and pulls her tiny boy closer. Each time the taut silhouette under the descending clouds pulls his bow tighter. And now that intoxicating taste is flooding through me again. How do I so easily forget it? I thrill to the great spirit of the wild as, out of the virgin wilderness sky, it reaches down and brushes me. Nod shudders and I know he's been captured too. I am also full of gratitude and love for Lucas. Lucas of the silent ways. Lucas who hides behind his own Sepik wall of reserve. Lucas who could hardly look at me when we greeted each other, yet who is so full of human love and a yearning to communicate that he writes to me all the way to Lawshall Green and signs himself 'your brother'. Lucas who is risking this overfull boat for us tonight.

Later, much later, when our aching behinds are screaming at the hard wet floor, when even the wide-eyed boys are falling asleep, we slide out of the tunnel of grass and part the waters of the huge black lake. Far away, the faintest shadow of the primal forest looms. An eighteen-month terror loosens inside me. We have been blessed with stolen time. The bird of paradise trees are still standing; we are not too late. At the foot of the forest, there is an even fainter, yellow light which I might have mistaken for a rising star if I hadn't known it was Wagu.

From Nigel's journal. Wagu. Sunday 31 December 1989.
Here I am, sitting at the edge of Wagu crocodile lake on the eve of our bikpela wokabaut into the forest. It's dark and late but I want to get something down before we go off tomorrow.

We waited so long in Ambunti for Lucas. Rick got a splitting headache and had to lie down all afternoon, eventually resorting to some Aspros. I went off right down to the other end of the village. I walked by the river, past the timber mill, and sat and talked with a round-bellied friendly Ambunti man who works for Air Niugini as an engineer in Port Moresby; he's here on leave. We spoke half English, half Pidgin. He told me how much he likes his own village and how he dislikes the crowded, dirty Moresby. But he has to earn a living. He wants to go to England one day. He was very interested to hear about our journey upriver, people usually go downriver from here: 'It is *plenti* hard, *plenti nat nat, plenti pik* (pig) *plenti plenti snek* (leeches)'. I'm not sure if he thought I was brave or stupid. A good time on my own. Good to be my myself and to discover.

Then the scary, unsafe journey in the dark horse's canoe. I should have spoken out and refused to go with someone who was drunk; I remembered our unbalanced journey with Jasper in Borneo and cursed myself for agreeing. Fortunately we were rescued by Lucas. He could hardly look at me when Rick introduced me, but I remembered Rick's warning of his painful shyness, and felt relieved to be in safe hands. A hair-raising journey up in the dark for over two hours. I managed just to trust Lucas, even though we kept crashing into sunken logs. The dim torch-light was hardly adequate with such an overloaded canoe in the pitch black. The moon gave an occasional splinter of light; I could just about make out the silhouette of the mountains and the tall grass. The chugging motor also added to my sense of security. My ears pricked on long stalks for the sound of a crocodile splashing into the water. Then we got to the bank to let off the old woman who had been huddled in a crumpled ball behind us. The mosquitoes that Rick warned me of descended thick as a cloud so I could hardly breathe. Now, here, they are not so bad. I'm glad that we have chosen the wet season for our visit. Last time Rick came in the dry season, the worst time for mosquitoes.

Tonight we gave our first performance in Pidgin. Today is Emanuel's birthday. Maria cooked all day, preparing. She killed and plucked a big white duck and made a feast for about sixty people. We sat on the patch of coarse grass by their house on a big blue tarpaulin and Maria spread the food around the edge. We were given a plateful each. After eating, a collection was taken for Emanuel; we were confused whether we were expected to contribute or not, so we put in two kina each. The dark horse, noticing our contribution, made a point of donating five! While Maria was preparing the feast, Rick and I played 'bikpela pukpuk' (big crocodiles) with Ringo, Jerome and Keith in the men's creek. Their squeals of delight brought other villagers running to watch.

We made up our impromptu play this afternoon. It was about an old man who couldn't manage to carry his cargo. A young boy (me) passes by. He is crying because his parents have no food left. He helps to carry the old man's cargo. The old man (Rick) then turns into the Spirit of the Forest: the cargo is transformed into a big bag of food for the boy's family. When I cried, the audience absolutely shrieked with laughter. When Rick turned into the Spirit waving a palm frond, they squealed with terror. And when the boy got his reward they applauded with delight. Under the swaying sago palms we had a hit! At the end there was a stunned silence; I think they have never seen white men being such idiots before. Later, Ringo and Keith took it in turns to play the boy and the Spirit; whooing and crying alternately.

After Emanuel's party, we had a big discussion about our seven-day expedition. Waga insisted that we take three guides: himself, Habe and a man called Tom. With some gentle confirmation from Lucas, we agreed. It means that we won't have to carry anything; I'll probably have enough to cope with anyway. The area in which we are going to walk is called the Hunstein Range. We have to cross Mount Samsai, one of it's two high mountains and the home of the King of the Wallabies. I'm glad we're not going over the other one, Pyramid Mountain, where, it is said, lives a monster with one thousand legs! I wonder how I'll fare?

It just turned midnight. The New Year. A great clinking and crashing of pots, drums and cans went on for about ten minutes, and Lucas lit a flaming torch and circled the house, to chase away the bad spirits. Now a *singsing* (traditional celebration) has begun up in the village, I can hear drums being beaten and a strange sound of singing. Even though it's late and we have to get up at dawn to begin our *tripela de bikpela wokabaut*, (three-day trek) how can we miss it?

III

Day One
Nod and I wake up early. Singsing is still going on and on, like a wailing cry through the dull half-light. Last night we went to have a look. Towards the top of the central thoroughfare between the two rows of bush-material houses, the huge oblong village drums were placed. One of the men was beating them: a slow, methodical rhythm; and around him, in a circle, a few of the villagers were pacing slowly, deliberately, chanting a plaintive, repetitive chant. There was no light except from the stars; and the dark figures and the wailing chant cast a ghostly spell. Other villagers seemed indifferent to the goings-on and continued to chat and go about their business as if it wasn't happening. But slowly, one or two more joined the plodding circle of chanters; dragging their feet on the baked earth. It was almost as if they were yoked, pulling the village with them, pulling their ancient traditions out of the shadows, out of the murmuring star-sprinkled trees.

As we climb out from under the mosquito net and finish packing our gear, Waga is already calling up, asking if we're ready. Ready? I have been ready for eighteen months. I have been ready ever since I first heard about their remote and mysterious sister village, Gahom – three days' walk through the forest. And now, today, on the first day of January 1990, we are actually setting off for it! Yes Waga, *mipela redi* (we're ready)! Under the house a big discussion is in progress. Jerome, Lucas's first born, has broken the only lamp and last night's search for batteries is still on. Next, no one has woken Habe. Yelled at, he answers gruffly from his close-by hut on crooked stilts. Solomon has come to offer a few last minute 'number ones' and, exuding fatherly goodwill, he apologizes for not joining the wokabaut. As Joseph confided to me last year, he is on the edge of becoming an old man. We are also introduced to Tom, our third guide. He is younger than Waga and built like a lithely ox; he speaks some English and will act as interpreter (rueful Frank from last year is away at another village).

Soon we are in the canoe with our equipment and Lucas to drive us, chugging out into the lake. Between the banana trees on the shore, Maria and children and villagers are waving goodbye. No mention of breakfast today, not even a cup of tea; but at least there's a bunch of bananas which we savour, every mouthful – precious energy for the day ahead. Across the lake, the forested hills are almost completely submerged in cloud. The ever-present giant egrets flap away, contracting their long white necks into loops. Flap, flap, over the glassy water. Flap, flap as we glide through the tall Sepik grass at the lake's end. Before us, a great wall of forest rises to meet the clouds, and overhead the dome of silence is deafening. Clumsily, we clamber out onto the mud and help carry our cargo up to the edge of the trees. 'Nice place for a little walk', Nod laughs nervously as Lucas heads away for the safety of home. And so by 8 a.m. we are on our way.

Now we are slopping barefoot through a black-mud grove of sago palms. Waga leads, swinging lightly with his back-breaking load: one of our rucksacks; a large leather bag of food and utensils; the big canvas sheet for our camps; and Nod's bulging sports bag slung at a daunting angle across his right shoulder. Nod follows, then me, then Tom with the other rucksack, another large load of supplies and a handful of spears. And finally, Habe takes up the rear, with two smaller bags and the broken lamp. Thank god they persuaded us to bring three men so that we don't have to carry any gear ourselves. '*Rot long Gahom!*'(the road to Gahom) exclaims Waga, with his bright, laughing eyes. But, as we begin to climb out of the mud and ascend a steepish slope, the track is barely apparent, and already he often has to cut our way with his sharp long-bladed machete. Our shirts are soaking. The humidity is extreme. I try to breathe out the fear that is tightening my hips. I hold my father's image above me to give me strength. Since his death he has felt very close; now he is beaming at me with incredulous encouragement.

We walk for four hours, firstly through tall, narrow, moss-covered trees and giant ferns, ropes and palm fronds – some with sharp spikes; underfoot a sponge-like litter of rotting leaves and logs; overhead the raucous shrieking of sulphur-crested cocka-toos. We stop every hour for a short rest. Tom and Habe light up their homemade roll-ups. Waga bends over a stream and drinks like a dog, lapping up the water with his tongue. We devour some more of the bananas, already over-ripening in the heat. Then down the other side of the hill; here it is steeper, darker, damper – lots of slimy black stones and walking through streams. Tiny fish. Nod is stung on the leg by a small plant with very rough leaves; the pain is severe. We both get thorns in our feet. Are we crazy walking without shoes? But it's such a relief not being loaded up in our sturdy boots, something that I was dreading. The humidity is worse. Our clothes are drenched. Sweat slides down our faces like hot wax; drips from our noses, drips from our ears. It fills my eyes, stinging, blurring my vision. 'Don't wipe it off,' I keep saying to myself, 'it's a cooling system; it's helping us.' Heart thumping, legs aching, fear is clamping me. All the old garbage. Fear that I don't have the strength. Fear that my varicose veins are going to explode. Fear that I should have listened to the voice inside me that said I'm still too weak from malaria. Keep breathing, Ricky. Breathe out the fear and let the sweat pour.

We stop for *kaikai* (food) at the *bikpela wara* (big river). This is the river I was brought to last year. It's extraordinary to be here again: a familiar corner in a primary rainforest! 'I'm done in already', Nod says with frantic eyes. So am I, but I make light of it, as we strip off and lay our dripping clothes on the beach of hot white stones. A dip in the fast-flowing water and our spirits rise. Ooh yes! Cool, soothing ecstasy! Either side, a gorgeous tangle of dense jungle cloaks the river banks. There are loud parrot cries from the high trees and those electric-blue butterflies which I remember so well are over our heads. The underside of their wings are velvet black, so that in flight they seem to flash and momen-tarily disappear as the dazzling blue upper surface tips away.

Lunch is pawpaw and slabs of tasteless, baked saksak which we manage by flavouring each mouthful with a bite of the last bananas. Also, we replace some sweat with the gastrolyte powder we've added to our water bottles. Luckily, there are large clouds over the sun, which means we can safely stretch out for a while on the stones. Then we're off again up the forest basin through which the river winds. There are some giant trees now with wide buttresses. Others, with roots hanging down twenty to thirty feet, are like great limbs with gnarled claws scooping into the mud. We catch a glimpse of a large cassowary dashing between the trees and then the outline of a couple of wallabies (though not royal-looking ones). There are also mounds of loose earth where wild pigs have been rooting for food. But as yet no birds of paradise. The undergrowth is scanty and we're swinging along at quite a lick; feeling easier too, knowing we're over half way for today. We must remember this stretch, it'll give us heart for the journey back. *'Richard diwai'* (Richard's tree); Waga points to one of the biggest trees with buttresses. Tom explains it is the tree I photographed last year. Yes, I remember it – but this is as far as we got. From now on it's new territory.

We cross and recross the river several times. Now it is up to our thighs and the current is pulling fast. Waga waits patiently as we waver and dodder; and when we slip and stumble he always says *'sori'* as if it's his fault, and holds out a steadying hand. Waga, our rock, a dancing smile with big white teeth, invincible in the middle of the river, holding our cargo over his head; his tattered green vest, more holes than vest, showing off his rippling, rock-hard physique. Sharp stones, hot stones, jagged roots. Our feet are suffering and, finally, we put on our boots. It's better. Now we can look up into the trees without having to negotiate every step; and as we promptly cross the river again our feet stay cool anyway. We come to an old camp left by the men of Gahom. Our guides want to stop here, but, although we're aching with fatigue all over, we insist we walk on. It's imperative to reach the foot of the mountain so we can start climbing first thing tomorrow, before it gets too hot. Now the river is getting narrower, glinting in the mellowing, after-noon light. We disturb a pair of hornbills and see them perfectly as they thunder up with startled cries, winding along the channel of sky between the treetops. Huge beaks, reddish heads, massive wide wings thudding the air. 'This is our country – how dare these tiny mortals intrude!'

Finally, we reach our first day's destination, a river beach at the base of the mountain. We have been walking for seven hours. Habe and Tom start to cut a clearing for setting up camp, and immedi-ately it starts to rain. Soon it's pouring and we squat awkwardly under our groundsheets: *'Tupela liklik lapun!'* (two little old men) we call out. Waga laughs as he sets up a fish trap of large leaves and rope that exudes a white poisonous juice. Habe and Tom cut stakes, wedge them into the ground and throw the canvas over them – our roof. They carpet the ground with big palm fronds and build a small slanting roof of matted leaves at one end of the canvas. We creep in out of the rain and lay out the groundsheets on the cushion of fronds. Habe and Tom strip sticks and logs to light the fire, which flares up fast. Phew, this is fun!

Later, the rain stops. Through the high canopy there are patches of blue, and tiny swallows the size of butterflies somer-saulting through the last, hazy shafts of sunlight. Our clothes are hanging to dry over the smoky fire on a rope that Habe has cut from a nearby tree. The three wonderful men are squatting, chatting quietly in their tokples as they bake the fish that Waga has caught and boil the rice. Our forest camp has no walls and all around us the jungle noises are getting louder and louder: high-pitched cicadas, screaming like electric wires, giant crickets, and millions of frogs; all merging with the babbling river. All rolled up in the soft, damp, vanishing light.

Before we eat, Waga prays in Pidgin. He is a Christian brother, though, he admits, not a good one. 'O Papa, thank you for bringing us safely through the forest. O Papa, guard us as we sleep through the night. O Papa, give us strength to climb the mountain tomorrow.' Tom fixes the broken lamp with a piece of soup wrapping and the little wick glows brightly. Later he curls up on the leaves beside us without even a cloth or a mat, naked except for his earth-smeared shorts. He groans as his square body twitches to rest. Waga is out like a light on the other side of the fire under the sloping leaf roof, while Habe, the oldest one, sits up smoking his *brus*, his furrowed face and distant eyes gazing silently into the fire. Much to Habe's intrigue I pull out my anti-insomniac kit and do some yoga. Then I curl up next to Nod: happy, hopeful, letting the pulsating din of the forest cradle me, and wash right through me. Thank you Nod for coming along with me. Thank you Waga and Habe and Tom. All is dark now except for the lamp which Habe has turned down but left on for our sakes.

Day Two

All night the noisy wet jungle pulsated around us, but we both got a few hours sleep. And now, in the first light, our friends are already blowing up the fire and boiling more rice. It's difficult to swallow, but essential for our strength and we insist on a cup of tea as well, with sugar. Then we pack up fast, leaving a bag of rice hanging from the roof of the camp for our return. '*Bikpela maunten*', declares Waga, gesturing towards the mountain, his eyes laughing; and we set off in the same order: Waga, Nod, me, Tom and Habe, always so quiet, trudging along at our rear. Already it's steep and Waga is cutting our way deep through the dark green dampness. We struggle over fallen trunks, under and through giant masses of upturned roots, over and through giant piles of rotting logs, branches and leaves and big wads of fleshy fungi. Tom and Waga cut us sticks, and again, when we slip and stumble, their immediate response is 'sori', so concerned that it is their fault. Now there are lots of leeches. We have to stop every ten minutes to flick them off our boots, our trousers, our shirts. Extending and looping their narrow bodies they can move alarmingly fast and always up towards our faces.

We pass a pair of upright sticks cut to the same height – the spot where someone killed a bikpela snake. Yesterday we passed two sticks with a couple of cross strips wedged between them: that was the place where a pig had been killed. And, later, a rock is pointed out where last year Waga speared a cassowary. We are beginning to learn the language of the forest as well as Pidgin. At a hole in the forest wall, where several trees have fallen, we catch a brief glimpse of the valley below, up which we walked: now it is buried in snowy cloud. Azure forested hills rise all around and, except for mysterious bird calls echoing across the void, the silence is profound, inexorable. Suddenly there is a harsh cry above. 'Kumul – bird of paradise,' Tom says, 'different one, red colour.' 'Quick, let's follow it', I plead. But the high canopy is thickly foliated and it's already gone.

After several hours heavy walking with hardly a stop, we reach the tree-covered summit: wet, close to the clouds and there's nowhere even to sit that is safe from the ever-ascending leeches. No sign of the Wallaby King, unless the collapsed roof-shelter of leaves is his palace in disguise. Our sweat-soaked clothes go cold. Waga has goose pimples. We had planned to celebrate with the one treasured pineapple but it's too inhospitable here and we are all keen to move on, only waiting for Tom and Habe to have a quick smoke. 'Lukim yu bihain, Wagu hap long maunten' (see you later, Wagu side of the mountain). Now we're on the Gahom side. The descent is even steeper, sometimes almost sheer. Tom leads now, hacking a way through the treacherous undergrowth. Against the shifting stones and slippery roots, every foothold has to be negotiated, and amongst the knotted vines, some with lethal spikes, every handhold has to be consciously chosen. Steady breathing, will-power, a hundred per cent concentration on the job in hand. It's hot and we are sweating sheets again, wobbly, depleted, hardly able to control our legs. I am exhausted and Nod is losing heart; I feel the weight of trying to carry his flagging spirit as well. 'We've got to climb up this side on the way back', he says with horror, tripping up; 'I can't control my legs any more, I've got to stop'. But Tom is determined to continue: *'Malolo long wara'* (we'll rest by the water). 'Listen', I say, 'you can hear it down on the right, we're almost there'. But we're not, and we stagger on and on and only slowly, ever so slowly, does the river get closer, louder. Keep breathing, Ricky. Every step is closer. Keep breathing, Nod. At last, at last the babble grows and crescendoes into a roar. Now it seems to be on both sides and finally we reel out of the trees and onto a burning rock at the point where two rivers meet.

Phewww! We've made it, and what a place! Split by colossal round boulders, the rivers are thundering torrents, crashing, dashing from deep ravines. All around the vertical jungle topples, sky-high, a chaos of liana and ropes and enormous leaves. On our left, from a sheer cliff, a magical waterfall cascades into a blue-green pool, above which an overhanging tree spreads its tiny oval leaves like a fan. Ahead, the double river roars away. Balancing from boulder to boulder we jump into the pool: it's cold and crystal fresh; while in the baking sun our strewn-out clothes are covered in giant, swallow-tailed butterflies, their sculptured wings an intricate lattice-work of sky blue, white and crimson. 'The harder the conditions, the more together you get', Nod sighs. And he's right. In the city he is often the one who has to hold our duo together; while, here, I am in *my* element.

But then the moment of rapture flips into crisis. Nod collapses. Panic. He's turned white and he's feeling sick and cold and can't face the saksak and tinned fish that we must eat for our strength. I lay out a groundsheet and bring him under our laplaps and plain sheets which have proved cooler and more versatile than sleeping bags. Waga and Tom make up a fire to boil him some water for tea. I rummage through the medicine boxes and give him everything in sight. One of his big toes is swelling up and a cut on his leg above it is swelling too and starting to go septic. I begin him on a programme of antibiotics and reassure him that the same thing happened to me in the Himalayas and that the antibiotics sorted it out in no time. So much for walking barefoot – how stupid could we be? I coax him to drink the tea and quickly boil up some noodles. He isn't eating enough; this morning he gave his rice to Waga. Every few minutes I dose him up with 'Rescue Remedy'. Now it starts to rain so I cover him with the other groundsheet and jump the boulders to save our clothes. Tom and Waga look anxious but I assure them he'll be OK; I don't want them to panic as well. 'Can we camp here?' But they are reluctant; it's too cold at night and we need to walk on. So I say we'll give him two hours, till three o'clock, and see how he is then. Water collects along the folds of the groundsheet and Nod has gone completely silent. I sit by him, silent too; knowing he is using all his will to regain his strength.

At three o' clock the rain has stopped. Nod emerges. He's warm again and, better still, there's colour back in his face; let's hope it was simply exhaustion. Later, as we put on our clammy, damp clothes and wedge our feet back into our wet boots, we are covered by a swarm of orange wasps, all up our legs and arms and on our hands. Nod hardly seems to notice, and I breathe against my alarm and continue steadily to tie up my boots. One of them stings me; the pain is sharp, but I don't let on. I say that they're harmless; and, as we set off, thankfully we leave them behind.

It's flatter country now. We walk slowly for another hour and a half. The river widens and winds, and lots of other rivers seem to join it and fuse with it; or is it just the same river looping back on itself? We cross it and recross it ten or twelve times, and sometimes we just splash along in the middle. In the golden light of late afternoon everything is aglow and shimmering. We pass stretches of white sand, sun-flecked shallows, darting fish. The high fringe of forest canopy on either side is translucent, full of birdsong and the whirring of hornbill wings. Some of the trees have coloured leaves: red, purple and white, mimicking flowers. And there are endless cascades of delicate vines, tumbling down and trailing the water's surface. Deep in the shadows, some of the trees are immense, towering with grotesque, hanging roots and wide, wing-like supports. And here there are large pink flowers blooming up their stems in whorls, which we later learn are found nowhere else in the world. This is a wonderland. As the pure gold deepens, I drink it in, and keep willing strength into Nod. Finally, we reach a wide pebble beach. Two more rivers converge and on the opposite bank we can just see the matted leaf roof of a little shack, almost completely buried in a slope of tall green grass. This is our home for tonight: Nod sighs with relief and lies down, still weak but OK.

We're just in time to lay out our clothes to dry in the last sun. After a wash, I sit dipping my feet in the satin water. There are no mosquitoes, no biting flies, no wasps and no stinging ants; just the forest, rising all around, and the increasing chorus of birdsong and frogs. Lots of visible birds too, crossing high over the river in the fading blue; the tiny swallows again and fat orange parrots with lilac-grey wings. And, hanging from a tree near the shack, a spray of creamy, purplish orchids. There was another scare today when a leech got onto my face and started creeping up towards my eye. But now, with the birdsong, river-song, jungle-song and quiet murmuring song of Habe and Tom raking up the fire for supper, I am a peaceful fellow. Waga comes to join me as I am writing my notes and he stretches flat out on the stones, peaceful too. 'Brada bilong mi Waga' (my brother Waga), I tell him. 'Brada bilong mi Richard' he replies, and his laughing, shining eyes are full of brotherhood and pleasure. After we've eaten, he and Tom go fishing in the dark with the only torch; we're still awake when they come back with no fish but twelve turtles. Silently they smoke them over the fire in the dim lamplight: acrid smoke, nauseous smell, and it's stiflingly hot. And on the hard ground there's lots of ants and other crawling things and flies. Aching with tiredness, we lie awake.

Day Three

Up with the dawn again, smothered in bites. There's no more saksak and we need to save the rice for our return, so it's turtle legs for breakfast! They're as tough as leather and only half cooked; we chew and chew, desperate to extract some nourishment. I trusted Lucas and Waga to know what quantities of food we needed for the trip: a mistake. We've only a couple of tins left and the sugar is running low. Nod has trouble pulling on his boots; one of them has split and his foot is still swollen and sore.

We set out down the zigzagging river. It's beautiful at first and still quite cool. I suggest we take it very easy: a short rest every half hour and a good gulp of gastrolyte solution. But my watch stops, gummed up by the humidity, and our friends are keen to keep moving. The ground soon gets muddy and the forest gets wet: muddier, wetter; muddier, wetter. Everywhere is dank and rotting and we wade through stagnant water. Next we leave the river altogether and head out into a swamp. No one is looking forward to this, but it's the only way to reach Gahom. Waga leads again, using rotten logs and trunks as causeways, but they are slippery and often break and then we're knee-deep in foul-smelling black mud. Small, twisted palms and thorny scrub, mounds of roots and no protective canopy above; the heat is fierce and the humidity asphyxiating. Then Nod gets his leg sucked down thigh-deep into the mud and it takes three of us with all our strength to pull him out. The split in his boot is worse and he's going pale again. I can feel when his spirit wanes and I have to will us both on; I'm exhausted too and hungry and it's still getting hotter. Both our spirits are sinking into the mud. Apart from a few blue butterflies, incredible beaker plants with cups full of water the size of my fist, and fungi of all descriptions, some like open white flowers and some like orange stars, this is pretty like hell. Prey to the vulture mud, lost to the cackling sun; I feel as if I am going to faint.

At last, Waga turns with relief and says, 'Swamp *pinis*' (swamp finished). He is tired today too, with a cough and a nasty gash on his foot. He wants to get to Gahom and has been racing on, reluctant to pause and wait for us to catch up. But he does stop to pick a yellow fruit from the ground; it's called *molli*, and looks like a cross between a lemon and a grapefruit. It's delicious and we suck every vitamin going. Another hour and we stumble onto a clearing with a cultivated patch of pineapples. We must be close! In fact, we're there: there's a path and a youth standing laughing; eyes almost falling out of his head with astoundment! Then we're balancing along a narrow pole spanning a wide, deep ditch – and we're out of the trees and into Gahom. A cluster of simple bush houses on high wooden stilts, short green grass and a wide surrounding arc of flowering bushes, pineapple plants, coconuts and banana trees. I never dreamed it would be open and spacious like this. The youth is running with the news and people are already stopping in their tracks. We walk to the house at the village centre. From it, large oblong carvings are hanging, painted white and orange and black, while under it, round a charcoal fire, the villagers gather to meet us. Old men, almost naked, with incredible lined faces, sunken eyes and massive hands. Young men, peering, open-mouthed. A tiny woman in a grass skirt, with shrivelled pointed breasts and the brightest, bird-like eyes. Dumbfounded children in loin cloths. Mangy dogs; a baby cassowary. Flies and smoke. And we are shaking hands all around. *'Nem bilong mi Richard'; 'nem bilong mi Nigel'; 'mi amamas, lukim yu'* (I'm pleased to see you); *'gutpela, gutpela tru!'* (good, very good). Black eyes dance, wide lips crack into grins, and welcomes break into rocking laughter.

Waga, Habe and Tom disappear to visit their wantoks and we are taken to the river to wash. The bank is high and steep and wide-eyed little boys are peeping over the top as we strip and plunge in. It's deep and fast and we have to swim hard against the current to stop being swept away. Simeon, one of the elders, helps Nigel wash his clothes, but the sun is too hot to stay for long and we go back to look for 'our house'. We are to stay with Thomas, the elected leader of the village. He is not married yet and his house, on extra-high stilts, stands close to the arc of flowering shrubs. The ladder is precarious, with the rungs very widely placed. Inside, the house is almost empty. The floor is of springy, wooden strips with gaps between them. Two of the sides are open, and there are just a few belongings dotted around: a pile of old clothes, a chest with a padlock, an empty drum of kerosene, a couple of little carved stools and, hanging from the wall, a bundle of bows and arrows and spears.

Thomas is young and courteous, with an air of contemplative calm. He brings us warm, steamed sago wrapped in banana leaves. It is smooth and white and looks like tripe. Timothy, his broad, stocky neighbour, arrives from the forest with a slaughtered wild pig and presents us with two pineapples. He cuts us big, fat chunks and our bodies sigh with gratitude and soak up the juicy goodness. Later we rest, stretched out on the floor in the fly-buzzing heat. Tom is quietly telling the story of our trek, and the room fills up with boys and men, listening, murmuring, laughing, asking questions. On and on. Next it's waswas time again. Tom and Thomas and a group of the men take us to another part of the river, further down. This seems to be the official place where the men wash and it's reached along a grassy path between coconut and breadfruit trees. There is also a large molli tree and our taste buds quicken, but the fruit looks unripe.

In the early evening, we sit on the narrow ledge that runs from the top of the ladder along the outside wall of Thomas's house. Noiselessly, three young women appear, one behind the other, from the bush. They are wearing only grass skirts that swing gently to the rhythm of their even step. They are carrying heavily laden bilums on their backs, with a palm frond under each to ease the back-breaking load; they have been beating saksak in the forest. Nod jumps down to take a photo; the men call them to stop and they pause for a single moment. The middle woman has a tiny naked child on her shoulders; she turns with the shyest moon-like smile. And then they are moving again, running swiftly like deer, as if drawn forward by an invisible force; loads too heavy to allow them to break the momentum of their journey. Beyond the village, river and green jungle wall there are mountains turning deep purple-blue. And above, in the yellow-mauve light, there are overflowing bilums of feathery clouds. Two tame *koki* (cockatoos) are noisily flapping between the trees and the baby cassowary is scratching down on the ground. It has a long beak, brown and yellowish stripes across it's wingless body and big feet with three scaly toes. At a week old it is already one and a half feet high. Its three-pronged tracks are a miniature replica of the large prints we passed many times on the river banks.

Thomas has told us to ask for anything we need and so we request some *kumu* (green vegetables) for supper. Together we cross the narrow pole and walk to a small cultivated patch where he and an eager neighbour pick us a bunch of juicy leaves. Now it's already dark and our faithful Tom is boiling our rice in the little shack next to the house, and Timothy brings us two fistfuls of hot, wild pig which he puts in our hands. We invite him and Thomas to eat with us and, sitting in a circle up in the house, Tom says a prayer. In the circular glow from the single lamp, there is a warm, easy feeling of kinship. Despite the caterpillars in the greens, and a mouthful of fur when I bite into my piece of pig, we feel nourished and pass our leftover rice to our 'guests', who wolf it down with greedy eyes. When it has to be carried three days over the mountain, rice becomes a rare treat!

We walk to the river in the dark to fetch water for our tea. Then we sit out on the ledge at the top of the ladder again. It is still very hot. Every body movement we make brings out a sweat, so it's a relief to sit motionless. The houses are dark, except for the flicker of fires casting spectre-like shadows through the slatted walls. Fireflies in the trees. A large flying fox. And, overhead, pale misty stars. Youths are strolling around chatting gently – such a soft language. Women cross with flaming torches, and call to each other from house to house. Below us someone is singing, beating the rhythm with a stick, and someone is playing a tune on a bamboo flute. There are only about twenty houses in Gahom, only sixty or seventy people, including children. Such a tiny village in the middle of such a huge forest. Such a tiny hub of life under the laplap of tropical stars. It's time to creep under the mosquito net: our friends brought it for us from Wagu and we are grateful for the little privacy it offers. Sleep comes like a blessing. I am hardly aware of the men coming back and stretching out on the floor around us, filling up the room.

Day Four

Rest day in Gahom. We sleep late, then waswas in the river and wash our towels and spare clothes. Breakfast is pineapple and freshly baked saksak: the pineapple is delectably juicy and the saksak still warm. And with our precious cup of tea, we feel revived, though Nod's swellings and bites do not look good. Again the mountains are wreathed in clouds. A grass-skirted woman with a basket on her head is walking off to her jungle garden, a pet piglet trotting beside her. Waga leaves to catch fish. We go wok-abaut with Thomas. Crossing the river bed where we go to wash, and traversing a long wide stretch of stones, we reach the big river, the Sitipa, which meanders down to the April River, which in turn loops and empties into the Sepik. Because of Nod's split boot, we had hoped we could get back to Wagu by boat; but there's no fuel in Gahom, and paddling can take up to two weeks. The Sitipa is quite wide and we swim at a point where it sweeps round a bend and disappears between beaches of brilliant white stones. Beyond the stones the forest rises; overhead there are eagles and the sun is already high. The boys go to look for wild kumu; Thomas disappears into the undergrowth and we are left in the cool, fast-flowing water. The heat feels dangerous and we soak our hats to protect our heads; but they dry out fast and we have to soak them again and again.

On the way back the stones are unbearably hot and we cling to the narrow rim of shade at the jungle edge. In the village we stop to watch one of the young men carving out a paddle from a single piece of wood; he uses a big axe and works steadily with extraordinary precision. Then we stop at the house with hanging carvings and meet up with Tom. All the carvings are oblong, with a similar design of roughly hewn protuberances like beaks and eyes. They are all painted in the same white and orange and black; and yet each one is different too, bearing the individual mark of it's carver. Tom tells us about the village customs. The boys make these carvings during their initiation into manhood. The Initiation House is away from the village in the forest so that the women can't hear when they are shouting out in pain; the boys stay in the forest and their uncles bring them food, cooked by their mothers and aunts. This used to be when the holes in the end of their noses were pierced; these were kept open with the legs of the large bug that lives in the sago pith. At singsings, the long antennae of the sago bug would be placed in the holes and they waved up and down as the people danced; but these customs are dying out and now only a few older men keep their holes plugged.

Although Gahom doesn't have a mission, they have been strongly influenced by the missionary in Wagu, so beliefs and customs have been undermined and eroded. For instance, women were told not to wear grass skirts. When she sees us, one woman covers hers with an old towel. Others wear rags, hand-me-downs from Wagu, in turn passed down from the mission. In these tatters they look wretched, downtrodden; in their swinging grass skirts of the forest they look regal, full of dignity. And then there's the introduction of a dowry system. Tom had to work for three years to earn the 759 kina (about £500) demanded by his bride's father.

He did it by catching fish to sell at Ambunti market, skinning crocodiles and seeking help from his family and wantoks. But the Gahom people have no income at all and totally depend on their wantoks in Wagu. Here there are several young men waiting for wives without the means to raise a dowry.

Thomas brings us a coconut and, back at his house, breaks it open. We gulp the milk and chew the fleshy lining; then take a long siesta in the deadly heat. Tom and Habe are flat out. Later we sit out on our ledge. The humidity is unbelievable and it's still too hot to move; but then we are persuaded to go waswas again with Thomas. If in doubt, go waswas: what else is there to do? On the way we pass the oldest elder, sitting at a fire on a stool outside his house. His body is emaciated and his face is like a carving of an ancient map. His name is Malakas. Malakas is blind. He wears only a loin cloth, and when he walks he uses a staff and drags his huge gnarled feet behind him. 'Yes, yes, waswas. Gutpela, gutpela!' he affirms, beaming, and with joy he vigorously shakes our hands. His house is exceptionally small and at the entrance there is a naked baby boy sprawling; it seems that he lives alone with this baby. Yesterday, when Waga greeted him, they embraced with tender fondness. On top of the river bank, two of the young men are carving out a canoe; again it is from a single trunk and again they work steadily, chipping away with an axe. A crowd of little boys are watching and the idiot boy of the village comes by, grinning his idiot grin. He is totally naked and rubs himself with mud. The other boys throw wood chips at him and I shout at them to stop: 'Nogat, ples' (no, please). And he wanders off, grinning and muttering, into the bush.

Next, Simeon, the elder who boisterously helped Nod wash his clothes on our arrival, invites us up the ladder into his house. The light in the huge, single room is dim. Again the floor and walls are slatted strips of bark and bamboo; the sloping ceiling is a dense thatch, with strong, supporting beams and two massive uprights – whole tree trunks with intricate carvings around their tops. In three corners there are smoking fires, raised off the ground in circles of stones. Huddled around each fire are skinny women in grass skirts; naked children covered in scabies and ringworm; babies suckling shrivelled breasts; and mangy dogs with gaping sores. The women peek up at us in the grey, filtered light, and the children cling to their grass skirts in fear. Simeon proudly points to each group, explaining who is who in the extended family and which are his blood children. In the fourth corner a man is lying on a stretcher. Slowly he raises himself to greet us; saintly, cadaverous face and haggard eyes. He is sweating with fever. He explains that he used to be the elected leader of the village before Thomas, but now he has been sick for too long. Simeon beams upon his progeny. Ceremoniously he beckons us to sit on a metal chest; it is the only piece of furniture, except for one broken metal chair. Large bilums full of green bananas are suspended from the roof; arrows and spears and baskets are lying around. And close by there is a flaking block of saksak covered in flies. We are presented with a basin of hot brown bananas, and around us the huddling groups are whispering and nodding in the smoke. Someone is picking nits out of a child's head. The dogs are yelping, squabbling; one is shooed out. It is difficult to breathe: partly because the air is so thick and partly because we're afraid of imbibing some virulent, unknown disease. But Simeon beams magnanimously with his knotted, pitted face; his nose is wide-splayed, his eyes are sparkling auspiciously. He is proud of his world, proud to welcome us to it.

On our way home there is a cloudburst and we shelter under the house with hanging carvings. It is the Boys' House and one of the youths takes us up to show us inside. When a boy reaches adolescence, he leaves his family and sleeps here right to the time he marries. Now there are 20 boys and young men here, and also an old man whose wife has died; he has come back for the company. He staggers in, wet, with a bundle of sticks and lies down panting on a raised palette that serves as his bed. The boys and youths follow him in out of the rain and sit down, asking questions. Back at our house, Thomas is wearing a pair of bright red trousers. We show him Nod's broken boot and, using a metal spike and a piece of old nylon cord, he stitches it. In the middle of another cloudburst there is a loud cry, high and resounding: a group of men have arrived from Wagu. The village erupts in noisy greeting. Laden with spears and bags, they are soaked and weary, and clamber up into the next house. They have spent only one night on the way, walking twelve hours each day. Then, with great delight, Thomas teaches us some words in his tokples: *souana*, woman; *ima*, man; *yaya*, hot; *dokineewa*, cold; *denyeah*, sun; *yagoo*, moon; *doo*, star; *hagee nai*, the rain is falling; *un inoo kanima*, see you later.

Evening brings huge piles of billowing clouds over the mountains, touched with orange and, later, an eerie, luminous green. Two women carrying bilums return from the jungle. The young one crosses to meet a tall Wagu man; she is weeping. He holds her briefly, then leaves her to walk on. Something is astir in the village and as dusk falls there is rising agitation all around. One of the Gahom men wants to marry his sister but this is decried. She is distraught. And anyway, he already has a wife. There's a big meeting under the Boys' House, voices raised in anger, confusion. The debate continues and we are forgotten. What are we going to eat for supper? No one has killed a pig today. Waga failed to catch any fish. In the forest, Waga cared for us scrupulously, but now he is turning into a bit of a wag. He has gone off with our salt and sugar and is speeding around with Nod's sports bag slung jauntily over his arm. He is also coughing a lot and has threatened that he is too sick to start the trek back tomorrow. So I rub Olbas Oil on his chest and cover his gash with Savlon and a plaster. But we have to be very surreptitious. Everyone wants medication; there is a lot of sickness in Gahom. Our precious supplies are dwindling and we have to guard them for our own survival.

Only now does Tom remember us. He is apologetic, so sorry, because all we have is a bag of rice. But I insist he finds someone to sell us some kumu; rice is not going to build our strength – and so he goes off into the dark with the torch that is almost dead. Sweating, we make up the fire in the shack, improvise a holder for the pot and start to boil the rice. One boy comes and brings us sticks and, finally, Tom returns with a bunch of leaves – but that is it for tonight. Suddenly there's violent, electric lightning and menacing thunder. When Tom says grace he asks Papa for no more rain: if the rivers swell any more we will not be able to leave. We wash the pots in the river with pebbles and then sit out on our ledge, still sweating and exhausted, but at least with a cup of Milo for comfort. It is still far too hot to sleep. Sheets of electricity – white and purple – light up the outline of the mountains and the dogs go crazy – baying, howling – picking up the tension and unrest of the village.

Day Five

It didn't rain in the night and everyone is up early and on the move. Throughout the night the floor was covered with sleeping bodies, but now, as we climb out from under the mosquito net, the room is empty. We sense it is going to be a big hassle to get away. And it is. We already know our men are reluctant to leave. Waga is nowhere to be found. He still has Nod's bag as well as the sugar and salt. We have asked Thomas to arrange some fruit to take but nothing has materialized. No breakfast either. The atmosphere is tricky. No one is looking at us straight. The man who gave us the kumu now wants payment for it. Timothy wants payment for the pineapples. Fine. But no one will change any money. Does anyone have any money? And no one will help us find Waga.

We express our extreme concern to Tom. It is essential we leave today because of our commitments in Wewak, and it is essential we leave soon so we can cross the swamp before it gets too hot. We do not have enough supplies to stay longer; neither do we have enough strength. If Waga is sick he can stay behind and we will take someone else. Thomas promised to find us fruit: he is the leader of the village; it is his duty to look after us. We are strangers from another country, another climate; we are dependent on his help. Tom nods his head, consternation in his eyes: our faithful friend. We know that he will do his best for us. And he does. A bunch of bananas and pineapples arrive; a slab of saksak; and Waga too, plus bag, plus salt and sugar, though what is left is overrun with ants.

The villagers are milling around us and, already dripping with sweat, it is a struggle to concentrate and organize the packing up. Thomas stands at a distance looking away. He doesn't join the group when Nod takes photos. Just before leaving we are able to catch him up in his house, alone. He is very sad that we are going so soon. Why can't we stay here longer in Gahom? *'Mi sori, mi sori. Gahom gutpela ples. Gahom, gutpela ples'*, he says. There is pain and, somewhere, a foreboding of defeat in the eyes of this young chief, handsome in his prized red trousers, proud to show us his finely carved spears – this young chief of a tiny village too far away, too near the swamp, too full of fever and sickness. Thomas has been to school in Ambunti. He's glimpsed the glittering enticements of the modern world; a world in which Gahom has no place, and against which it has no power. *'Mi sori. Gahom gutpela ples'*. We give him a hug and two kina as a gift. He accepts both with a smile. Thomas Yanwe, you have done your best for us; perhaps there just isn't kumu and fruit to spare. And perhaps we have offended you. Perhaps in your culture it is a discourtesy to visit for so short a time?

By eight o' clock we are ready to leave, and we shake hands all around. A group of women are standing apart, holding babies and tiny children, and when we cross to shake their hands their faces shine, so dark, so shy, so bright. Thomas stands at the edge of the village to give the final handshake of farewell. And then we're over the pole, across the ditch and into the forest. The villagers call after us – high, mellow, birdlike cries – and Habe calls back again and again, until we can't distinguish any more the villagers from the real birdsong.

Men and boys of Gahom.

Women of Gahom.

Thomas Yanwe, Gahom.

After the swamp, we walk at a good lick up the bouncing river. Suddenly Waga stops dead. There's a cassowary round the corner. All three go into action: Tom darts into the undergrowth with his bows and arrows, Habe follows him and Waga crosses the river and disappears. We edge into the river ourselves and catch a perfect view of it: light brown, youngish, about four feet tall. Bending over to drink, it's unaware for a moment and then gone. They miss it. Soon after, a disturbed hornbill crashes up out of the trees. Again we stop dead and all crouch. The giant bird circles overhead and, as it approaches us again, Tom stands with his bow pulled ready. Feigning ignorance, Nod also jumps up to warn it and the bird veers away, saved. Then Waga stops us again. He has a sixth sense. There is a *goanna* (a large lizard) close by. Instantly he is dashing up the river with his spear raised. He hurls the spear and shouts in triumph: a three-foot reptile is dead on the stones. Crimson blood gushes from its pierced side, incongruous against its black, scaly skin. '*Gutpela kaikai*' Waga exclaims, salivating as he cuts off its head and hangs it, dangling, from the corner of Habe's bag.

Homeward bound feels easier; the pressure is off. We stop several times as Tom and Habe dive for fish and turtles. The deeps are green-blue, the shallows golden; sun-splashed trees and sun-splashed bodies. Waga is himself again – laughing eyes and perfect action. We pass the shack where we slept before and walk on. The late afternoon is iridescent. A huge gamebird, a *gurea*, deep blue and grey, with a spectacular crest, thunders away. We set up camp close to the mountain, but below the waterfall. Waga and Tom cut a clearing just above the river and Habe skins the goanna in the last moments of sun.

While they're cooking supper, I sit out on a stone in the river a hundred yards downstream. A purple kingfisher flashes by, and chubby birds with white wings and red faces shout overhead. All around the looming jungle darkens; before me it towers, so high, fantastic layer upon fantastic layer, that I fancy I am facing a mountain. And below this mountain, where the silver river curves away, there is a pebble beach, a bank of grass, a slanting palm, and a gap: bordered by huge descending ropes, an entrance leads into the darkness, into the primal night. The route between Gahom and Wagu, along which Waga and Habe and Tom and their wantoks pass, is no more in width than a tiny hair. Either side and through the entrance opposite, the virgin forest stretches undisturbed, as it has stretched for aeons of time. Watching this magic I slow down. I let the river into my blood. I cup this moment in my hands. This is it. This is what I came looking for. Tiny man on a tiny stone. My feet are in water as pure as starlight. The air is as sweet as liquid birdsong. Far above me, the moon, like a pale glow-worm, creeps slowly out of the trees; and stars like silver ants prick out of the wing-like clouds. Around me, the circling ocean of croaking frogs soaks up the sinking purple light, and behind me, a narrow ribbon of smoke curls up from our fire. In a cold, dark galaxy, there is a fabulous jewel called planet Earth. This is what it used to be like . . .

Nod calls me for kaikai. Supper is turtle and turtle eggs, with rice and jungle greens which Waga has collected for us. The eggs are cherry size with leathery shells, which we split open, squeezing the dense yellow yolk straight into our mouths. With this rich protein and a cup of Milo as well, we feel pretty good. Afterwards, in the dark, we see Waga sitting out in the river gorging himself. The goanna: obviously too much of a treat to share. We fall asleep quickly, but wake shortly after with heavy rain. The canvas holds, we don't get wet, but having woken I can't settle. My thoughts dwell on a moment of panic earlier today: Waga saw a leech sliding into my right eye. Nod has to get it out. He can't; it's small, impossible to get hold of. Very quietly, I tell him to take his time. He tries again. It goes deeper, right down under my eyelid. Absolute panic. But we must stay calm. I have visions of it getting right behind my eyeball, swelling up and bursting the main artery to the eye. And we are still two days' walk from Wagu. What is going to happen? I am going to go blind. Nod tries again. It's worse for him; he has got to try to deal with it. Big drops of sweat are falling from his face. Waga wants to have a go. Nod tells him no, and tries again. But the more he tries the deeper it goes. 'It's hopeless, I can't get it'. He has gone grey with fear, his eyes white with terror. There is a ghastly pause. Then Waga steps forward and with incredible, unbelievable dexterity (he has big, rough hands), somehow gets it between his nails and whips it off my eyeball and out. 'Are you sure? Are you sure?' I keep saying. Yes, Waga's sure; yes, Nod's sure. Wooooooo – that was a close one. It's a long time before we can even mention that moment.

Day Six
The others are already up with the half light making a fire. I hardly slept and I am cold and full of dread for the big walk ahead. I try to breathe myself through the fear, try to breathe myself warm; but I stagger up, feeling like death. Breakfast is rice and the last tin of fish, and the end of the tea. Last night Habe found an especially

strong rope to fix up the camp with; now Waga plants it so it will grow for others to use. We walk to the magical waterfall and refill our water bottles for the climb.

I am feeling as if I can't make it. As we start ascending my heart feels like a ball of lead, as if it's going to conk out, as if my chest is going to break. My legs are so achy and stiff that my knee joints are surely going to snap. I breathe, steadily, evenly, trying to smooth through the fear, the tension; trying to exercise my flagging body, my flagging will. Slowly, slowly, step by step, I get into the swing. We're already dripping with sweat and it's already getting steep. From time to time we stop for a life-giving swig of waterfall water and salt solution. On the mountain top we hear a new and amazingly beautiful birdcall far below; a perfectly melodic phrase, bell-like, descending in a minor key.

At our old camp, with the last bag of rice hanging, waiting, we have a heavenly swim, upstream in a shadowy pool. We all devour the last of the bananas and the precious pineapple that we hassled for back in Gahom; and then we all crash out in the shade. But soon it's 'Malolo pinis' (the rest is finished), and we're off down the easy stretch we remember from day one: the gushing river, the big trees with wide buttresses and spreading overground roots, lots of winding ropes and lots of birdsong. Hornbills crashing, sunlight splashing. We come upon four types of exotic fruit trees for which our guides have no name:

1 A slim tree with a mass of shiny, green, tomato-like fruits: sharp, juicy, fresh-tasting.
2 A larger tree hanging over the river, with round dark leaves and big purple fruits, a bit like soft, fleshy aubergines, but white inside like a pithy guava. The taste is sharp, strong and acidy.
3 Large red cherries, but with small pips instead of a stone: again very sharp and fresh-tasting.
4 A large brown oval husk. Broken open, the fruit is divided into segments; the flesh is yellow pink. It smells as sweet as mango, but Waga insists it is only for pigs and we musn't eat it. It's hard to believe with such a delicious aroma.

There are also lots of berries, all colours and all sizes: *kaikai bilong pissin* (bird food), again not for human consumption. We see a black poisonous snake and giant centipedes nine inches long. We get another view of the blue gamebird, and, on the beach, a very special butterfly: it's wings like a paper cut-out, as delicate as lace; the colour like an intricate batik in fading mauve and gold. We stop where the river is wide and, under the over-hanging trees, it's deep and slow. Waga cuts a new spear and dives for fish; it is hard work and he emerges from time to time, shaking off the water, panting. He manages to spear four large ones, each time hurling them up onto the stones. Habe and Tom tie rope through their mouth and gills and carry them dangling, still half alive. We walk for another hour; back past the mounds of dug-up earth left by foraging wild pigs. One mound is very fresh and Waga shoots off in pursuit. But no luck. Here it is difficult to find a good camping site; there has been a lot of rain and the river banks are steep without any easy access down to the water. We agree on a site. It's already getting dark and they set to work fast, cutting and clearing and making the camp.

We scrape the numerous leeches out of the crevices in our boots and anoint our bite-covered bodies with tiger balm. 'There's no room for any more bites', jokes Nod, 'they'll have to bite on top of bites from now on!' Then, for the last time, we sit out on the stones again, our feet in the wide river; the reward at the end of the day. Here the beach is also wide. The light is duller tonight: grey, almost brown, and thunder growls in the distance. A bough hangs over the stones, full of white, star-shaped flowers, gleaming in the gloom, fragrant with sickly, sweet perfume. As dusk falls, a couple of large kingfishers whistle by, a huge eagle swoops overhead and clouds of small bats tip out of the trees on the opposite bank, like a mist, like falling leaves in a strong wind. They come on and on, thousands of them, missing our heads by inches. And higher up, larger ones with fat wings and long ears are crossing between the treetops.

Later, as we're doddering about, Waga calls us his *pikinini* and he's right. In Port Moresby, an expatriate woman complained about the Melanesian people being like children; but that's only in our world. Here, in *their* world, we're the children, utterly vulnerable, their liability. Tom calls us proudly, holding out an enormous, long, fat eel that he's just caught and baked together with Waga's fish. We all enjoy our supper. Next, right after supper, it starts pouring down with rain; all the while the thunder has been approaching and now it crashes overhead. And the lightning: great sheets of electric blue and purple light up the trees. The rain cascades down and blots out the chorus of frogs and cicadas, and Waga and Tom, who have gone hunting wallaby, return, soaked and empty handed. It is as if a great bucket of water is being tipped over us, a bottomless bucket, on and on. It's too heavy for our canvas roof, and the water comes through and sprays in from all around. Nod and I huddle together, closer and closer, squatting under the groundsheets, burying our sheets and towels and everything else in sight in a great big bundle between us. At first it is thrilling and, after all, we can't complain – this *is* the rainforest. But then we wonder if it is ever going to stop. And is the river going to rise and sweep us away? Suddenly I remember that my boots are still down on the beach. Waga dives out into the steaming torrent and reclaims them. The water level is rising fast; tomorrow's walk could be in jeopardy.

One hour? It must be at least two hours before it finally begins to lessen. And as the rain at last eases, the roar of the river and the roar of the forest surge back. Fireflies are sparking again on the river bank and a pale fluorescence glows on the ground all around us. Miraculously, our sheets and towels are still almost dry. We wipe down the groundsheets and curl up relieved. The oil is finished so there's no lamp tonight. Except for the ghostly fluorescence, everything is pitch dark.

Day Seven

And now it's the last morning; only one more hurdle to safety. Habe is making up the fire again with the first light. We have the last helping of rice for breakfast and the rest of the eel – tasty, sweet white meat, though the slimy, black skin is not recommended. While Tom, Habe and Waga dismantle camp and pack up, we have a last sit out by the river. It's swollen in the night and the beach stones are almost covered. The rush and roar of the water seems to encircle us from all round. And, despite the hardship, the fear and a body smothered in bites, I feel a pang of sadness to leave the rivers, the forest walls, the cry of the hornbill, the cry of the tumultuous wild.

We walk for hours through the lovely forest basin, but it's hard work crossing the rivers: fast, swirling water; slippery stones. Once we wade up to our waists. We get a good sighting of two blue-green parrots with red heads and elaborate crests, and spot a shiny, black butterfly on a stone with a perfectly-shaped orange heart on each wing. There are trees with big, heart-shaped leaves; others with leaves like great, hanging tongues, and some the size of tea-trays, and bigger. I pick one of the enormous leaves off the ground. It is hard to register just how amazing it is. Somehow in the context of the forest it is not extraordinary at all. Waga stops at another molli tree and picks a fruit for us. It is a different variety from the one near the swamp – a larger, rounder fruit with thicker, spongier skin and sweeter, pinkish flesh.

We stop on the beach where we had our first kaikai. There is a small shack here and a couple of pawpaw trees. Waga picks a pawpaw fruit and slices it up for us; and, although it is not quite ripe, it's excellent sustenance for the last lap of our journey. Only a few hours to go as we set off back up along the warm streams and the steep slippery stones; it seems much further than we remembered and we're sweating sheets again. The downward side seems to go on forever and we're both walking on sheer willpower now. All along the trek Nod has been yearning to see a bird of paradise, and now we pass the grove of trees where I had my spell-binding sighting. These graceful trees with whitish bark and delicate high boughs are the bird of paradise's favourite; but now they are empty – their fruit out of season? This is the one great disappointment of the trek; I hadn't realized quite how lucky I had been. 'So where are they?' we ask. Tom and Habe can't answer; they gesture vaguely: 'Another part of the forest.' Then Tom is beating a large hollow tree trunk with a stick; the sound resonates loud and deep like a drum. 'They hear this in Wagu. They know we are coming.' The telegraph of the forest.

'*Wara klostu; wara klostu!*' (we are near the water). At last, at last we catch a glimpse of the lake below us. And at last, at last, we're down on the flat and slopping through the sago palms. A canoe – thank god – has been left for us as arranged, saving us that extra two-hour trek round the lake. As we glide out onto the crocodile water, the finest rain begins to fall. All is silent and the surrounding hills are lost in their ermine clouds. Waga, Habe and Tom stand upright along the canoe, their strong black bodies rippling as they pull with single long oars. The giant white egrets, keepers of the lake, and thin black cormorants watch from the trees on the shore. Low in the Sepik grass, a woman and a boy are fishing; and as we pass a fat sago palm, Waga and Habe discuss it at length: who does it belong to and is it ready for harvesting? Maria is the first to see us as we land on the mud, and she greets us with bubbling laughter and smiles: 'Oh Richard! Oh Nigel!' She is so happy that we are safe. Immediately she takes our filthy clothes to wash them in the lake; and soon we are sitting with Lucas and the children as she stuffs us with the juiciest pawpaw and the sweetest coconut milk. Later, we wash in the creek, playing 'bikpela pukpuk' with Ringo and Keith; and then, as we rest on the mattress up in our own airy, rickety room, we are in the very lap of luxury and Wagu feels like a five star hotel!

IV

WE DID IT! Nod, you have reached a remote village in dense virgin rainforest in Papua New Guinea – and survived to tell the tale. I think you can now call yourself a 'traveller'. No more safe tourist holidays sprawled out on a white sand beach under a plastic umbrella sipping chilled, freshly-squeezed orange juice – well, maybe just occasionally.

I only have one small regret, that I didn't take any journal notes on the way, but I guess I had enough to cope with: collapsing by the waterfall, getting stuck in the swamp, and my foot swelling up; I felt more like a liability to Rick than a companion. Waga, Habe and Tom must have thought me a real weed at times, but they didn't show it. I hope I thanked them enough for their attentive patience. I hope the kina that we agreed to pay them will reward them for their strength. Waga, with his incredible hunting skills. Habe, who was so delighted to be with his wantoks in Gahom, flitting from house to house telling them the story of our bikpela wokabaut – how they all must have laughed when told of the antics of *tupela* (the two fellows). And Tom, constantly on the lookout for us, helping us in Gahom when no one else could. Thank you, all three.

So this changes things a bit. I wanted a new perspective; now I certainly have one. No longer going along for the ride: having experienced the forest and its people, I now have my own conviction to spur me to do something. As fate would have it, I have already begun. Tonight as we walked through Wagu, we came across Joseph sitting on the steps of his house; he is one of the elders that Ricky had the meeting with last year. He invited us into his big house. In the corner next to the smoking fire sat his blind father. We sat with them and had the follow-up meeting Rick had long been awaiting, about their concern for their forest. Lucas translated patiently. Solomon 'number one', Petrus and many other villagers piled in too. We begun by repeating the same warning that Rick had given them last year: about the danger of big companies coming in to log; about the necessity for an environmental plan and a replanting scheme; about the risk of the big logging companies tricking them with false promises, as has happened all over the world. I stood back and listened to us all and realized that here I was talking to the people that it mattered to most. I looked around at the faces and the house and caught a sense of excitement and urgency in my heart.

They told us of a man called Harry Sakaris from the College of Forestry in Lae. He had been the leader of a team who had spent several weeks doing an ecological survey in the Hunstein Range; Petrus had been one of the cargo carriers. So now there was a person whom Rick could legitimately contact for the information that he had peviously failed to obtain. Even though Harry had not crossed Mount Samsai, he had given the same warning to the Wagu people that we were giving. They had heard about a meeting that is to happen in March to decide which company would start logging. They asked us to find out more about this in Wewak and let them know. In response to their questions, we told them of our connections with Friends of the Earth in England. The Rainforest Campaigner, Simon Counsell, would be happy to offer some advice and guidance if they wrote to him. We impressed upon them that FOE only act if asked directly by local people.

Later at Lucas's house, when he had written a letter to FOE, Solomon and Joseph came to sign it. It was just getting dark and Lucas had lit the kerosene lamp which was hissing wildly; we were all sitting cross-legged on the floor. Lucas signed it. He then invited Solomon and Joseph to do the same. Solomon leaned over and put his hand flat on the top of the pen while Lucas wrote his name, thereby effectively signing it. Joseph in his turn did exactly the same. These people are illiterate: how on earth are they going to cope when it comes to reading and signing contracts with the ruthless logging companies? My heart rose into my mouth with the thought of their utter vulnerability. The precious letter is now safely tucked away for posting in Wewak tomorrow. My resolve to help these people to protect their forest in any way I can deepened at that moment. These are quiet, patient men who trust us. I cannot let them down. It seems they have no clear notion of what may be their fate. No one could shed any light on the mysterious Billimer company that Lucas had written to us about. It looks like we are going to be kept pretty busy in Wewak. How will we fit all this into our tight workshop schedule? Good old Trust and Patience will have to come to the rescue.

It occurred to me after the signing that the dark horse had been absent from these discussions. I wonder if he is off somewhere plotting against us or peering at us from the shadows. But there is no time to worry about that. Tomorrow first thing we are off to Wewak, sadly – I would like to spend more time here in Wagu. I need more time to build my own relationship with the villagers. More time for that must be written into our next visit. Because there surely will be another.

From Nigel's journal. The police house, Ambunti. Mon. 8 January.
This morning it took an age to get here from Wagu. Lucas's engine
kept spluttering and cutting out. We bobbed around in the hot sun
while he fixed it. We phoned Anton from the DOIC's office.
Mistakingly, he had come in a truck to pick us up on Saturday and
he cannot come again until tomorrow. *Stuck.* Leanne, the DOIC's
secretary, came to our rescue; a gorgeous, round-faced, round-
bodied woman with a red hibiscus flower in her hair. When we told
her of our interest in the forest, she merrily explained that she has
a sister, Cathy, who works in the Department of Forests in Port
Moresby, and gave us the name of Martin Golman, the Forestry
Officer in Wewak. What a stroke of luck and exactly what we need!
I wrote down this important piece of information and put it safely
away. Leanne also helped us with accommodation and arranged
this police house: one double bedsprings with no mattress and no
other furniture. Once we had settled here, I shot off to the trade
store to buy peanut butter, crackers and corned beef for lunch and
a couple of tins for supper. I bumped into Waga who came back
and shared our lunch.

While we were enjoying the luxury of familiar food again, he
asked us if we had given Habe and Tom the same 'present' for
guiding us through the forest. We confirmed that we had. He asked
us to buy him some batteries for his torch – so back off to the trade
store we went. There his brightest of bright eyes fell upon a big
silver torch. Could we buy it for him? And the transistor radio
beside it, could he have that too? We apologized and said the
batteries were what we had agreed to and nothing more. If Waga
could be pulled towards indiscretion over batteries and a torch,
how on earth will he fare with the empty promises of a mercenary
logging company? Again my heart jumped into my mouth at the
enormity of what we had taken on. How to help them regain
confidence in their own wisdom and belief in their own ways, and
yet not to deny them the 'development' that they so desperately
seek? We gave a warm goodbye to Waga, but sadly not to Lucas.
Like last year, Rick tells me, he just disappeared. When we went
to look for his canoe it had gone. After all his kindness I feel not
to bid him farewell makes the time with him incomplete; I have a
nagging feeling that perhaps we did something not quite right.

But tonight it is a relief to be alone here. We lit a fire outside
and cooked the baked beans and curried chicken in their tins. We
even had to borrow a tin opener from a willing neighbour and

spoons to eat them with, having left both behind in Wagu: talk about bad boy scouts! We sat by the glowing embers of the fire looking up at the glittering stars. A dog came and settled cosily by my feet; funny how dogs know I like them and always come to find me. A rest point and a moment to reflect at the turn of events. A time for preparation for the new part I am to play. This role feels even more demanding than playing Richard II or Jimmy Porter, up to now my two most challenging parts. Here I am in a real-life drama that is going to test all my old and newly acquired skills. So tomorrow we start back to urbanization and meetings and workshops. It's very sad that, because of our heavy schedule, we will not be able to visit Ilahita on the way. Again something to come back for. I feel that I'm planting seeds here that are going to take a few years to flourish.

From Nigel's journal. Raun Isi campus. Wednesday 10 January. While Rick was leading his Daring To Write, I was taken to meet Martin Golman, the First Assistant Secretary for Forests in the Department of East Sepik. The offices are set high up overlooking Wewak at Kreer Heights, where Rick had gone originally to find out about Wagu: a spectacular view of the sea and harbour, and, to the west, the forest gallops down to the edge of town. Martin's office is in the top deck of a two-storey, wooden-walled, louver-windowed building. I approached a shaky door (reflecting the state of my tummy!); on it a tatty sign hangs from one rusty drawing pin: *Department of Forests*. Acutely aware of my lack of technical knowledge and afraid that Martin might think me ignorant, I reassured myself it would be all right 'as long as I don't pretend to know what I don't know'. I took a deep breath and knocked on the door.

Martin is six feet tall, well-built almost to the point of running to fat, mid-thirties and with the most amazing pair of hands I've ever seen: long, tapering, strong, yet delicate fingers that he uses expressively. He wore a bright turquoise short-sleeved shirt. As we sat and talked he constantly wiggled his legs from side to side. We sized each other up and within about thirty seconds I decided that I liked and trusted him. I also saw that he was as scared as I was; suspicious and curious. This helped to allay some of my own nervousness from knowing that I couldn't afford to mess up this important meeting; I knew this man had some vital clues that we needed. His office was small and tidy and overlooked the car-park. Because of our mutual shyness, this car-park received a lot of attention throughout the half-hour we spent together.

I told him of my theatre background and about our work with Raun Isi. He was impressed with my story of our bikpela wokabaut, which felt like a good start. He is a local of the Hunstein, living in Malu, the village where the dark horse nearly catapulted us into the river. I said I had come to see him at the direct request of the Wagu villagers, to satisfy their questions and fears. He listened attentively. He confirmed that there was indeed a logging project underway called 'The April River and Salumei Project'. He explained that it was a plan to log *selectively* half a million hectares (which we later worked out to be two thousand square miles); this consisted of highly valuable kauri pine, the wood that Rick had tried to find out about back home. Martin told me that his department was carrying out a survey into the tree species of the area; this was independent of the Harry Sakaris survey. It was certainly too soon for the plan to be out to tender yet as the villagers mistakenly thought, and he knew nothing about the so-called Billimer Company. Concerning the dangers of a big logging company coming in and causing mass destruction, Martin reassured me by stating very clearly that he would *never* allow logs to cross Wagu Lake. He confirmed the uniqueness of the forest's flora and fauna, and was acutely aware of the specialness of the Hunstein Range, particularly of Mount Samsai, over which we had walked. He endorsed our concern for the effects of bad logging; the effects of erosion and the damage caused by carelessly floating logs downriver. He wants the area to be guarded as much as we do; after all, it is his homeland.

Having established a good level of mutual trust, I alarmed him by telling him of my Indonesian experience and warned him of the notorious record to date of the big international logging companies – as exposed in *The Barnett Report*. I also questioned him on the Executive Adviser that Rick had met. Martin admitted that he had initially agreed with the plan, but on closer examination he discovered that it had no environmental safeguards, no reforestation contingency, so he had revoked it. Finally, I encouraged him to to continue his environmental stand. I surprised myself with the force and conviction with which I spoke. The strength that I had discovered on the trek to Gahom was still with me. I was grateful for Martin's empathy and I respected his own love for his forest. I saw that here was a man who feels for his people and his forest, and yet is still a forester; it is his job, after all, to cut down trees. I believed after this meeting that he wants to do it well. He offered me the visitors' book to sign and I noticed Rick's entry of last year, 'tourist' next to his name. I was tempted impishly to sign 'environmentalist', but instead I put 'Green Light Productions'.

❖ ❖ ❖

Martin Golman was clearly not the indifferent forester who had first pointed me to Wagu. But, irrespective of the qualities of the individual officers, a forestry department as an establishment had, in my mind, always posed an indubitable threat. Rightly or wrongly, I had always imagined it to be on the other side of the fence from that of the environmentalists. So, all the more credit to Nigel for strolling into the lion's mouth; for winning a level of trust and for proving my prejudice to be at least partly unfounded. The identification of the April/Salumei region, the vast area to be logged, was a new key piece of the jigsaw and the fact that it had not yet gone to tender meant that time was still on our side. The news of the collapse of the ex-Executive Adviser's mega master-plan was a relief (so I had been right about those panther eyes) and the confirmation of the ecological survey indicated that the crucial missing link was now tangibly in reach. 'Sherlock Holmes and Doctor Watson' left several messages for Harry Sakaris at the College of Forestry in Lae. They dismissed the Billimer Company as a red herring. They posted the precious letter to Simon Counsell with a covering note. They asked Anton to try and set up a meeting with the Premier of the Province: if they were going to be of any use they would have to raise their profile and enter the murky corridors of politics.

At the same time, we now had the privilege of meeting and learning more about the Sepik people through our workshop programme. I had always had a yearning to be more than just a traveller. Drifting and observing was fine, but how much richer to be able actually to participate and share with other cultures in a work arena. My aspirations were rewarded. The following days were extraordinary and, despite the difficult conditions, many doors were opened. Our endeavour was not to impose *our* methods and values – rather the reverse, to learn from *them* and to encourage the blossoming of their own rich ideology, artistry and creativity which has been so quashed and discredited by Western influence.

A two-day Daring to Write took place, with seven writers squeezed around a precariously rickety table in the hard, uncomfortable Raun Isi 'studio' next to the rat-infested kitchen. Before I had even concluded my brief introduction I was sweating buckets. The group wrote powerful stories in a mixture of English,

Pidgin and their own individual tokples: stories about the day-to-day life in their villages, about the legends of their ancestors and about the dilemma between the traditional way of life and the white man's call for development. One participant's work immediately stood out: a young man called Denis Waliawi. Throughout the course his attention never flickered and his burningly intelligent eyes absorbed everything. He was engaged in a story about police brutality. The hero, a young innocent from a Sepik village, was mistakenly arrested on his journey to Port Moresby to pursue his further education. His resulting imprisonment and mistreatment totally changed the course of his life and he lost forever the wisdom and ways of his ancient and spiritual heritage.

On the first morning of the three-day Mastery of Acting workshop, Nod got up early to boil the urn. It took so long, we had always had our tea an hour after our breakfast; that morning we would have the luxury of drinking it *with* our bread and fruit. When I emerged from the single-drip shower, he was sweeping the studio floor with a single-twig brush: 'Why do we always have to do *everything* ourselves?' he sighed, already drenched in sweat. But then, Alice brought two large bunches of flowers and leaves which she put into old Nescafé tins as vases. We started with nine Raun Isi actors. Three more participants, including Anton and Denis, whom we had especially invited, turned up late, having been stranded in town. And shortly before lunch break, the only two female members of the company were discovered hiding in the kitchen, too shy to come in and join us. Nigel worked with delicate skill; little by little disbanding the shyness, gently encouraging humour and a frank rapport. The actors responded like wallabies hopping out of a wood, eager to play in the sun, yet easily frightened away. Their work was physical, intuitive and colourful.

The short individual pieces they had prepared took the form of mime and improvisations and stretched to ten minutes, fifteen minutes and more; once imaginatively involved, their concept of time dissolved. Their stories, as with the writers, evolved around village life and around tradition and legend. Dominic's mime was about the stealing of a giant watermelon. Alex was a boy playing truant from school who went into the forest to hunt birds with his catapult. Josine, the newest and shyest member of the company, came into her own depicting a timeless, day-to-day story about her village and her grandmother who cast a spell on the young man whom she loved. The work of Lucas Kou, one of the senior members of the company, stood out particularly. Lucas was partially deaf; his father had once beaten him so severely that one of his eardrums had burst. His story was about fear. It centred round a puppet-maker who was plagued by a Pig Spirit. Lucas played both, totally changing character as he donned the mask of the Spirit. Initially the puppet-maker was overcome with terror, but eventually he found the courage to shoo the Spirit away and complete his singular and comical little puppet. Lucas's performance was both dramatic and humorous, and his miming, using every muscle of his body, was both sharply accurate and evocatively soulful. Like Denis, he had hungry, burning eyes. He was ravenous to learn more and improve his craft; he felt deeply thwarted by the company's financial and structural problems which impeded its work and stifled its growth.

Possibly that proved to be the most valuable part of the workshop: the open discussion. Actors daring to air their dissatisfaction. Like everything else in modernized PNG, Raun Isi is rigidly hierarchical; again, its form is an out-dated copy of colonialism. To sit on the floor with Anton and Larry and share ideas and concerns had clearly never happened before. These actors seemed unused to expressing feelings. Was this further inheritance from the colonial tight-lipped rule? Or was it their own traditional way? Maybe an uneasy marriage of the two? Whichever, Nigel approached this area of the work with caution; especially after the raucous response my earlier demonstration in the kitchen had received. His instinct was right. Beneath the reticence and reserve there lay volcanoes. During an acting exercise exploring a variety of emotions, the division between exercise and reality quickly blurred. When it came to anger, we literally had to hold the actors apart. One of them picked up a spear that was standing in a corner and had to be forcefully restrained from hurling it at his partner!

During the weekend we also began to learn how this volatility was a mirror to the rawness and volatility of their lives. On the Friday night, Anton announced that half the members of the workshop had been invited to provide the music for a large party at a nearby village. These gigs provide the main income for the company, so we couldn't refute their decision to go. On Saturday morning they were ready to start on time; but they had been playing all night – outside, with drunks from the swirling crowd hurling bottles and abuse at them. The transport that was supposed to have brought them back had not materialized. The only early-morning bus had been going in the opposite direction; so they had hijacked it and demanded it turn about and bring them back to Wewak. But then the fuel had run out and they had

had to walk to another village which had the only working petrol pump in the area. Unperturbed by these events, they were quite ready to embark on another day's work.

Then on Sunday, Denis was missing. There had been a wedding in his family and the previous night there had been a wedding feast. His younger brother had got drunk and driven off in the hired car; the car had been found wrapped around a tree. Denis had spent all night traipsing the highways and byways, searching for his brother. On Sunday morning he had had to play mediator between the different, heated factions of his family. Like us in the exercise, he, in real life, had literally had to hold them apart. Again on Sunday morning, the woebegone mother of one of the female Raun Isi members arrived. Another family feud was raging and, before we could continue the workshop, a vociferous debate with much wringing of hands took place. Afterwards, a revived mother with her wantoks and friends stood at the mosquito-screened window and roared with laughter at the white men's antics. Then, after all was over and we had even escaped for a swim in the warm, viscous sea, Lucas was missing from the celebration feast that Anton and his wife Nancy had prepared. He arrived late, harassed and angry. His big uncle had wanted to sell his sister for a video; Lucas had confronted him and had been attacked with an axe. Now his uncle threatened to obtain a gun and shoot him. The conflict of old and new, between traditional values and Western materialism, was not only a topic for the Daring to Write stories and the Mastery mimes, it was being played out in real life before our very eyes. I remembered William's story of his last exchange with his mother. These people had also travelled thousands of years in a lifetime, been wrenched from the forest, wrenched from their own ancient Gahoms. I thought of Waga in the trade store. Of course he wants those shiny things. But where does craving end? The forest felt more vulnerable than ever. And the protection of it even more vital.

The feast was delicious; served outside on the grass. It rounded off our programme well. Several times we had felt like giving up. When people hadn't arrived; when people had fallen asleep; when the heat and the sweat had got too much; when I had had a flaming row with Joe Mande, Anton's boss, the Provincial Secretary of the Department of Culture and Tourism. But now we were both relieved that we had seen it through. Respect and trust had been built all round and the actors' eyes were alight with enthusiasm and rekindled fire. Even Joe Mande arrived, plethoric and bountiful in a large laplap, and was placed in an even larger chair to watch *Brukim Bus*, a Pidgin video on logging. He also gave a formal speech of thanks. Nod made a return speech, acclaiming the talent in the company and urging that it be used to its full potential. Under the stars we both knew we had done our best. Under the stars Joe was keen to watch another video. Now our only mission left in Wewak was to tackle the Premier.

❖ ❖ ❖

From Nigel's journal. Wewak. Monday 15 January.
Anton came to pick us up for the meeting with the Premier. As we drove up the hill, he said that he had one 'small disappointment' to tell us – the Premier is not in his office today. We will have to meet Bella Seiloni, the Acting Secretary, instead. At the Department offices, ready to express our displeasure, we were met with hushed tones, he was in after all and would see us! So Anton, I, Rick and Bella were ushered into an air-conditioned office with comfortable bamboo chairs and pictures of the National Cabinet hanging below an imposing portrait of 'the Chief' – Michael Somare, PNG's first Prime Minister and a Sepik. Behind a large, polished wooden desk on a high-backed swivel chair sat Bruce Samban. He smiled politely, exposing betel-nut-stained teeth. He wore shiny black trousers, an immaculate white shirt and blue tie; his hair well-cut and oiled. An attractive, charismatic man, about forty. Implacable. Impeccable. Nervously we introduced ourselves and gave a run-down of our work with the Raun Isi company and in the writing workshops. Joe Mande crept in sheepishly late and slid onto a chair.

We congratulated the Premier on the high level of talent in Raun Isi and encouraged him to use them more. We observed that the company had become stagnant and disillusioned and requested a truck for them – after all they are called Raun Isi *Travelling* Theatre, but how can they travel without a truck? He listened attentively as we had been primed he would, but did not respond; his eyes somewhat dull and implacable as ever. Next, we moved onto our bikpela wokabaut long Gahom, and introduced the forest issue. We reiterated all the points I had raised with Martin Golman. We ended by stressing a point that Rick and I had been discussing: that if his Province really implemented a sustainable (regenerative) forestry plan, they would win world acclaim. The world was waiting on tenterhooks for such a project – and with it he had the opportunity of bringing his backwater into the international limelight! At this there came a tiny flicker into his eyes. Then we asked for his comments.

Silence – uneasy silence. We held our breath for a long moment. Bella Seiloni, the round-bellied Acting Secretary with a glorious chuckle, saved the day with the news of a new Land Act that ESP (East Sepik Province) were trying to get through Parliament to safeguard the local people's rights to their land, ensuring that all transactions passed through the provincial offices. He told us that ESP has innovative ideas, ahead of other provinces. Finally, Bruce piped up. He thanked us for our recommendations, observations and suggestions. He said that few people took the time and trouble to go and report to him. He was happy that we had had such a rich experience in his Province. All very diplomatic and correct. Then a slight chink appeared in his armour. He told us that he was writing a play about the election process in PNG. He asked us if we would read it when it was finished and give our comments. Of course we would. In the past he had been a very popular radio announcer and story-teller; when he is out and about people often still ask him to tell his stories. For a moment his eyes cleared and came into focus; so he is an artist masquerading as a politician! We had found a gossamer connection. After an hour the meeting was closed, handshakes all round; we promised to write and send him a report of our trip. We left. Joe was happy; Anton was happy; and we felt that we had penetrated the Premier's implacability for a moment.

As a reward, Joe put his Department's vehicle at our disposal for the afternoon and we were taken on a guided tour of Wewak by Anton. Then a view of the Premier's residence and garden, plus a trip to famous Wom beach where the Japanese surrendered in World War II. Afterwards, we were taken back to Raun Isi and a farewell meal prepared by Alice and Larry. As we were packing in our room, Larry and his children came to watch. There was a knock on the door and Alice and her friend tentatively entered. Alice handed me a beautiful bilum that she had made out of cuscus fur; the nameless friend presented Rick with a bright red and yellow bilum; we both also received 'Paradise Beach' laplaps. And, graciously, they said goodbye.

V

From Nigel's journal. Port Moresby. Wednesday 17 January.
'*Tupela yu lusim sampela weit*' (you've both lost some weight),
remarked William when he met us at Port Moresby airport
yesterday morning. Back at his house we moved into the big room
that has a bathroom attached – shorter for Ricky to run! He has
chronic diarrhoea. A few hours to rest and recover before another
and last crammed week of workshops and meetings. Today has
been hectic; didn't know life in Port Moresby could be so frenetic!

8 a.m. Met with the National Secretary for Culture and Tourism at
the big Waigani Central Offices. Gave him the run-down of our
work with Raun Isi and our proposed programme here. His main
question was: can we be effective in a two-day and a three-day
workshop? He spent time telling us about his recent initiation; it's
unusual for an older man to decide to get initiated.

9.30 a.m. A recorded interview for NBC, PNG's national radio. A
veritable shed. One microphone suspended from a cup-hook on
the ceiling, two very squeaky chairs and a tape that has exhaus-
tively been recycled.

11 a.m. Meeting with the President of Friends of the Earth, PNG.
Took Rick home first, otherwise likely to be a nasty accident! The
President is just recovering from a serious bout of malaria. Knew
nothing about April/Salumei Project. Promised he would come to
the 'Environment Day'.

12.30 p.m. Quick lunch and check on Rick. Then to William's office
for a series of phone calls to set up tomorrow's meetings. Also still
trying to reach Harry Sakaris. No luck.

2.30 p.m. Visited the Head of the Literary Institute where Rick is
supposed to do his Daring to Write; but, bad location – an open
courtyard with doors from all the offices leading on to it and close
to heavy traffic. Not suitable. William will have to find another
venue.

4.00 p.m. Westpac Bank Manager who is the MTG (Moresby
Theatre Group) President. He has offered us the Arts Centre for the
Mastery. Wiry, pale, tight, expat Australian. His attitude summed

up by his comment: 'Oh we will do *South Pacific* – we can use all our National members in that; as the chorus they won't have to learn any lines'. It was hard to be gracious.

6 p.m. Invited to observe the recording of a new radio play, *Warriors of the New Dawn* at the NBC. Chaos. Two of the leading actors who had been at a two-day conference decided to stay on and get drunk. Consequently I was asked to play a part. Hasty rewriting of the script produced the part of an Australian expat adviser to the rebel government. So, among peeling soundproofed walls, three rickety chairs and a three-legged table with one multidirectional mike, again hanging from the ceiling, we recorded the first part of the play. Part Two to be continued tomorrow; so I have recorded my first radio play for Papua New Guinea national radio!

11 p.m. Home to attend to Rick and to scribble down these notes to relieve my scrambled brain.

From Nigel's journal. Port Moresby. Thursday 18 January.
William and I had two important meetings back-to-back. First, with Cathy Munagun at the Department of Forests, the sister of Leanne who helped us out when we got stuck overnight in Ambunti. When I phoned her office she had been immediately welcoming and happy to meet us. We drove to the Department of Forests which was quite unlike the one in Wewak: it occupied the whole of a single-storey building. We waited in the wide entrance hall that had a map of PNG made out of samples of their indigenous timbers. Cathy came to greet us and took us into the large neon-lit office: big drawing tables, large maps hung on the walls. She gave me a *strong* handshake and greeted William warmly. Bright, alive eyes, a squarely-built woman, 5 feet 4 inches, with well-defined jaw; a very rich, throaty laugh, and a strong conviction in her voice and manner. She was delighted that we had met her sister. She told me she too has walked in the Hunstein Range; she is a landowner there and knows it well, although she has not gone all the way to Gahom. She verifies its uniqueness and is herself awaiting the results of Harry Sakaris' survey. I repeated the points I had made to Martin Golman. She nodded in agreement. Yes, she too is strongly in favour of environmental safeguards, reforestation and careful extraction of selected timbers. Cathy was affected by William's powerful presence and referred to him a lot. He is of course a famous and well-respected actor and director; she had seen his plays many times.

She explained that in a remote area such as the April/Salumei, monitoring was the biggest problem. There is new satellite photographic technology that can be used, but it is very expensive. She also described a way of extracting the logs using a suspended pulley system to lessen the damage of heavyweight machinery on ground level. All in all she gave me the impression that she had a deep concern for things to be done well for the benefit of her people and her country as a whole.

We shook hands and I promised to keep in touch with her. I was pretty pleased with myself for conducting my second meeting about a subject that I still had very little knowledge of. This new role I had taken on was certainly testing my mettle as an actor; not that I was acting, but that I was able to put conviction into a subject that I was not familiar with. I felt like I had made a firm contact and, with the current state of play here, that is important. The situation is hotting up and I sense that we may need to be back pretty soon. This feels like a crucial year, the economic strains are showing and the urgency of the Government to raise revenue may force them into some hasty decision-making. Their valuable trees are, of course, an obvious target for creating that revenue. Getting stuck in Ambunti was a blessing in disguise.

Next off to NBC for a live interview with Francesca Samusa on 'Community Hour'. She is another amazing woman; another strong handshake and direct eye contact. These women have had to work through so much to get themselves to high-profile positions, as Mary Sundrouwau had pointed out to Rick on their first meeting in Wewak. William, Francesca and I share one microphone, the co-presenter is on the other. For the third time in short succession, I talk about the forest, our trek and the need for environmental care – this time with thousands of people listening. I stressed Green Light Productions' interest in culture and how rich PNG is with all its varieties. I feel completely easy and confident. William talks wonderfully about his bird play, *Conference of the Birds*, that Rick saw on the beach last year; how it entertains and informs people about the need for respect of birds and animals. So, all in all, we cover in half an hour exactly all the topics we want to.

While Nigel was vanquishing Port Moresby, I had to lie low and eat nothing; only boiled water and gastrolyte salts. I was even reduced to watching *Around the World in Eighty Days* with a fairly unimpressed Ani; to counting the strips of the louvered windows in our bedroom, and to tapping out the lacklustre rhythms of the early-evening mission singalongs. Still, great news that we now have a friend in the National Department od Forests as well as the Provincial. And great news too that these forestry officers are people in tune with the land, people of the land, and people with environmental awareness and understanding.

In retrospect I think it was opportune that Nod had been left to conduct these meetings alone. Together we would have leant on the remnants of my 'archaic' biological knowledge; alone, he had to depend on his own intuition. Having reached my destination at last and lived that moment in the starry river on the fifth night of our trek, I was feeling raw. Rainforest devastation was no longer just about the collapse of the earth's 'lungs'; it was also about something deeper – the loss of something at the core of existence – the 'mystery' that I had cupped momentarily in my hands. And the people of the Hunstein Range were not just examples of an old culture, but the guardians of this mystery: yet guardians who had no concept of the monumental dangers stalking them. I had always sensed this. It is what drew me to the primary forest in the first place. It was in my Jakarta poem. But now it was no longer an idea – it was an experience; an experience that was alive and kicking. Little wonder I had acted so oddly at that first rainforest encounter with Mr. Uno on the Garuda flight. How could I have explained what I was really after? Would he have understood the contents of my poem? I hardly had myself. In our meeting with the Premier I had felt my emotions rising and had had to work hard to keep the lid on them. Would he, and the forestry officers, have been impressed with the ramblings of a sub-romantic poet? Thank you *pekpek wara* (diarrhoea), I think you incapacitated me at just the right time!

On our first evening back (before the pekpek wara had got too bad), we met Simon Pentanu, the other Vipassana meditator that William had told me about on my first visit. Simon was the Clerk of the National Parliament and arrived in a suitably lavish car; but his manner was far from ostentatious. Black as William, Simon was bearded and had the stoop of someone who had been held ransom at an office desk for too long. His soft handshake and reserved speech belied the smouldering fervour in his eyes. Up in the bedroom, we meditated together. The four of us. Both men were under a cloud and heavily weighed down; for their home island of Bougainville was in strife. There, the kind of destruction we feared for the Hunstein Range had already happened. Bougainville has one of the biggest copper mines in the world. In November 1988, the local people blew up all the power lines and shut it down. This was done in response to the mining company's refusal to recognize the environmental deterioration that the mine was causing. The beautiful Jaba river had become seriously polluted; the fish in the sea were dying; the trees along the river banks were also dying. And, worst of all, the flying foxes had disappeared.

William was the chief of the Flying Fox Clan in his village and their passing had wilted the spirits of his clanspeople. But the revenue from the mine had provided a large percentage of the nation's income, and it's closure had had a disastrous effect on PNG's economy. Recently, under both national and foreign pressure, the PNG Government had sent in the army; their aim was to flush out the so-called militants who were holding the mine. Partly due to the mountainous terrain and the dense jungle, and partly to the stoicism of the Bougainvillians, the operation was failing. But the island was presently stricken with bloodshed and extremist propaganda. Far away from their besieged families and wantoks, William's and Simon's spirits were also wilting. And yet there was pride in their sorrow; jubilation in their pain. For their homeland had defied the so-called march of progress and, against the incredible force of multi-national interests and international pressure, had said, 'No'. A people to be reckoned with. A people who valued the health of their land more than the wealth in their pockets. An environmental inspiration to the rest of the world. Not least to the people of the Sepik.

Originally William had planned to take us to Bougainville over Christmas; but due to the troubles, travel there was now restricted and entry by non-nationals was prohibited. Sadly, our visit would have to be postponed. For the present, we urged William to try to share his suffocating burden, and to find a way to turn his concerns into action. When he introduced himself in the Mastery, with a deep sigh he expressed his anguish to the full. In his performance piece, he portrayed his own youth; his untrammelled boyhood; running free in the lush and pristine forest.

The Mastery in Moresby, was a challenge. It was the most difficult first evening that Nigel had ever encountered. It was held in the smart, expatriate Arts Centre; and, to start with, a large stray dog threatened to maul the participants to death as they arrived. The range of people was the widest possible: from two loud expatriate amateur actresses to timid villagers who had come straight from tending their tapioca gardens. The great divide between black and white was immediately apparent. The Westpac

Chairman's attitude was still clearly part of the general atmosphere. And one of the white actresses admitted, in no half terms, her fear and mistrust of the national people; even their smell she found obnoxious. Later, she was clearly moved when her partner in an observation exercise, and the shyest of all the group, whispered in monosyllabic Pidgin how happy she was that the white woman had looked at her and smiled at her, and even touched her. Later still, after a physical limber, she involuntarily shared her towel with a big sweating national actor. The walls from both sides wanted to come down. So much. They only needed a very little shove. The final resolve of the workshop was to create a performance that would be called *The Bridge*: a joint effort between the national actors and the white expatriate group. Later we heard that this performance was a big success. There was even a picture of it in the Air Niugini magazine.

One sadness for William was the absence of Nick Dukoro. He was the Director of Bougainville's Sankamap Theatre and had been booked to fly to Moresby for the workshop, but he had been detained at the airport and held in custody for questioning. Great was William's joy when he finally arrived on the Sunday afternoon. Nick was a cross between a sea elf and a poet king. His slim, quicksilver body was always on the move. His dreadlocks were tangled. And his eyes were as bright as the *sankamap* (sunrise) itself, and yet hinted knowledge as deep as the ocean. While Nigel and William travelled out to work with the Community Theatre Group in a Motu-speaking village along the coast, Nick had joined me for Daring to Write. In a form similar to Chinese proverbs, he sketched delicate pictures of his partnership with the sea. To Nick, the ocean was an underwater forest and he could read it like a map. He knew its contours and all the regions where its different riches lay. Once, when diving into a coral cave, he had come face to face with a giant monster sea-cow. And once while fishing in the moonlight with his father, a gargantuan sperm whale had thrust itself up thirty feet at least out of the water, only a few yards away from their tiny canoe.

With Nick's arrival, William's spirit lifted; for Nick had brought good news. One night recently his mother had been crossing from the jungle's edge to the house and, looking up, had seen two black shadows crossing the full moon. She had called Nick excitedly: 'Quick, look – there are flying foxes in the sky'. Nick had not believed her; 'You are deceived – they must just be sea birds'. But as soon as he looked himself, he knew she was right. There they were: two flying foxes gracefully swooping through the shimmering moonlight. Nick and his mother watched them with streaming tears. Their spirit kin were returning. The closure of the mine had brought back hope.

William responded to this news with two powerful letters. One to all the people of Papua New Guinea, and the other to the Prime Minister. He ended the second letter as follows:

In Bougainville we have realized from our own personal experience with Bougainville Copper Ltd. that preserving a living land for future generations is our utmost responsibility and task. Even if we don't have economic development, so long as our natural land is alive, and clean, we know we will never lose any of the real happiness which we are so ignorantly losing today.

Please tell the world why we in Bougainville will oppose any moves to open the Panguna Mine – to protect and to keep our living land alive – we want to keep Bougainville a traditional land it is. The world can laugh at us and call us stone-age or primitive and backward, that is all right. We are so strongly convinced that the best way is the natural way. In Bougainville we know of the Paradise they said was lost.

Shortly after writing this, the Prime Minister summoned William for a private audience.

On our last day we held Green Light's first environment workshop. The idea for this had been growing in me for some time. The purpose was to take a fresh look at our daily lives and to see how effective we can be in making a positive difference; also to recreate a rainforest situation and to increase understanding of the different factions involved. For this Nigel and I constructed what we called 'The Rainforest Game'. We pinpointed a particular morning in a typical PNG village; it was the morning on which the logging company had come to ask the villagers to sign the contract. A member of an environmental group had arrived to warn the villagers; and the village missionary was also in the thick of it. Each participant was given a card. On it was written their character and their major objective in the game. Some of the villagers were for the logging – some unsure – and some against. Simon played the Elder of the village. William was the white logging company's Operations Manager, and one of the expatriate actresses from the Mastery played the missionary. We divided the National Theatre's run-down studio into four areas – the village, the mission, the loggers' camp and the environmentalist's camp. We checked that all seventeen participants had understood their cards. And then it was over to them: ready, steady, go. They had forty-five minutes to try to resolve the situation. After a low-key start, the studio began to come alive. Soon the participants were no longer acting, they were living their parts. Many of these people were from the forest themselves. What was it to be? Trees or torches? Money or wood? Canoes or cars?

At the end of the game no solution had been reached. The Elder wanted more time. The loggers were threatening violence. The missionary and the environmentalist had found themselves in a sticky quagmire. An animated discussion ensued. Everyone was affected by what they had experienced. The vulnerability of their people was suddenly staring them in the face. The gamble of the forest was suddenly their own gamble for life. Nod and I were also affected. Before our very eyes we had just been shown a glimpse of what we were going to be up against. A game of frightening similarity might well be played out in Wagu – and sooner rather than later.

That night, as we packed up for our workshop tour in the other countries, we made a promise to return to PNG as early as possible in 1991. Sherlock Holmes and Doctor Watson had unravelled some important pieces of the jigsaw; the only one missing was the forest survey and the elusive Harry Sakaris. We also realized our new trek had only just begun. Ahead lay many unknowns: some scary; some unsurmountable? All we could do was to take it one step at a time . . .

In Melbourne I met up with Campbell again. He had left Air Niugini and moved to Australia. He had bought a small property on the northern border of New South Wales, but everything had gone disastrously wrong. His white brother had betrayed him in complex and horrible ways and he was now feeling lost and almost suicidal. I found him staring blankly out of a window on the top floor of a block of flats. He was spending his time wandering the streets and writing his own story which he had called *The Cassowary Man*. Campbell came to spend a morning with me. He was feeling so low and lost that he just lay down, flat out on the floor. His mind was all knotted up. He just didn't know what to do. After a long silence he found his own answer. Above all and beyond all he needed to go and visit his mother. He had neglected her for too long. His heart was burning with shame and guilt. If she should die before he had returned he would never, ever forgive himself. I remembered her plea to me: 'Tell him to hurry. Tell him I miss him every day.' And so I did my best to encourage him to follow this deep wish. I watched him heading off towards the tram. The troubled cassowary man on his own bikpela wokabaut back to the forest.

PART FOUR

RAINFOREST HOPE

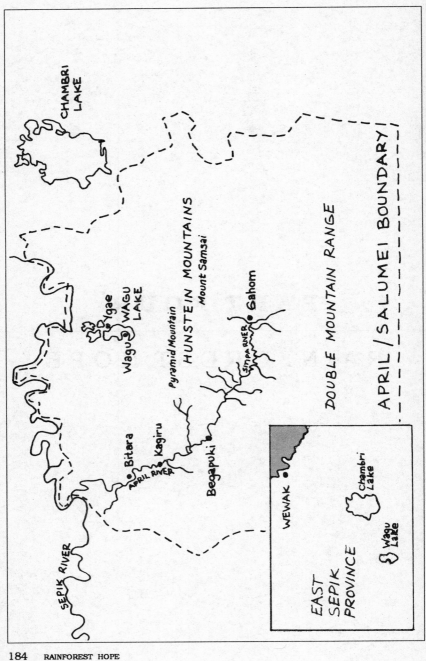

Green Light Productions, Newsletter, 14 May 1990

Dear . . .

We've just got back from our five month tour of Australasia leading courses for performers and writers. Most exciting was our work with other cultures which included the National Theatre of Papua New Guinea, a troupe of young Maori dancers and a large group of actors on the island of Lombok, east of Bali. Part of our long-term aim is to bring you plays encapsulating the richness of these cultures and already there are some wonderful possibilities.
This summer we have the following event to offer you:

Monday 4 June at 8 p.m.   *New End Theatre, Hampstead*

The Severed Head of a Toucan

This is a dramatized reading of our search for virgin rainforest. Using our journals and letters, we take you into the heart of Borneo and then up the great Sepik River in Papua New Guinea.

The reading is our contribution to the FOE Rainforest Festival.

Tickets: £6.50
Rainforest Festival Box Office: 071-490 4670/5210

Our Rainforest Benefit last October – An Evening of New Writing - played to a full house and raised £711 . . . .

Lastly, until we acquire long-term funding, we are in need of some voluntary admin assistance, so please give us a call if you can help. Hope to see you on the 4th!

Best wishes, Richard and Nigel.

I

Our 4 June performance took place exactly two years after my first arrival in PNG. The set was very simple: a log each to sit on, our trekking gear piled between us, and a backcloth of the maps we had used on our adventures. A few green and red gels over the lights to give a forest effect and a rainforest soundtrack to complete the atmosphere. In the first half Nod told the Mahakam story and I described our trek to Gahom. In the second half we told the audience about the logging project, about the threat to the local people, and about our desire to help them. We also suggested that if they were interested they could write a letter to Premier Bruce Samban; just to tell him that they had heard about his forest and to ask him to take care of his precious environment.

We repeated the performance in Stroud a week later, and once again at the New End Theatre in the autumn. From the three performances, nearly a hundred people wrote to the Premier. They all received replies. Many of them phoned or wrote to us excitedly, not really having expected one, especially from the Premier's office with East Sepik's logo on it: a crocodile, a shark, bikpela drums and a haus tambaran. After my previous attempts at PNG letter-writing, it was also a big surprise to me. The letters were congenial and inferred that the Premier was sympathetic to environmental concerns. They also proposed the formation of 'Friends of the Sepik' – a group to assist the Province and lobby for international support. All were signed by Graham Campbell, the expatriate Executive Officer to the Premier. But no letter came directly to us, even though we had written twice ourselves and enclosed the reports on our cultural and environmental observations as promised. These had been completed in Melbourne and copies had also been sent to the other PNG officials with whom we had spoken.

As soon as possible we met up with Simon Counsell. Yes, he had received the letter from Wagu village and yes, he had replied. We showed him our environmental report. In it we did not decry logging altogether, but recommended the inclusion of environmental safeguards and replanting schemes as an integral part of all logging plans. In principle, the Friends of the Earth Tropical Rainforest Campaign was against any cutting of primary forest whatsoever; but Simon could well appreciate the urgency of the situation in the Sepik and how a sustainable plan would at least be far better than a major commercial operation. He was also enthusiastic at the thought of setting up a sustainable model. We knew Simon had a hundred and one campaigns screaming for his attention, but we hoped that we had captured his imagination.

During the time of the Rainforest Festival, a large ensemble of Papua New Guinea dancers arrived in London. Three groups were represented: one from the Highlands, one from the Trobriand Islands and one from East Sepik. The organizer of the East Sepik group was Ivan, a member of the Department of Tourism and Culture, whom we had met in Wewak. Ivan brought Sabena, one of the Highland dancers to lunch. There was almost no free time in their schedule and so we took them shopping on Portobello Road. Both were enraptured by Woolworths and bought plastic flip-flops for their children; they also enjoyed strawberries for the first time. Our friend Ray came to lunch too and they were intrigued to meet a black American. Ivan immediately called Ray his wantok.

We saw a performance of the dancing for schoolchildren in Richmond Park. It was a cold, drizzly afternoon and it left a question mark in our minds. From the outside it all seemed to mean very little. Fantastical headdresses, colourful face-paint, monotonous rhythms; but we were given no real clues as to what lay behind this pageantry. The children were curious, even titillated, but was this perpetuating our deluded notion of the primitive savage? Without any insight into the wisdom that lay behind these dances, where was the door to a deeper and fuller understanding? In the large marquee which served as a changing room, we shook hands with all the Sepiks. They were from the Chambri Lakes of the Middle Sepik some way below Wagu and Ambunti. Patrick Stephenson, who had helped me with my initial investigative efforts, was with us, and his face flushed as he shook hands with the Sepik warriors: something very different from the world of facts and figures, from the concept of the forest, from campaigns. Patrick shared our frustration that the jigsaw puzzle was still incomplete: Harry Sakaris and his ecological survey still eluded us. Following the fruitless phone calls, I had sent him a copy of our environmental report. But, as yet, there was still no reply.

By late summer, Nod and I were swamped again with our next Green Light production. This time it was my drama, *Warriors in a Wasteland*, based on a true story of two of the young homeless people with whom I had worked. They were another kind of warrior: young urban warriors fighting for their dignity and independence, though in a way this was what we felt the modern Papuans were also doing. The play was booked for a four-week run, again at the New End Theatre.

Coinciding with the beginning of rehearsals in early September, our friend Simon Pentanu, the Clerk of the National Parliament, arrived in London; he was on his way to a formal Parliamentary conference in Luxembourg. He took off his shoes and socks and stretched out on our Notting Hill flat carpet with a sonorous sigh of relief. He shovelled down our simple vegetarian nosh and enjoyed a walk across Hampstead Heath, marvelling at the frequency of the planes passing overhead. Simon had been profoundly affected by his experience of the Elder's dilemma in the Rainforest Game; he had subsequently organized an 'Environmental Walkathon' and, with William, started a group in Port Moresby called *Indigenous Environmental Watch*. He had brought with him a copy of the PNG Government's recent White Paper on Forestry Policy. He called it 'the White Paper with the Yellow Cover'. It forcefully propounded the need for sustainable development, and that national people should be used to log their own trees; also that the revenue accrued should remain in the country and not disappear overseas as had been exposed in *The Barnett Report*. In theory, Simon agreed, this was an excellent step forward; but in practice would these new ideas be executed? However, we could now quote the Forestry Department's own ideology back to them. We could no longer be written off as greeny extremists.

During this period we also wrote ourselves to Graham Campbell, Premier Bruce Samban's Executive. We were wary. Why had he written to our audience, but not to us? Until we could meet this man we should not give too much away. So we simply asked him how he saw 'Friends of the Sepik' operating and what more precisely he would like its function to be. If we were really going to get something up and running, the format should come from East Sepik and not be imposed by us. We received a reply, but the *Warriors* were already running riot and we hardly even managed to glance at it. Producing another play on a shoestring budget meant that once again, for a while, the forest had to lie low.

However, our 4 June reading also rebounded on us in another way. Two members of the audience, Brian and Celia Wright, wrote a full report for *Green Farm Magazine* on the evening and our Sepik endeavour which they entitled 'Rainforest Hope'. They also brought *us* hope. They had been particularly heartened at receiving a reply to their letter to the Premier and, in the middle of the *Warriors* whirlwind, we received a phone call from them. Brian and Celia belong to an organization called *The Network For Social Change* which sponsors new initiatives, both cultural and environmental. They recommended we approach the Network for some funding to set up this 'Friends of the Sepik'. But a full application was required, accompanied by a full project proposal. With my head already bursting with actors, mail-outs, posters, programme notes and party bookings for sponsored youth groups, how to find a space for this important application? Though sympathetic to my plight, they urged us not to miss the opportunity.

A few weeks later, two members from the Network came to interview us at the flat. They seemed more nervous than we were. But once we had clarified why in the world two theatre people were trying to save a rainforest, we got on very well and had an interesting meeting. Both interviewers became enthusiastic and promised to recommend us to their group. Meanwhile, Celia had suggested that the *Toucan* reading should be turned into a book. Yes, of course; but what about agents and publishers? I had never had any luck with either. Celia admitted that they had their own small publishing house. Would we like *them* to publish our stories? Yes of course, but – 'No, no buts,' Celia laughed, 'what better way to spread the news of the endangered forest?'

When we finally got to consider Graham Campbell's letter we were astonished at its openness, breadth of vision and sincere tone. He emphasized the pressure that the Premier was under to accrue revenue and outlined several ways that Friends of the Sepik, which he now called FOTS, might help in establishing alternative rural developments to mass logging. But a letter is only a letter. Sherlock and Watson had barely begun to tiptoe down those labyrinthine corridors of power; they couldn't be sure of a man they hadn't met. And so my reply was brief and non-committal: I acknowledged his ideas and recommended we postpone decision-making until we met.

Nod was to fly off first, after *Warriors* closed in mid-November, for another workshop tour of Australia and New Zealand. My plan was to write for a month in Suffolk and join him in the New Year. On the day Nod left for Perth we were both so busy that he forgot to pack! When our friend Diana came to pick him up to take him to the airport, he quickly threw his belongings into a bag and was ready. Once again we were overstretched and overworked, and in the cold corridor outside the flat he wished me well with the start of the book and I urged him to find at least one quiet time for himself each day. A few days later I was in hospital with a malaria relapse. Luckily we caught it early and the drugs worked fast. I was out within a few days; but it still brought all the horror back. I still had to close my manuscript and put it away once again; and once again, I was tempted to cancel everything. But this time I couldn't. The grapevine had already confirmed that the Network application was successful: our first major funding was on its way!

The original plan had been for us to work with the National Theatre of PNG on a special two-week project in January – we were still keen to combine our FOTS research with our theatre work. But William had written to say that the company were performing in Thailand and would not be back until the end of February, so at the last minute we had had to rearrange everything. Now it looked like providence. The new plan would be to use the full month of January to work on the book together in New Zealand and begin our Friends of the Sepik research from there. My flight to Auckland was on 30 December. I gave myself a little bit longer than Nod had to pack but, at the last minute, I discovered that I had misplaced my small rucksack. What could I put my cabin luggage in? When Nod met me at Auckland airport, I was carrying our old green plastic laundry bag: 'Isn't is going a bit too far, crossing the world just to go to the launderette?'

The pounding breakers on the vast black beach of Murawai seemed to roll away forever and mingle with the foaming sky. The small, sculptured hills around the farm were sprinkled with white daisy flowers and also seemed to fold into the sky. Pukekos – large water fowl with long red legs – scurried into the narrow swamp. A strange song issued from the branches of the old, gnarled tree – an operatic warble deteriorating into the clunk of a cracked bell. The ranch-style farmhouse squatted discreetly in a grove of eucalyptus trees; behind it loomed the shadow of a tree-covered 'Pa', the dome-shaped hill which was once a Maori settlement. We leant against a gate into a meadow in the warm evening glow: the eucalyptus leaves shedding their oily fragrance into the fresh, clean air and the cows and horses standing on the hillsides as still as statues. This was our haven for January. The farm belonged to Barry Hart, one of Auckland's foremost criminal lawyers, who had been on Nigel's first Auckland Mastery, two years before. What a boon that he had invited us to use this magnificent place to write. There was even a pool to help me wake up in the mornings.

During January, as well as writing, we began to put out feelers towards the new kind of Papua New Guinea journey ahead: an introductory fax to John Seed of Australia's Rainforest Information Centre (RIC) in Lismore asking for advice and help; another letter to Graham Campbell to confirm the date of our arrival; a note to Campbell who had sent me a Christmas card with his new address in Port Moresby; a fax to Simon Pentanu for visa help. But most important, one more letter to Lucas. This time we had received no news from him whatsoever; no answer to my several letters. I had even written to Solomon asking what had happened, and asking him to get Andrew or the schoolteacher to write me back. Had we somehow offended Lucas? Was Lucas sick? Had Lucas left the aid post? This horrible unknowing nagged me daily. We would, of course, find out the truth on our return; but it would be daunting to arrive in Wagu not knowing why or how the communication between us had broken down.

Prior to our PNG departure on 20 February, we had two hot workshop weeks in Sydney, staying once again with Sandy in his lovely leafy house. Time also for acquiring more forest information and making further contacts. John Seed of RIC was particularly helpful. We had hoped to meet him in person but had to make do with a long phone call to Lismore. Firstly he solved the Harry Sakaris mystery. Harry Sakaris is Harry *Sakulas*. He is not the Director of the College of Forests in Lae, but the Director of the Ecology Institute in Wau, near Lae. Maybe that was why our phone calls and letters had received no response. Seizing on this new clue as if it held the secret to eternal life, Sherlock and the Doctor faxed the newly arisen Harry Sakulas immediately. And lo and behold, a response! A Sepik man himself, Mr Sakulas showed interest in our endeavour, invited us to come to Wau to meet him, but warned that the East Sepik Provincial Government was going through a rocky stage and might be on the point of collapse. John's second point of help was to put us in touch with two colleagues who had recently made an environmental awareness tour of Papua New Guinea and the North Solomon Islands. They sent us an excellent series of large colour photos depicting logging destruction. Thirdly, he told us about RIC's own sustainable project in the Morobe Province, a region already ravaged by disastrous logging, and he answered my query on the validity of something called the *Wokabaut Somil*. This is a mobile saw that can be carried by four men and has revolutionized small-scale village-based logging. It means that trees can be planked on site and transported out without using destructive heavy machinery. However, the wokabaut is controversial because, without proper safeguards and monitoring, it can cause local havoc. Despite the dangers, John's argument ran: 'It's without a doubt the best way we know, and the cheapest way, of buying time for this particular piece of paradise, in case the human race wakes up in the next decade or so and decides it wants a bit of biosphere here and there after all.'

We also faxed Sasa Zibe Kokino of the Village Development Trust in Lae which runs a programme for training in the use of the 'wokabaut'; we should visit him and obtain his perspective too. An introductory fax also to Kembi Watoka of the Department of Conservation and Environment in Port Moresby. It was time we introduced ourselves there, and gleaned what information we could about their approach to the forest. Back in the autumn in England, I had tried to gain the interest of the World Wildlife Fund (WWF), but Francis Sullivan, their rainforest expert, had admitted he had little knowledge of PNG. A Pacific Co-ordinator would be appointed in December; better for us to meet up with him in Sydney. And so we did: his name was Peter Hunnam. The Australian WWF office was in the city centre, on the tenth floor of a skyscraper – no wildlife in sight! I felt back at university again as he drew abstract diagrams with his red biro. There is no example of a sustainable project. There is no proof that such a project would be successful. But he was interested in our grass roots approach and endorsed Simon Counsell's view that the setting up of a 'working model' was a good idea. He even began to spill a drop of his wry humour and was amenable to the possibility of giving us a small discretionary grant if we set up a local NGO (Non-Government Organization).

Finally, I spoke to Graham Campbell to give him our change of flight. With a light Scottish lilt, he told me that the Provincial Government were all on the alert for our arrival. He had briefed all the Departmental Secretaries. He had even informed the Premier of the next province. Help! Excitement and fear bubbled up inside me. We really were being taken seriously. But what if they found out that it was only Nod and Rick?! I breathed deep. The circle had swung round again. For me a third trip to PNG, for Nod a second; but this time the stakes were much higher. We had funding and we would travel by the invitation of the Provincial Government of East Sepik; (even if it was on the point of collapse?). While Nod shot off to Melbourne for a last Mastery, I clarified our purpose ahead.

Our objective for Friends of the Sepik was not to impose another white scheme on another third world people, but rather to learn from the people themselves, from landowner to politician, to find out what they wanted/needed/dreamed of. And to discover how their knowledge could be used to protect the Hunstein Range and the whole half-million hectares of the April/Salumei region. What skills did the local people have? What riches other than timber did the forest contain? How could alternative revenue be accrued? And how could the cultural heritage of the area be revitalized rather than decimated? The focus of our trip would be a *Toktok* (discussion) Tour of the Hunstein Range. We would again travel up from Wagu to Gahom, but this time by dugout canoe along the remote and winding April and Sitipa Rivers. There we would stop off for toktoks at the isolated forest villages along the way – to warn the landowners of the logging threat and seek their solutions. Either side of this tour we would meet as many government personnel as possible from district to national level. We would gather their solutions to the problems and seek their views on how best Friends of the Sepik could help. One thing only we had already decided: through the ethos of Green Light Productions, Friends of the Sepik would emphasize the link between forest and culture – a link that William's *Conference of the Birds* had first inspired me with – and a link that we knew was close to the Melanesian heart.

The very day before our departure, the longed-for letter from Lucas arrived. It contained the solution to the mystery; a solution that had never crossed our minds, though Sherlock would doubtless have chortled, 'Elementary, dear Watson, elementary!'

Dear my two brothers,

Yes I've got your letter already but there was something wrong between the Government and us the Community Health workers. We didn't get any pay for three to four months. That's the trouble and that's why I didn't write to you. There was no money for me to buy stamps and envelopes. Stamps and envelopes are now very expensive, that's why I couldn't write letters. Bikos of this liklik mistakes only and that's why you didn't receive any letter from me to you.

So brothers I've nothing much to tell you here in the Sepik, and Wagu Lake is a big high tide, and we haven't seen any makaus [a kind of fish]. All the makaus from the rivers and lake have gone. We never eat makaus. You cannot see any fish at all in the lake. Because the last day is coming closer and everything is changing. So brothers I am just waiting to hear from you and about your coming to Wewak and your journey to Wagu. Just waiting for your message to arrive at Ambunti to Wagu.

So I think I've nothing to tell you now. I think that's all and sori for not replying to your letter and Merry Xmas and happy new year . God bless you.

Your brother Lucas.

Our relief was immense. This was the real visa to our trip. It would have been a devastating blow to have lost Lucas's trust, and though the content of the letter was ominous, there was at least no mention of logging. Time seemed still to be on our side.

II

We arrived in Port Moresby on Wednesday 20 February at midday. The Takaku household welcomed us with their usual radiant easefulness: William, now with dreadlocks to his shoulders as a traditional sign of mouring for his besieged people; Puele, with their new son Leka on her hip, a naked shiny-skinned baby with pixie ears; and Ani, now at school gobbling up her A B Cs with careless excellence. We only had forty-eight hours in the capital before our onward flight to Lae and Wewak, and we had hoped to complete the mundane business of money transactions and air tickets that afternoon. But William was in the middle of a day-long meeting with his department, so we were left vehicleless in the scorching afternoon heat. At the airport we had passed a large new poster which shouted: 'Papua New Guinea – Land of the Unexpected'. We had forgotten. Nice neat plans were made to be broken. The poster proved itself further – we learnt that there was a curfew in the city. Following a wave of violence, everyone had to be in their homes between 8 p.m. and 6 a.m.

Puele asked Nigel to remind her what he liked to eat. He mentioned pitpit, kaukau, breadfruit, ibica and corn. For supper we got them all! Plus long-nosed fish which William cooked on an open, coconut-shell fire in the garden. But it was a late meal; by the time it was ready the city was already long silent, the Mission singing had already petered out for the night. The electric cooker was broken and Puele had to crouch on the kitchen floor over a small kerosene stove which belched nauseous fumes. The toaster was also broken, and the kettle. The television too. Puele admitted sheepishly that 'someone' in a tantrum had thrown something at it. William had placed it outside the fence for anyone who might want it. But a policeman had arrived vexed – what was it doing there? Had it been burgled? William had offered the television to the policeman, whereupon he had become even more perplexed. He could only accept it if William would accompany him to the police station to sign papers. William and Puele found this story side-splitting. And anyway they were happier without the television. Technology seemed to be a joke. When it breaks down, throw it over the fence; make a coconut fire instead.

After our feast William updated us on the Bougainville situation. The PNG army had failed to flush out the Bougainvillians holding the copper mine and had withdrawn from the island. A cease-fire agreement had been signed, but the Bougainvillians had refused to give up their arms. In retaliation, the PNG Government had imposed total sanctions on the island: food supplies, medical equipment and all communication had been severed. Media headlines stated that the island was in dire straits; but William knew that this was not the case. William's wantoks were reverting to their traditional life. Their gardens were bearing bountiful food, the Jaba river was sparkling clean again and the flying foxes were hanging as thick as luscious ripe figs from the trees. A traditional government was being formed and the people were keen for William to return and start an institute of traditional arts. But his loyalties were divided: family and work on the mainland, the call of his wantoks from home. As he spoke, the internal tug of war showed in his body, his eyes smoked as darkly as the embers of his coconut-shell fire.

On Thursday morning we opened our PNG bank account for FOTS, and then drove in the National Theatre's brand-new 4WD Toyota to meet William's new boss, Mr Abanetta. He peered at us from between the piles of boxes in his office; a light-framed man sporting a straggly goatee beard, his bifocal glasses swallowing up most of his face. Mr Abanetta had read our reports and had congruent ideas. He would do all he could to support our work with William and the East Sepik. To show his good will he invited us for lunch at the renowned Golden Bowl Chinese Restaurant. In the afternoon we went to meet Kembi Watoka at the Department of Conservation and the Environment whom we had faxed from Australia. His office was tidy but dark. A large, brown-painted fridge stood in the middle; dog-eared folders were piled on top of it and an orange extension lead fed through the ceiling tiles. The atmosphere was dispiriting and Mr Watoka spoke in a husky whisper as if he expected eavesdroppers. At first he seemed evasive, his eyes more interested in the files than us. Was he paying lip service to conservation? Was he humouring us? But eventually his sincerity emerged. Indeed he longed to protect the forest, indeed his job was to do just that. But how often, I wondered, did the recommendations and proposals that he and his colleagues put forward blow down those labyrinthine corridors ignored and even unread. Nudging towards us, Kembi gave us valuable advice: we should always remember that the local people are the official landowners of the forests, and so they always have the last say as to whether a tree is cut or not. Environmental education is thus of paramount importance. The local people need to understand the jump in technology from their traditional use of timber to the multi-national projects. Even as he spoke an idea germinated: perhaps we would produce an environmental play with Raun Isi; a forest drama that could be taken upriver. At our cordial parting he warned that if we wanted to win trust, we should never make promises that we were unable to fulfil.

'Of course I remember you' Cathy Munagun had said when Nigel phoned. 'Of course you may come and talk with me again.' And so on Friday morning, a few hours before our departure to Lae, together with William, we piled into her office. Flamboyant clothes, braided hair and a watermelon smile, Cathy welcomed us back to PNG and was delighted to hear about Friends of the Sepik and our endeavour to help the forest communities of her Province. Concerning the April/Salumei project there was presently some dispute as to the boundary-line circumscribing the region. This had delayed the signing of the Timber Rights Purchase (TRP), which is the contract whereby the landowners agree to lease the logging rights of the forest to the Government. Only after this has been signed can the Government put the logging operation out to tender. Although the project was one of those exempted from the recent moratorium that had been imposed by the National Department of Forests, it had not as yet received the go ahead.

Nod and I gulped. As long as the TRP remained unsigned there was still tangible hope for the forest. But Cathy informed us that this TRP did not necessarily have to involve big outside logging companies. It could use a local company formed by the landowners themselves; it might even involve the use of wokabauts shared between a group of village communities. Cathy was keen that women should play an active role. In such a set-up they could be trained as monitors, to check that environmental guidelines were not violated. So already possible alternatives to mass logging were being seriously considered. This was good news. Cathy recommended that, on our toktoks, we meet and speak with the village councillors. They had done a lot for their communities in pushing for the improvement of services, and they had the welfare of the local people at heart. She also warned that some of the remoter villages along the April River were inhabited by semi-nomads. We would need to inform them by radio that we were coming, otherwise we might find the villages empty. Cathy's brave water-melon smile left us heartened, though, as with Kembi, we sensed she was caught up in a maelstrom of conflicting energies.

Before our departure we sought some advice from William. If we challenge people, could we get ourselves into danger? Might they do the 'Sanguma business' (witchcraft) on us? 'Not if you always come from the truth, with only the pure intention to listen and learn – then any hostile spirits will melt away when they come in contact with you'. William counselled us further:

'Go to the people, apologizing for the white man's mistakes, saying you have come to learn. Ask them what they want. And tell them stories of what you have seen and experienced in other countries. Tell them the story of the crossroads:

'Ahead is a long, straight bitumen road with a single row of flowers bordering it. Ahead is America, Britain, Australia. But either side is nothing, emptiness – everything has been used up. All the trees cut down.

Before this road, to the left is the road that leads to the PNG Government and to the right the road that leads to the mission-aries. Behind is the road to the village, the forest, the traditional wisdom of the Melanesian people – but you have your back to it. So why not turn round and embrace it before it turns into the wasteland on the other side of the crossroads?

'Tell the Bougainville story; the people who recognized the danger just in time. And if you mention your love of the forest, then *explain* that love. It is a word used too much; they have heard it a lot from the missionaries and others. Go deeper, and give them your feeling of the love. Love is a feeling. For the beauty of the beautiful nature. The beautiful food in the jungle; better than tinned fish. The crystal-fresh water, better than Coca-Cola. And it's best that you take a Sepik man as a translator, otherwise they will think, 'Who are these outsiders coming to tell us things? What gain are they after?' And it would be wonderful for Raun Isi to go with an environmental drama. Drama is the best communication; it is natural to the people. If you speak like that you will reach the Melanesian hearts – then they will listen and think about it.'

❖ ❖ ❖

From Nigel's journal. Klinkii Lodge, Lae. Friday 22 February.
Matrius, Sasa Kokino's assistant at the Village Development
Trust, said he would meet us at the airport which is a long drive
from the town. We had been warned that the road was particularly
notorious for rascals. We looked at each black face and waited for
the raise of a questioning, expectant eyebrow – but nothing. It
became obvious, when the luggage had been unloaded and most
passengers had dispersed, that we had been left high and dry. Rick
goes off to phone. No reply. Rick asks the security guard if there
is a PMV. No, finished at 6 p.m. The mosquitoes whine and start
to attack. The guard suggests we ask the driver of the crew bus to
take us into Lae. The driver asks for 25 kina (£38) *each.* One of the
Australian pilots says, 'That sounds too much but I don't want to
get involved'. Rick does one of his outraged speeches. 'OK we'll stay
at the airport' I say, hoping that this will provoke some compassion. We stand and watch them drive off.

Just as they do so, the other pilot sticks his head out of the
window: 'They are going into Lae – they'll give you a lift', referring
to the airport staff who are locking up for the night. A round-faced
National woman asks where we are staying.

'Klinkii Lodge.'

'Oh we can drop you there.'

We are invited into a dark-glassed minibus – caged to prevent
the windows being smshed by vandals – and are driven along the
dark empty roads towards Lae at high speed. Broken-down cars
with punctures are spread along the road. Multi-coloured lights
decorating enormous trucks hurtle towards us. Dimly-lit neon-
light buildings flash past occasionally. A crowd of young people
disperse before us on the road – a street party with accompanying
bonfire. We arrive at Klinkii Lodge without mishap. An old man
carries my bag up the caged stairs to the first floor and into a pink-
painted, twin-bedded, torn-sheeted bedroom; a hatch in the wall,
a dangerously low fan and mosquito-proofed windows. But no
message from Sasa or Matrius. And again, no answer on the
phone. I wonder why. We had planned a meeting with Sasa
tonight. It's odd because he has been so conscientious in his faxes
to us; he's sent us lots of good info on the wokabaut and his work.
He did, though, complain that he often felt used only as a
database. Let's hope he'll call tomorrow, before we leave for Wau.

From Nigel's journal. Saturday 23 February.
Breakfast put in the hatch at 7.01 a.m! Bottled lime-juice, one tea,
one coffee, toast, cornflakes, three sausages and a tomato each,

plus two little green egg-cups full of marmalade. No sign of Sasa or Matrius. The new day porter takes us along to the bus stop for a Wau PMV. After a long wait, a bus comes. Broken plastic seat coverings spew out manky foam rubber. Fold-up seats are folded down and we're full up. One woman carries a large, white, dead chicken and bottles of kerosene which spill on the floor. The tarmac road quickly turns into rough, pot-holed gravel and squatters' camps: shacks made from old tin roofs, or cardboard cartons and bits of bush material; plastic bags adorn the road; 'Trukai' trade stores with bands of yellow red and green painted planks. The jungle soon takes over. A rich assortment of trees. Bright yellow flowers; scarlet hibiscus. Then up and up through elephant-hide grass-land hills. The blue beyond forested mountains always decorated with cotton-wool clouds. The road now just the width of the bus; the mountain falls away down the steep ravine. Dust engulfs us as trucks and buses pass in the opposite direction: brown hands quickly reach up, reflex-like, to close the sliding windows.

We arrive at Wau around 1.30 p.m. and I see a sign pointing up the hill saying, 'Ecology Institute 25 Kilometres'! Oh you can walk it easily, we are told – it must be 2.5 kilometres. Phew! We trudge up the twisty road, in the midday heat, of course. On and on, winding up into the hills, passing wild angel trumpet bushes. Confronted by an unsignposted crossroads, fortunately we guess right and, finally – the Ecology Institute. We walk down the track to meet an old man.

'Harry goan antap haus bilong em' (straight on, the top house is his).

'How far?'

'Two, three minutes' walk.'

There is a truck that we eye hopefully.

Mi nogat ki, mi no ken draiv you.'

Eric, an Australian project worker, appears and offers to drive us up in his truck. Steep, winding, bumpy drive, as we suspected much longer than two minutes' walk! We pull into the driveway – no car! No Harry! Nobody home! Eric tells us there has been violence overnight in the town. All the Government offices have been burned down. The unemployed Chimbu youths who have settled here from the Highlands are angry and have come to express it. Women at the market had their food smashed up. And a local civil servant had screamed hysterically at Eric to drive him home before they murdered his wife and children. Maybe Harry has gone to deal with all that. The house overlooks the entire Wau valley: fertile, lush, flat plains; grassland hills, edged by thick blue mountains. Some slash and burn fires smoking. 'The best view in the Province', Eric says as he explains his project. 'The most fertile valley – I could grow enough vegetables and fruit here to feed the whole of PNG. And I could employ all the local youths; that would solve the rascal problem.' A brilliant, fluorescent-green butterfly with bright yellow body comes fluttering by – then three more: 'These are the males', Eric tells us, 'look out, the females will be coming soon'. Sure enough, a moment later two delicate cream ones with black trimming flutter by – the three males chase them trying to mate.

Slightly exasperated that we may have come this way for nothing, we write Harry a note and leave it jammed in his door. Eric suggests we stop at the Pastor's house – he always knows where Harry is. So we wind down the hill again. The pastor is having a shower. He comes out wet, his large Afro hairstyle glinting in the sun, and points us further down the hill. Eric spots Harry's blue Mazda. He is visiting family. As we wait for him to come out, his son shows us some giant stick insects hanging in a tree. Clever camouflage. Knobbly, brown, bark-like bodies with a flash of moss-green on their backs.

In the well-kept garden of the Ecology Institute stood a long house on stilts. Mr Sakulas graciously ushered us through the door. We laid out our Sepik maps and began our discussion with the man we had been trying to contact for over a year. Poor Mr Sakulas would clearly have much preferred to stay with his family down the hill. In recompense he had brought his smaller son with him. His little boy wore bright red shoes of a similar size to those that we had seen strewn over the balcony up at their house. Harry informed us that he had a fetish for new shoes. He just couldn't get enough of them!

Already whacked, Nod and I tried to pull our melting brains out of the heat haze and give some credibility to our presence. As well as being the Director of the Ecology Institute, Harry Sakulas was also the Director of NANGO, the umbrella organization that serviced all PNG's non-government organizations. Like us, he looked tired and over-extended. At first he was cautious, reluctant to impart information. Who were these do-gooders? What were their motives? But gradually he became more amenable. This man carries much of Papua New Guinea's environmental conscience on his shoulders; no wonder they look a little weighed down. His ecological survey had been sponsored by *National Geographic Magazine.* Unfortunately, the cameraman had spoiled the photos, hence the delay in publishing. Harry refused to comment on the number of new species they had found. Plants – yes, amphibia – yes, insects – yes; but taxonomic analysis took a long time. It was being carried out partly in Germany and partly in Hawaii. And so Harry offered no lists, no charts, no documents: the survey remained enshrouded in mystery for the present, though at least he assured us that sooner or later his findings would be published. However, the Hunstein Range was certainly unique, certainly worth protecting. And recently a second survey had been carried out looking at the medicinal properties of the indigenous plants. As to the Double Mountain Range beyond the Hunstein and also in the April/Salumei region, there was no news. This remote forest remained uncharted and unsurveyed. Because of its altitude, science might assume that the fauna and flora were the same as that of the Hunstein, but, Harry agreed, there could well be some surprises. Imagine if it was logged and destroyed before we even knew what was there?

On a practical level, Harry was not categorically opposed to the wokabaut, although he agreed it required stringent monitoring. His advice followed on from Kembi's: not only should we deliver what we promised, but we should deliver it fast. A Raun Isi tour would be fine, but the landowners would only be won over by *action.* Their infatuation with the idle promises of the logging companies would only be assuaged by evidence of action, and evidence of aid. Wagu village needed a *haus sik* (hospital). People came from the surrounding villages to be treated, but often Lucas was away, and they would have to stay with their wantoks. It was in this way that their infections spread: a haus sik where they could wait would greatly improve the health of the community. The district also needed a tanning centre for crocodile skins. Crocodile hunting and crocodile farming were part of the local culture and so would not be an imposition; but the skins would need to be tanned for the local people to receive even only the minimum wage for them. With the Sepik high tide a large percentage of crocodile eggs were wasted anyway. If the eggs were caught and the crocodiles farmed, the wild population would not be depleted. Harry also mentioned the Sepik blue orchid. This was of great value. In Port Moresby, orchids were imported from Singapore; if these could be farmed here too, there was potential revenue. Nod and I smiled as we thought of the Sepik Blues flowering outside Lucas's house. Did he know of their economic value, we wondered? By now, our brains had solidified back into focus, and Harry's wall of caution had melted. And when we described our Sepik story-telling in Britain his lucid eyes shone. 'Beautiful', he said; 'beautiful', he repeated.

❖ ❖ ❖

From Rick's journal. Sunday 24 February.
  'You go long Lae?'
  'Yes.'
  'Wanem taim you go?'
  'Nau, nau.'
Just time for Nod to get a couple of soft cake rolls from one of the brightly painted stores and we cram onto the dusty, early Sunday morning minibus As we set off, women and spruced-up boys carrying guitars wave to us on their way to *Lotu* (church).

We wait outside a crumpled bush house for a second driver who appears, eyes swimming, out of sleep – tangle of dreadlocks, smoking an emperor-size newspaper roll-up. Bump, bump and we're off again. One puncture. Two punctures. Bump, bump. But the breeze is delicious, the grassland hills like soft creased velvet, and new thoughts and ideas are flying through my mind.

Back in the stifling heat of Klinkii Lodge, still no message from Matrius or Sasa at VDT. Immobility has overtaken us and we leave it too late to finalize how we are going to get to the airport. The Klinkii minibus has gone off to a plantation. The local taxi will charge too much. It's too late for the bus. The receptionist on duty is drunk; incorrectly, he promises us that the minibus is on its way back. We wait. 4.30. It doesn't arrive. We insist he has to help us get to the airport. How? It's up to him. His mouth drops open, red with betel nut; silly drunken grin on his face. Poor wife shouting at him. Finally he goes to the adjoining house. A young bearded man comes out. It's now 5 p.m. The flight leaves at 5.40. The man has no petrol in his car. He has to sort out someone to look after his baby because his wife has gone to market. But yes, he will take us: 'Fetch your bags'. We buy him 10 kina of petrol and soon we're speeding down the road, overtaking everything in our way. The young man is the son-in-law of the lodge owner. He points to the steep wall of shadowy mountains rising out of the plain. He has land up there; full forest land, which he is proud of. Suddenly we're blinded by smoke; people are burning the grassland, chasing out mumuts (large rodents) to eat. And then we're speeding again. We screech up to the airport at 5.32. 'Sorry, plane full up.' Histrionic reaction from us: 'The Provincial Government in Wewak are waiting for us – it is essential to the Government that we get on the plane!' Alarmed, the check-in clerk rushes out to the plane and we dash through the gate – ignoring the demands of the security guards to stop. We dash right up to the plane. A drunk is being removed down the steps. We leap up into the cabin and wave to our driver, standing dazed at the fence.

In the hot black dark, no Anton, but Graham Campbell is there to meet us. 'Raun Isi haven't got their act together – so you're lumped with me'. And so off we drive in the Government Landcruiser, making light chat; down the familiar, palm-fringed coast to Graham's house in a high-wire cage, his two little half-caste boys, Jamie and Jack, chattering in Pidgin. Graham quickly spills the beans. His wife has left him, gone to Australia – 'Oh well that's life'. His business went into receivership and he lost all his investment. He has the offer of a job in the private sector in Lae; and after three and a half years as adviser to the Premier he is ready to move on. 'No, no – Bruce's Government won't be suspended.' There had already been six attempts to remove him! 'He sticks to his beliefs and so he's bound to create waves and dissension. But the investigations into his conduct have only found inefficiency – not direct mismanagement.' Nervous forced laughter all round and we are all saying 'excellent' and 'brilliant' too often. Awkwardly, he shows us his basic house, the basic spare room, we eat a basic supper of cabbage, potatoes, overcooked rice and venison. Lonely man. There's something so poignant about a single dad with little boys. Mummy has left such a gaping hole, a hole that the nervous laughter makes more painful, not less.

After a beer, leaning against the verandah, we all begin to relax and Jack and Jamie fall asleep on cushions on the floor. We had both hoped not to have to talk business tonight, but there is no way round it. Graham is full of ideas. And has schemes a-dozen up his sleeve which he pumps out with all the vigour of a bagpipe player. He is adamantly against clear-cut logging and agrees we have got to reach the landowners themselves. Of his own volition, he suggests an environmental play by Raun Isi, and endorses Harry's suggestions of crocodile farming, a tanning plant and the husbandry of the Sepik blue. He also recommends the growing of rice and soya on the Sepik plains, and postulates the possibility of a paper-making factory using the Sepik grass; apparently such a plant is already operating in India. Memories of the choked channel and the strenuous grass-cutting on my first trip to Wagu flood back. If all that grass could be used: paper without the loss of a single tree!

Graham talks with humour and frustration. So many ideas, but as yet it has seemed impossible to implement them. Why, I wonder? Especially as, on our behalf, he has acted fast. Already he has arranged meetings tomorrow at 9 a.m with Premier Bruce and the Provincial Secretary; then at 10 a.m with all the relevant Departmental Secretaries. Phew! 'We'd better get our heads together', Nod whispers under his breath. Then we both say in unison: 'But no – we already have our heads together.' We know why we're here. We just need to be truthful. In at the deep end. Why waste time? In the basic spare room, Nod stuffs the hole in the mosquito-netting at the window with my dirty underpants; and we try to slow down the ideas racing through our over-stimulated brains.

Outside the Premier's office up on Kreer Heights, the driver nodded when Graham asked him if the boss was in. At the same moment, a Japanese delegation arrived who had been on the plane with us the night before. Five obsequious bowing men with cardboard tubes, maps and samples of tinned fish. They were here to win fishing rights. Their plan was to fish off the East Sepik coast, ship their catch back to Japan for processing and then sell the tins back to PNG. We were diverted to the Secretary's office, whereupon Bruce Samban himself appeared and, smiling a warm, red, betel-nut smile, promised he would see us in fifteen minutes. In the Secretary's office, we sat with Graham around the polished table, phone and fax close by and a large map of the Sepik on the wall. Appointed last August, Alois Jerewai was a Law man; he had been to England and visited the Inns of Court. He faced us with reserve and a touch of judicial austerity. He had not been primed and didn't seem to know who we were. With nervous, syncopated interjections, Graham filled him in. But just as he was becoming interested, the telephone rang – it was the Premier summoning us; and once again we found ourselves sitting in his air-conditioned chamber.

This year there was no implacable wall. He welcomed us with light-touch informality. He was startled and flattered by the number of letters he had received; the idea of being a celebrity in London as well as in Wewak obviously appealed. We updated him on our progress and our suggestion of a Raun Isi tour. The stage lights in the Premier's eyes came on. A very good idea. It was clear that he would like to be cast too. And concerning his own play – 'Yes', he affirmed shyly, shifting like a schoolboy in his chair, 'it is finished. But I have misplaced it. It must be back at the house. I will find it and show you.' Graham, with an eye on his watch, then informed Mr Samban of our meeting with the Departmental Secretaries. 'Very good. They will present my policies to you and we will speak again later.'

Around the long table in the conference room, six brown faces and three empty chairs were awaiting us in silence. We filled the chairs and Graham introduced us. He explained that the meeting was a forum for sharing ideas, a chance for them to convey to us the needs of their Departments, and offer suggestions as to how FOTS might be most beneficial to the Province. The faces I knew, Joe Mande, Anton and Larry, looked mildly stunned that we had become so 'grand'. The faces I didn't know looked mildly scared, though Martin Golman gave Nigel an encouraging smile. Patrick Hokmori, the Provincial Planner, welcomed us formally in a hesitant half-whisper and, talking rather too loudly, Nod and I explained our purpose and our brief. The circle of brown faces listened obligingly. But a certain dull turgidity seemed to be infiltrating the room. The louder we talked the more it settled until Nod stopped and changed course. Had they heard of Robin Hood? Yes. Had they heard of Sherwood Forest? Yes. Nigel retold the story of the robber rogue and painted a vivid picture of Sherwood Forest. The addenda to his story was the tragic fact that this once-glorious forest was now reduced to no more than a small wood. Like all our forests in Britain, it had been cut down long ago and now the British people were so sorry. As Nod spoke, the veil of dullness lifted and we were suddenly surrounded by a circle of eyes as bright as the sunshine splashing on to those lost Sherwood trees. Now the circle was with us; now the circle was alive. As William had said when we had asked him for advice: 'The Melanesians love stories.'

Joe Mande spoke first. His dream was to build a cultural centre with five wings, one for each of the Province's Districts. Anton added that Raun Isi needed the finances to tour the rural communities with awareness-raising campaigns. Vincent Sale of the DPI (Department of Primary Industry) spoke next, sitting in for his boss, John Wasori, who was unavailable. The most pressing need was to find a cash income for the rural communities. He reiterated the ideas of crocodile farming and rice-growing, and stressed the need for financial assistance in researching other crops such as chilli, cardamom and ginger. Patrick Hokmori, the Planner, followed. He emphasized the need to explore the economic use of natural resources: the rivers and the forests held many riches. He also stressed the need to organize the selling and exporting of local artefacts; a networking corporation was needed to capitalize on the skills and crafts of the rural Sepik people.

Finally, Martin Golman spoke, giving us the sobering news that in the Angoram district, in the lower Sepik region, a logging project had already commenced. The contract that had been signed was not the TRP that Cathy Munagun had explained. It was an LFA – a Local Forestry Agreement – which is made solely between the local landowners and the logging company. This agreement had been pushed through by certain National politicians who had obviously been offered personal rewards. Martin had been unable to intervene. And now a Malaysian company had started work. Certainly the Province's magnificent flora and fauna needed to be protected. In the Torricelli Mountains, for example, near Maprik, there were species of tree kangaroo found nowhere else in the world. The environment needed to be policed and monitored, as did the logging operation already underway. But Martin had no funds and no workforce to do this. Here a despondent edge crept into his voice; and the circle nodded in assent and empathy. They were all hampered and rendered helpless through the same lack of finance and equipment. How could Martin safeguard the Province when his Department only had a single truck? Yes, they needed a Friends of the Sepik. Yes, they were agreeable to working with us. Yes, they should remember Robin Hood and not lose *their* Sherwood Forest. These men were unused to talking together; sharing their visions, sharing their concerns. Generally, they worked in isolation, hidden from each other beneath their separate piles of papers and reports; now they were flushed and clearly affected by each other's honesty. Already this was one salient thing that Friends of the Sepik could encourage. Martin concluded the meeting with a special vote of thanks to us for coming and talking with them and making our intentions clear. 'Too many white men', he said, 'sneak into the Province after their own ends and show us no respect.'

❖ ❖ ❖

From Nigel's journal. Graham's house, Wewak. Mon. 25 February.
Crashed out back at the house – these meetings in this heat really take it out of me. We arranged for Anton to call round to discuss

our Raun Isi ideas. Waiting for him to arrive. He finishes work at 4.06 – like all government workers throughout PNG. The fortnightly pay structure left one hour missing, so they added six minutes on to each working day to make up the time! At six, still no sign of Anton, so I phone Denis Waliawi instead. Back in the autumn he sent us the completed story about police brutality that he had worked on during Daring to Write. His family live just a few hundred yards away, over the strip of wasteland. He is very surprised to hear my voice.

'I heard you are coming to Wewak.'
'I am in Wewak'
'You're in *Wewak?*'
'Across the road.'
'Across the *road?*'
'At Graham's house.'
'At *Graham's* house?'
'The kettle is on, come and have some coffee.'
'I'm busy right now helping mum cook supper.'
'Can you come later?'
'I'll come later.'
'See you later.'
'See you later.'

We sit on the balcony smothered in RID (repellent), the warm breeze wafting over our hot skin; dogs prowling and barking. Suddenly we see a figure walking across the wasteland. I say to Rick, 'That looks like Denis – I'd forgotten how dark his skin is'. Beard and a clean green vest and shorts, smoking a tightly-rolled newspaper cigarette which he places carefully on the bottom step after we have unchained and unpadlocked the front gate. The ten-foot high chain fence to keep the rascals out, makes me feel trapped.

Denis tells us of his bad year. It turns out that his short story was prophetic: he has been wrongfully arrested, imprisoned for three weeks, beaten severely, thrown into a cell – no clothes, no blanket – for two nights lying on the hard urine-soaked floor, bleeding. He was then transferred to Wewak prison. Sixty men in a cell – sleeping body to body. No books or magazines allowed; only the Bible. Disgusting toilet – unusable – but they have to use it. Today he was in court again and his case was adjourned; the police haven't yet prepared their case against him. He has to return a week on Thursday. He has a good lawyer, to whom we offer to write a character reference for him. He is a deep, serious, twenty-two-year-old. Real wisdom in his spirit. He listens keenly and relates his tale well. All the time he is speaking I am assessing if he is the right man to do what we are about to ask him to do. With every word he verifies my trust in him.

We tell him what we have in mind. Travelling with us, up the April River on our Toktok Tour as our interpreter. He is pleased. He will do it. He has never travelled upriver before. It has always been his dream. He has never been in a dugout canoe. After he has digested this request, I put our second proposal to him. As a result of the meetings we have had so far, it is clear that the best possible way to encourage environmental awareness is through a drama using the Raun Isi. I ask him if he would consider writing one. 'Oh certainly, Nigel. I would like that. I would like that very much. Oh most certainly, Richard. Yes. Thank you.'

Later, at his house, we sit in his family's big kitchen, cob-webbed ceiling, lino floor; old carvings hang on the walls; big central wooden table; torn mosquito-proofing at the windows. We meet his sisters, Rhonda and Glenda, and his little adopted brother, Alius. Rhonda offers to make tea – Glenda whispers into Denis's ear and giggles. 'Sorry, no milk'. As we sit sipping the strong, milkless tea, dogs howl wildly outside. 'Oh, the Masalai [spirits] are restless tonight. We had better beware.' I'm not sure if he is in earnest or just trying to scare us a little!

From Nigel's journal. Tuesday 26 February.
On the balcony of Graham's house about six-thirty: Anton has made it tonight. He tells us that last night he came to the gate as arranged but could not *singaut* (call out) for our attention, he was intimidated by the white man's house. As always, it's something we hadn't thought of. At our request he has brought Lucas, the actor who impressed us with his puppeteer and pig spirit story last year. Denis is here too. We explain that we have called the three of them because of the plan we now have in mind. And when I really look – what a trio! Anton, with his deep-pool, heavenly eyes that look as if they've already seen Nirvana. Lucas, with his strong-boned, cropped head and whiter than white teeth – no betel nut stains in his mouth. And Denis, with his dark skin and piercing eyes. Lucas has written down the idea for a play about the forest already; it could be blended with the play that Denis has been working on since last night's meeting. He got so excited after our talk that he stayed up writing all night. We begin to unravel the plans: a play to take on tour up the Sepik with a maximum of four actors; a play to remind the people that their forest is precious and to warn of the danger of loggers coming in to destroy it. Denis and

Lucas exchange confirmatory glances. They could work their ideas together. The links are beginning to make the chain.

In the dog-barking, mind-spinning night, I am disturbed by Rick, creaking on his yoga mattress twice through his routine; the dogs howling every ten minutes. The Masalai are moving around. I ask myself, suddenly full of doubt and anxiety: 'What are we doing here?' Trapped in a small bed jammed against Rick's mattress. Trapped by the wire concentration-camp fencing. Trapped, not being able to walk about freely for fear of rascals. No access to my sea that I always yearn for and hear tantalizingly in the distance. We seem to be taking on the decline of the whole Province. This place is in total danger of being sold out to the highest bidder. The Malaysians already have a foot-hold. They will bribe and cut, bribe and cut, eating away at the forest, while the corrupt politicians get richer and send their kids to school in France, buy property in Bali and stash money in the Gold Coast. *Greed is the devil that is eating this planet.* How do we combat that? How to wake the world up to the knowledge that enough is enough. The Gulf War, the billions of dollars and pounds that are being rained down on the desert: blasting, burning, destroying, shaking. The Earth cannot take any more. Yet the earth is all these people have. Martin Golman said he would go back to his land. Lucas said, 'Maybe I will go back to my land' William Takaku says, 'Perhaps I'll return to my land'. And yet if they give up the fight, the gobbling Malaysians, Japanese and other multi-nationals will come and devour this last precious area of forest and spirit home. So we have to go on. But will we learn to look after ourselves, to jump off the spring before it coils too tightly? One small step at a time. We are only two tiny dots on this huge planet, two tiny leaves in this big forest. Look out! If we don't, the bulldozers are waiting to flatten us too.

We had hoped to leave for Wagu on Thursday, but as expected in the 'Land of the Unexpected', things did not go to plan. Transport to Pagwi was a problem and there was a maze-like confusion over the number and size of petrol drums that we should take on the Toktok Tour. Where to acquire them at anything other than a rip-off price was also a major stumbling block. Meanwhile, Graham continued to be an excellent and considerate host and planned more meetings for us.

On Tuesday morning we met Valentine Kambori, a businessconsultant in the private sector. A cordial gentleman with fine social skills, he welcomed us into the comfortable chairs facing his tidy smart desk. Mr Kambori had already heard about us from Denis who is his nephew. He, too, is a voracious lover of stories and has read all of Denis's writings. 'Most talented', he confirmed; 'just some character problems because of his youth.' As sweet coffee was served in unchipped china mugs, we asked him how he would approach development in a remote rural area such as the Hunstein Range. 'Tourism and crocodiles.' They were the answer. 'Not though, of course, that one should be fed to the other!' There should be local guest houses in the villages for tourists who want to see the Sepik nature. But first and foremost, he repeated the crocodile idea. There were big crocodile farms always on the lookout for baby crocs. Friends of the Sepik could provide the villagers with materials such as netting and he would arrange for them to be trained in crocodile management. Then he would send a colleague at regular intervals to buy the young stocks and transport them back to Wewak. 'How?' we asked. 'No problem. Crocs can be carried in big bags with their mouths tied.' We agreed to propose this idea to the Wagu villagers and, as we turned to leave, Mr Kambori affirmed that our meeting was not over: 'It has just been adjourned.'

On Tuesday afternoon we were supposed to meet Martin Golman, but as we drew up we saw him dashing off down the hill in the opposite direction in his yellow van. Instead, Graham took us to meet Damien Sarawabe, the Provincial Minister of Finance. He was a small, timid man who had a special fondness for Robin Hood, and he was mortified to hear that Sherwood Forest is no more. Damien believed firmly that the answer to the Province's problems lay in revitalizing the village communities and creating rural developments to slow down the ever-increasing tide of urban drift. To show that he practised what he preached, he and his wife had recently returned to live in his village and were now happily ensconced in their own bush-material house. Mr Sarawabe said, 'Very nice of you to come and talk with me'; and he offered to set up a meeting for us with all the Ministers on our return from the Toktok Tour.

When we finally caught up with Martin Golman on Wednesday afternoon, he apologized for his previous absence. He had had to go to stop his electricity from being cut off – the 'Land of the Unexpected' once again! Nod and I had first come to the Department of Forests individually and now we were there together. This was the most important meeting of the week and I was keyed up, feeling sick. I did not want to hit too hard, but there were facts that were essential for us to know. To help me, I had written down a list of questions. If we could really win the trust of the Department of Forests it would be a great stepping stone. Martin Golman was a precious creature, we mustn't frighten him off. His new office was full of unpacked boxes and he had to move them off the chairs so we could sit down. His manner was warm and friendly, only a hint of caution still hovering in his eyes. Martin showed us a letter. It was from the National Inspector of Forests, addressed to the Malaysian company, suspending their operation in the Angoram District that Martin had already told us about. Mosko Lumber had violated the contract on seven counts, including cutting into a special conservation area. Mr Sahui, the boss, was conveniently absent. Martin had delivered the suspension order on site and he had been shocked to witness the violations. The forest destruction was now no longer a foreign atrocity, it was happening in his own Province and before his own eyes. These Malaysians needed to be regularly checked, but Martin's money was frozen because of the recent crisis and his truck had just broken down. He needed to go to make sure that the suspension was being honoured, but he had no means of getting there. Good. FOTS' first undertaking could be to sponsor his journey; and if he hadn't been by the time we got back from the Toktok Tour 'we might just throw you over the mountain', Nod added, winking.

Next we steered Martin to the April/Salumei project and the Hunstein Range. Had he read our environmental report – did he agree with our sustainable ideas? Did he consider them viable? Yes, he did agree and yes, in theory, he did consider them viable. But such a vision was clouded by all the immediate problems in his way. How could we best support him on our tour? He seemed stumped. We could recommend careful logging, environmental logging; and warn the villagers against a repeat of the Angoram situation. He eased. Yes that would truly support him. To the idea of Raun Isi repeating our message in drama form, Martin responded enthusiastically: yes, yes, yes. Nod suggested one of the actors might play him: Martin waved his hands with a burst of coy and embarrassed laughter.

Finally, we questioned him on his attitude to the wokabaut somil. He told us there were twenty-four already operating in the Province. His problem, again, was lack of funds and transport. He did not have the wherewithal to monitor them and, consequently, he did not have the slightest idea as to how they were faring and whether or not the environment was being abused. He also informed us there was one in operation at Ygae, the village next to Wagu. So, despite our failure to meet Sasa in Lae, we would be able to see a wokabaut in action and judge it for ourselves. Before we left, Martin showed us on the map where the main Hunstein landowners live and advised us on the practical aspects of the journey. We were all surprised to discover that we had been talking for almost two hours. I was exhausted but exuberant. My mind had been working overtime throughout, trying to hold on to the thread of questions that needed to be answered. My sick stomach was gone, and I hoped that, in Martin, we might have the making of a trusty colleague.

For light relief from our schedules of meetings, Anton invited us to lunch at his house. In the shade of the tree under which he and I had first met, we sheltered from the blistering sun, while Nancy put the last touches to her 'light snack' of sandwiches, ibica, boiled eggs, chopped pineapple and cucumber, which she laid out on the floor of their simple bungalow home. While we ate, Anton told us the stories of his children's names. The eldest was christened Priscilla because of his love of Elvis Presley. Emmanuel because he had been born at a crisis in their lives and, though separated by necessity, they had both individually dreamed the same name. Next came Pamela, who was named in respectful appreciation of Nancy's mother. Then there was Newton, named after Anton's favourite scientist. Then came Ramus, christened in honour of the Indian pastor when he had left their church for promotion in the USA. And lastly, there was baby Young: the young Anton; the young Sakarai. As Anton spoke, the beautiful Nancy listened alert, hanging on every word, with her easy children around her, hanging on her.

Thursday was set aside as our day of preparation. The convoluted intricacies of the petrol drums continued. Denis and I went shopping for the Toktok Tour supplies while Nod wrote faxes and letters. The most pressing of these was a funding request to Peter Hunnam of WWF in Sydney. Would he sponsor the Raun Isi Environmental Drama Tour? This would be a first step to prove that Friends of the Sepik meant business. At dusk, our evening team meeting on the verandah had swelled to include Hendrick, Lucas's first choice for the Raun Isi tour. A young, slim man with a clean, clear spirit, Hendrick was Lucas's wantok; they were from neighbouring villages in the Middle Sepik between Ambunti and Angoram. While we were upriver, Lucas and Hendrick, and two other actors of their choice, would start preparing the environmental drama. Anton would encourage them and on our return we would spend some time working it together. Lucas's idea involved a young man who returned to his village to discover that the surrounding forest had been cut down. But all agreed there was an element missing. What was it? The inclusion of the forest Masalai. 'But the Masalai part has already happened' exclaimed Denis, with fire spilling out of his eyes. He had wantoks in the Angoram District and his auntie had arrived just that day with a true story:

Malaysian loggers had been cutting into a sacred area and a Masalai had appeared to one of the village elders in a dream. Next morning the elder went to tell the loggers to stop. They wouldn't. Next night the Masalai appeared to the elder again. Again he implored the loggers to stop. Again they would not heed his warning. On the third night the Masalai did not return, but a violent storm that raged on and on severely damaged the loggers' machinery. The next day the Malaysians moved on to another part of the forest.

Now we had the missing part of the play. And Denis had his story for the Toktok Tour.

III

From Rick's journal. Wagu. Friday 1 March.
'You came back. You came back', Petrus, one of the younger Wagu men repeats. And hugs me again. Threadbare, forest-stained, unbuttoned shirt, and threadbare river-stained shorts. Lucas is here too – striding to meet us across the Ambunti grass. Also Maria – 'God bless you', like last year – and Habe and plenty of others. All standing grinning gawkily. They have been waiting since 10 o'clock. They heard the toksave and came downriver to pick us up.

But the bikpela worry over the drums of petrol continues. They are too heavy to bring to Wagu with all the supplies. But where safe to store them? The boys who brought them up on a separate dugout canoe have shifty eyes. We suspect they've already siphoned off a few litres each for themselves. Precious juice for our trip – where will it be safe in rascal-infested Ambunti? Albert, from the fisheries section of the DPI, is very concerned. He accompanied us on the journey from Wewak and is an old school-mate of Denis. He is to loan us his driver – also called Albert – who knows the April River well. I ask to see the shed where DPI Albert offers to store the drums. But the walls are fragile, the padlock small and the position secluded. I am unsure. So is he. In his keenness to help he offers to sleep in the shed. Back on the banks there is much discussion and the shifty eyes are still watching hard. A barrel of fuel is worth 200K here (about £130). Big money. The storekeeper assures us it will be safe with him in a high-security area close to the lodge: 'No problem'. Lucas is satisfied. And the other Albert – Albert the driver – will bring the fuel upriver to Wagu early Monday morning ready for the start of the tour. We will use his engine, transferring it to Lucas's long dugout which will go faster than the council dinghy. Once negotiations have finished and we're all aboard, Denis tells us that Albert the driver whispered to him: 'Tell Nigel and Richard not to worry. I am trustworthy, it will be safe'. He is a lovely, big, easy fellow, whose eyes pop away with a high laugh whenever we smile and acknowledge him.

❖ ❖ ❖

From Nigel's journal. Wagu. Friday 1 March.
Off across the wide expanse of Sepik, we can see whirlpools spinning, curling the water down into its centre, strong and fast. The grass is about three feet shorter than last year, showing the height of the water level in this flood-tide season. We can see over it now, before we were cutting through deep channels. The Sepik eagles fly up wheeling and gliding, brown-winged above us. The light fades to lilac hues and, in the reflection, the blue in the clouds turns an oily dark purple.

The water has reached right up to the ladder of Lucas's house. We have to step carefully from canoe to the bottom rung of the ladder to avoid taking our muddy feet into the house. No big garden stretching out below. Banana and pawpaw trees are in several feet of water. The Sepik blue orchids have been moved back, up behind the house. Water laps under the store. Another big house has risen up beside theirs, and Maria has her own *haus kuk* building so that the old kitchen is now our room. Old spiders' webs dangle dustily from the high-woven, cross-poled ceiling. A QEX home audio system that cannot run off batteries stands waiting, unused, in its cardboard box; a tangled coil of extension lead lies redundant beside it. Maybe one day Lucas will run a generator?

From Rick's journal. Wagu. Saturday 2 March.

Back at my Sepik home we begin to learn of the current troubles and problems. As Lucas informed us in his letter, he wasn't paid for three and a half months. The health authority in Ambunti had their motor stolen, so they can't bring any more medical supplies upriver. He has no kerosene for the stove to sterilize the needles for injections; he used his own money for a while, then asked the villagers to help. They didn't. So he asked them to help him collect wood: they didn't. So no more sterilized needles. As he also said in his letter, there is no makau in the lake – their favourite fish. The people of the (relatively) nearby villages of Yambon and Malu, who have no fishing grounds of their own, have over-poached the lake. They were offered big money for smoked makau by a company, and so they got too greedy. Now there are none left. But most serious is the controversy surrounding the new school-teacher, Silus, who is suspected to be misusing the school funds collected by the parents for supplies. 1,000K is missing – and he has a brand new outboard motor.

Up in the depleted little aid post on the hill, there are a few bottles of cough mixture, a few jars of chloroquine and aspirin; dirty syringes in a tray and a packet of bandages and plasters. *'Nogat marasin bilong pekpek warra'* (no medicine for diarrhoea), a notice announces. And other peeling posters in Pidgin advocate dental care and drinking milk – How? From where? Mothers with their babies feeding from their breasts, scabby bodies, sores and boils. Lucas has tried to teach the people to have a mixed diet: but they still just eat saksak and fish or pig. The men just want to go into the forest to hunt and sleep. Waga and Tom are there now. And Solomon is there too, building a canoe. 'Didn't the missionary help with diet education?' Lucas feels he was only interested in translating the Bible. Now he's gone, the old traditions are coming back.

The *sik mun meri*– the young women who are in their first menstruation cycle – return with a scurry of excitement from the bush. The men and boys have to go inside and avert their eyes as they pass. A new haus tambaran is being built. And the youths are being initiated again. Phillip, who has finished school now, tells us about the singsings and the fights with sticks, the learning to beat drums and hunt. His spirit is sunrise, eyes full of anticipation. His initiation is yet to come; but he has already speared a 'greasy' pig.

Later, sheltering from the pouring rain in the haus win next to Maria's haus kuk, the women and youths and neighbours are talking expectantly. Silus came down from the school drunk and abused Maria. Everyone thinks there's going to be a fight. Maria, indignant with rage, is ripping off betel nuts from a big bunch and stuffing them into her bag; strong angry woman; strong angry voice. And then Lucas returns from the scene. Silus has accused him of slander, but he has held in his anger, despite an outpouring of abuse. A boy puts sticks on the fire to make good smoke to ward off the mosquitoes, and the children let down the grass tied up against the roof so it forms a wall, and we're dry. A large white duck, with enormous feet and red head, hisses and growls, extending its neck and trying to play with a skinny puppy who has fallen asleep in the ashes. In all the commotion one man is silent – Lucas. Staring inwards, gathering his power, holding his strength.

From Nigel's journal. Saturday 2 March.
Denis, our new travelling companion, is open-eyed and drinking everything in astutely, evenly. He is always respectful towards us, now he shows his good ways with the villagers too; sits patiently understanding it all. He is so ready for this journey and he is so ready to take a leading role. After the downpour, I take him up to the school to show him a view of the lake. We climb to the top of the hill. A man is there wearing a purple laplap; wide-bellied, large mouth with protruding teeth and bulging blurred eyes. He speaks sloppily. This is Silus. Matthew, a large-footed, big-eyed thirteen-year-old who now owns most of the forest, has come with us. Asked why I am here, I say lightly, 'Oh to walk in the forest and look around'. Silus tells me there is plenty of valuable wood in the forest and if anybody wants it, 'This is the one to speak with'. He slaps his hand heavily onto Matthew's shoulder, making it very clear that he would be prepared to act as go-between in any negotiations. Matthew's father, the principal Wagu landowner, has died, and now Matthew holds the land rights to a large portion of the Hunstein Range. This is it. The fate of the forest is on the shoulders and large feet of this thirteen-year-old boy!

Later, the drums sound, summoning the people to the village for a public debate on the Silus issue. This is the way things are settled in Wagu: an open forum in the village thoroughfare. Topics are discussed against the backdrop of general village life: babies screaming, children yelling, dogs yapping. The debate begins with Silus asking the school committee to speak out their case. First Daniel speaks. A pause. Then Petrus. A pause. Then Kim. A pause. Always plenty of time between speeches. Silus gets more like a rat in a corner, walking, pacing, flinging his arms around, showing everyone his guilt. The light fades fast. Petrus vents his anger and frustration by banging his stick hard on the ground. Earlier he made a very clear gesture as to what he could do to Silus, if necessary. Meantime Lucas sits silently. He is satisfied; there is no point in saying anything. The case will now go ahead and the inspector in Ambunti will deal with it.

When the debate was in full swing I was sitting on a shelf in the open-sided Men's House listening, and Matthew came and stood beside me. He stood dead still, his round bright eyes alert, listening and absorbing everything. I tickled his back and he laughed a short high giggle. This lanky lad is going to be pulled so many ways; how can we help his young spirit? How can we help him to understand that he must look after his forest? How can we help him not be seduced by 'West is best'.

Back at the house, when everyone had calmed down and Lucas has said that his mind is clear after the 'fight', we eventually get to speak to him about our plans; about Friends of the Sepik. It was hard for us to raise the subject with all the other village distractions, but we took a breath and plunged in. As I suspected, he is absolutely with us. And yes, of course he will join us on the Toktok Tour. It will also be a chance for him to take some medicines for the villages that have no aid post. We show him the photos of the clear-felling forest destruction that we brought from Sydney. Waga comes in and sees them too. They are silenced by the pictures. Waga's bright eyes turn inward. I underline how much he loves the bikpela bus – he has just spent several nights in it; what would he do without it? Maria, sitting apart as the women usually do, looks at them too. She sighs and lies flat on the floor in shock. Then she slowly goes down the ladder into the dark. We tell Lucas about our search for a practical solution. What could the villagers do? How can we help? But Rick's quick-fire questions are too much for him. He stands and silently follows Maria down into the dark.

From Rick's journal. Sunday 3 March.
Sitting in the haus win outside the kitchen, David, a visiting wantok of Maria, comes from morning Lotu to join us. He is from a village further up the Sepik beyond Yambon: smooth wide forehead, thinner nose; a strong man with an air of worldly experience. Feeling a little frantic at Lucas's silence and the

villagers' preoccupations, we engage him in conversation. What does he know about crocodiles? They have been over-hunted in the lake and river; numbers have gone right down. And crocodile farming? Lo and behold, David and Lucas have a little farm under our very noses in an enclosure under the store house! But the problem is stealing. They started off with twenty-six – now only seven young crocs are left. As they grow to a valuable size, they disappear. So what about a communal village farm? It would be the same, the crocs would still be stolen. But if a village farm had good security and it was noted down how many babies each man brought? No it still wouldn't work. These villagers don't do things together. If there are crocodiles already in an enclosure it makes the hunting easier! I remember Lucas telling me how he had stopped growing pineapples – they also disappeared. And maybe to these people it's not stealing, it's taking – taking what's on offer. Nod and I sigh. So much for our white liberal concepts of village co-operatives. So much for all the theoretical plans propounded in the Wewak offices. Oh well – are there any other possible small-scale industries? Yes, Lucas affirms. He has joined us now. Small chicken farms, or duck farms. But wouldn't they be stolen too? Maybe – but they could be used to feed the crocs and the villagers could buy cheap meat. But how can they earn the money in the first place? Plenty of ways, if they work hard. They can sell saksak, wild pig and fish in the Ambunti market. So, do the Wagu people have enough? Yes. If they work hard. It is up to them. There is plenty in the forest. And if the forest is cut down? Ah, then their livelihood will be gone.

Night has already fallen as Maria stretches the canvas out on the grass, and a full constellation of liquid stars are glimmering through the fronds of the sago palms. Lucas brings a single lamp and several of the bikpela men of Wagu gather round for our first toktok. Youths and boys peer from the dark behind them and some of the women are watching too from the vague outline of the haus win. Adapting William's story, I give a picture of three roads. Ahead of them and stretching away they have three choices. The first choice is the road that leads to a bad logging company; a company that will trick them and *gris* them and make them vain promises that will not be fulfilled. Such a company will cut down their forests, run off with the wealth and leave the villagers with a *bikpela bagarap* (big mess), a *bikpela nating* (big nothing). The second road ahead of them leads to a logging company with an environmental plan; a company that will listen to their needs. This company will ask them which areas to cut and which areas to leave so that they will be able to decide. Over here you must leave because these are our hunting grounds. And over here you must leave because here stand our sacred trees. But here you can take, and here you can take. But only if you take carefully, always leaving some trees and always replanting new ones. But even though this second road looks good, it is still unsure. No one can say how much the forest will be disturbed. No one can say if it will grow again. And no one can say whether or not the animals and birds will be frightened away. But at least there is a chance. At least the bagarap may not be so great. Lastly, the third road. Along this road there is no logging company. Along this road you have said: 'No, we will find other ways to make our kina, find other ways to use the riches of the forest. We will have no logging. And yet somehow, with careful thinking, we will still find a way to make enough . . .'. Denis stands beside me translating into Pidgin. Clearly. Strongly. And I ask him to emphasize that it is up to them which road they choose. We have come only to show them the options. It is *their* choice.

Next, in the glow of the single lamp, Nod shows the photographs and the men and boys crowd close. The first depicts a bulldozer removing a single tree. 'Nice big yellow bulldozer.' No one will miss a single tree. In the second photo a few more trees have been felled. In the third, a track has been made, muddied from the rain, but nevertheless impressive. In the fourth and fifth photos, more and more trees have come down, and by the sixth photo, across the whole muddy wasteland there is only one left standing. Like Lucas and Maria and Waga, the villagers are silent. For a while they just shake their heads and then slowly they begin to murmur in their tokples. One of the bikpela men present is Kaniofu; we had not met him before. He is Matthew's uncle and he is looking after the forest until Matthew is old enough. At first he watched us shrewdly, suspiciously, with a bowed head. But now he is murmuring too. And Matthew himself is standing, gawky and silent as ever, watching, listening, taking in everything. Only Petrus speaks out. His narrow sculptured face and watery eyes riven with passion. Of course they love and need their forest, but they are poor; they have no money for even the basic things like school fees. And things are changing. They have seen what the people have downriver. They want to come into the modern world too.

But now the concentration has gone. It is too late and people are falling asleep. Petrus agrees we should continue our toktok on our return from upriver. Meanwhile, everyone will think about the three roads and the many questions that we all have can be answered then. But my heart is low. How, what is the answer? We can't turn the clock back. Of course they want the good things that they have glimpsed. Denis has told us they are *dying* for them. But how – how to find the balance?

❖ ❖ ❖

From Nigel's journal. Monday 4 March.
Up this morning and ready to leave around seven. But no Albert the driver. So we have to go to Ambunti. At the last minute, Lucas insisted that we take Habe with us. He assured us, because of all Habe's wantoks *en route*, he will be our 'passport'. His wantoks will also feed him so he won't put a strain on our carefully calculated supplies. We had a frustratingly long wait at Ambunti as Lucas and Albert sorted out the fuel and engine. As we were impatiently waiting in the tree shade, hiding from the intensifying heat, some dramatic news was delivered: the Provincial Government had been suspended. Two million kina had been misappropriated. All our hard work down the drain; all that diplomacy gone to waste! It was not clear who had lost their jobs. No one could tell us if Martin Golman was safe. The second piece of news: Indonesia had invaded up by the Green River, not too far from our destination. This is a constant fear of the Papuans, and now it had come true.

So, into the mouth of the lion, eventually, at noon, off we all went. Albert driving; Lucas as shotgun; Rick and I settled on our blow-up cushions, smothered in factor fifteen; Denis in front of us on one of Maria's little carved stools; and Habe in the prow. The canoe loaded to capacity with six days' supply of food and fuel. The DPI motor powered us along against the strong current. We skimmed up the wide Sepik, no other boats around. Occasionally we passed a small village, but mostly it was tall Sepik grass and sky and water. Albert skilfully manoeuvred us through the swirling Yambon straights: strong, spiralling currents tried to suck us into their vortex. Because of the high tide we took many short cuts. We broke off from the main river and slid through narrow tracts between flame of the forest garlanded trees. Sometimes we got stuck, jammed in the grasping grass; stuck in the stagnant, stinking swamp. Ants, spiders and many unknown creepy-crawlies creepily crawled all over me. Plenty of birds wheeling, darting and splashing.

We turned off the Sepik onto the April River at a wide junction. And we chugged slower through the thickening swamp, taking more short cuts, the grass making narrow hall-ways for us to squeeze through. No sign of any villages. Relentlessly we chugged on for eight hours, the river getting shallower. We ground to a halt several times just as the dark closed in and Habe got out and pulled us clear. Logs littered the winding river and the darker it got the more scared I got. In the pitch black it rained heavily and visibility closed to almost nil. For two hours we struggled on, silent anxiety running between us, fearful that we may miss the lights of Bitara, our first-night stop. Just as I was resigning myself to a night sleeping, soaked, in the dugout, Habe shouted, 'Lukim yu – Bitara, Bitara'. The tiny dashing lights that I mistook for fireflies were villagers carrying lamps, excitedly scuttling down the steep banks and running along the muddy beach to help us in.

The rain eased off as, chattering, they unloaded the canoe and ushered us up the high bank into a large, dusty, creaky-floored house. About twenty men crowded in to look at the two pale and exhausted white men; a weird presence in the atmosphere. What did we want, what had we come for? Questioning eyes. Uneasy body language. Scratching, staring, gaping at us. One of the men showed us his carvings: shields, stools carved in shapes of crocodiles and turtles. He hoped that we were tourists and had come to buy; he wanted to charge us twenty kina for the night. Rick whispered aside to Lucas and asked him to tell the carver of our true purpose. As we ate our crackers and baked beans, Lucas came to us and proudly announced that he had cleared up the misunderstanding; they now knew we were on official business and entitled to a free night. We fixed up our troublesome mosquito net and arranged the food boxes and tool kits and bags around the edges to secure it. Now as I write, dry at last, the rain pouring down gives me a sense of comfort on the hard-ridged, downhill-sliding floor.

❖ ❖ ❖

From Rick's journal. Tuesday 5 March.
Fat tree trunks support the big house on the steep river bank. Albert leans against them languorously as he makes up the fire for breakfast, his eyes still popping away with a high squeal of laughter whenever we look at him or talk to him. Further up the hillside, the bush-material houses look out over the blue river winding its way through the empty forest. Sepik blue orchids are flowering and there is a big molli tree with bright yellow grapefruit-sized fruit scattered around beneath it. Some of the little boys carry armfuls for us and tip them into the dugout.

When the men of the village finally gather together in the shadowy, cavernous room in which we slept, the toktok begins. Lucas introduces us and then we repeat the same pattern as at Wagu, but here some of the older men do not speak Pidgin, and so our words have to be translated twice. First into Pidgin by Denis, and then into the local tokples, which is completely different from the language that the Wagu people speak, and which Albert nor Lucas nor Habe understand. A young man called Geoffrey is chosen as the second translator: dark, sultry eyes, a necklace of white shells, and a hand-me-down double-breasted jacket over his bare muscular torso. Nod and I tell our stories. Denis edits them into Pidgin, and by the time they reach Geoffrey they are down to a couple of sentences. What is being left in, and what left out? We will never know! The photographs, again, have a powerful effect. The men who have been stooping against the wooden pillars and sitting facing different directions, now gather closer to gaze at them, shaking their heads and tutting. Low guttural language with strong sliding vowels. Here, they explain, the landowners share the forest as a group. And yes, they will decide which areas to leave. And yes, if a company comes they will watch carefully.

The elected leader of the village, whom they call the Committee, is a wiry, elderly man who has been hanging on every word and now holds forth in answer to our questions about their welfare and their livelihood. Life in Bitara is difficult. They have no schools and they have no aid post. They have a motorboat, but no money for fuel. They gather plenty of saksak; they have a knack for catching small red parrots, and they make canoes. But when they transport these wares downriver to sell in Ambunti market, the income barely pays for the cost of the fuel home; and so they are back at square one, and no better off. The noble-looking but sad carver, also has no luck. For a time a buyer came occasionally and a few stray tourists arrived, but mostly his beautiful and original work accumulates unseen. The hopeful price tags dangle aimlessly and the painted patterns along the edges of his crocodile shields and chairs collect dust. And even if he could transport them, there is no outlet in Ambunti either.

The younger men have heard about the wokabaut at Ygae village. If there was a wokabaut at Wagu, could they come and help work it? Habe is unsure. It would be up to the Wagu people to decide. Maybe they could have their own wokabaut to share with the other villages along the April River. Yes, maybe. Then they could cut the wood themselves and would not need a company at all. All agreed that the major problem was transport. How to solve it? A road? They would love a road. But from where, to where, we asked? No one knew.

❖ ❖ ❖

From Nigel's journal. Tuesday 5 March.
Again we mistimed our departure and left Bitara in the heat of the morning. We had to douse ourselves constantly with water to keep cool. At one point I looked around to see Rick, resplendent in hat, silk scarf, laplap and towels – reminding me of descriptions of Cleopatra sailing down the Nile! First we stopped at Kagiru, a pretty, well-kept village bordering the river, where they were building a big new *por* (dugout); a clean, spacious village, with a feeling of serenity oozing from the people. Graceful, swaying coconut palms. Coconuts were shaken down for us, skinned and opened. A whole one each. The most welcome drink to relieve the harshness of crouching in the dugout. We sat peacefully in the Men's House. I wished we could stay and soak up the sense of harmony emanating from everyone, but no such luck. We told the people we were on our way 'up top' and would return for a toktok on Friday.

Back in the canoe and we reached Begapuki in an hour to find only two men there. They were completely taken aback by our arrival. These were the semi-nomadic people Cathy Munagun had told us about in Moresby. But no radios; they hadn't heard the toksave about our visit. This was a much smaller village, with only two large houses on the bank. We ruminated about whether we could make it all the way to Gahom – it was two-thirty then. How long? Maybe four and a half hours, maybe longer, depending on the flood-tide. Lucas already thought the water too low. We would try, and hope we wouldn't repeat the same dangerous situation as Monday night.

After two hours we came to a junction in the river. The April continued off up to our right and we entered the even narrower and twistier Sitipa River. Winding and twisting and almost doubling back on ourselves, we approached a bush camp. About twenty men, women and children clustered together in a tight knot, presumably for protection, as our motor canoe chugged up to the bank. These were some of the Gahom people living in the camp to collect saksak and hunt pig. It was a rare experience for them to hear a motor canoe, and even rarer for them to see two shrivelled white men (whom some of them recognized) sitting in it! They knew Habe – Lucas was so right to bring him – and were happy. The men came down fast to meet us and shook hands vigorously. It was decided that two men would come with us to help us up the shallow, dangerous Sitipa: an older man called Kiawi and a young man with severe skin disease, Isaac. Isaac bundled into the canoe six, large, white-bellied fish that had open, long-whiskered mouths. He had red face-paint around his jaws and temples; two bands of paint also decorated his arms. The river was too shallow now for the engine, so he took up the paddle and confidently punted us along. Flocks of wild ducks that they all wanted to spear skimmed away. Hornbills swooped low over us. Multi-coloured parrots and sulphur-crested cockatoos screeched overhead. More garlands of flame of the forest cascaded from the trees and small river swallows darted and twisted. As we travelled, Kiawi kept turning around and saying to me: 'Me postman, me postman', or so I thought; and I wondered how he managed his job. Lucas later explained to me that he is the *'Boss* man', the *Luluai* of Gahom. Kiawi is the wise man, the Elder and the main landowner. Last year he was also out at the bush camp and that was why we hadn't met him, but he had heard of our visit and was keen to accompany us this time.

At dusk we pulled into the bank and walked to a small bush hut where we spent the night. A rickety, bouncy floor with many holes and armies of ants and spiders marching over it. Habe got to work, made the fire and cooked the long-whiskered fish. Sweet and juicy. After our meal, while Lucas, Kiawi, Albert and Isaac went wok-abaut, Denis shyly sang to Habe, Rick and me a song that he had been composing on the river. He stood grasping one of the rickety roof supports to steady his nerves and sang:

If I was given a chance to take another step down my past,
Would you believe I'd see forgotten riches of society?

Are you sure enough, do you call yourselves Papua New Guineans,
Dressed in foreign clothes and different lifestyle, are you sure enough?

The time has come to identify and to rectify foreign mentality,
Do you not know without our identity we are nothing, nobodies?

Will you bow down to this unknown culture,
a culture where money talks much better?
Is it really true that the old man beside you
will never see the setting sun again
and cherish the simple life of his wise old culture?

You know traditionally our names mean more than anything,
With Western names you're just another Tom and Sue.
Lomonduo, a name, a legend, an identity.
Tom and Sue, a coincidence, the've heard it before.

The time has come to identify and to rectify foreign mentality,
Do you not know without our identity we are nothing, nobodies?

IV

From Nigel's journal. Gahom. Wednesday 6 March.
We're back in our beloved Gahom, feeling completely at home. This
time without getting stuck in a swamp or keeling over or splitting
my boots!. A clear, windy, sunny day – much cooler than our last
visit. We are staying in a different house this time, up on stilts not
as high as Thomas's house. Six main, big support poles, plus one
central cross-bar in the middle of the room. Two fireplaces. One
for the 'Boss man', Kiawi. He has a special board to sleep on tilted
at about twenty-five degrees. Pipes are being played in a house
next door, a simple, circular tune using about six notes repeated
again and again. Thomas Yanwe is here, warmly greeting us and
happy we remembered his name; but he didn't get the letter we
wrote during the year. There is no post here – further disproving
my mistake that Kiawi was the postman. The village church is still
being built and we watch a man carefully weaving some saksak
leaves to make the roof: laying three together, folding them over a
pole and sewing them with lianas – a simple and effective design.

As we wash our clothes in the fast-flowing creek, one of the
young men comes to collect water and we see his father, Malakas,
the old blind elder. His health has deteriorated since last year; it
is hard for him to shake hands – they are completely cracked – and
his balls have blown up to an enormous size. He sits in the harsh
midday sun scratching, his spine almost bent double. His son
explains he used to be a good strong man, but now look at him;
he has real tenderness and love in his eyes when speaking of his
father. Later, Thomas and Isaac invite us to listen to them playing
their traditional flutes. They begin with two-foot long bamboo
instruments and play a circular tune using about six notes,
following each other physically round and round in a circle in

Thomas's house; the sacred flutes are not allowed outside. They progress to larger and larger flutes, ending up playing eight-foot long ones that they can't lift. With our encouragement they become more and more ambitious and adventurous with their tunes.

Now, as I finish writing, Thomas is sitting silently observing us and, in the back doorway, Isaac is stretched out, asleep. Kiawi has lit a fire and now Thomas finds Rick's boots and remembers last year when he mended mine!

❖　❖　❖

From Rick's journal. Wednesday 6 March.
Everyone very keen for a toktok. Should we wait for people to come back from the bush? Or hold it early, because they have no lights? Gathering finally occurs early evening – in the unfinished lotu; an oblong of tree trunks around the edge for sitting. Kiawi, the Luluai, sits in the centre of one of the trunks and the men with their babies and little boys sit around him. Some have put on shirts, threadbare and torn, for the occasion. The women and little girls squat on the grass nearby.

This time Lucas translates into Pidgin. And Timothy, just back from the bush, the broad strong man who gave us handfuls of hot wild pig on our first visit, translates with verve and confidence into their tokples. The reaction to the pictures is extreme as always. A big crowd around Nod, squatting with the torch. Women and children behind, trying to peer over. Rapt, startled silence broken by sighs of the now familiar 'tt'ing and a shake of the head.

Next, Denis is introduced. The young men have been suspicious of him today and he has been finding it difficult. But he stands and tells his Masalai story bravely and with confidence.

Earlier, Thomas Yanwe, with his yearning liquid eyes, had begun to beg us to take him to Wewak. So Denis includes his story of town life; how it is not so good. How he was beaten by the police and locked up; how the prison was full of lost boys from the villages. After straying attention, with babies screaming, there is dead silence. Thomas doesn't ask us again. And now it is Kiawi's turn to reply. He speaks, strongly, forcefully; with authority and dignity. He is no fool. He will not allow the big companies to destroy his forest. He knows its value. But the people of Gahom have big difficulties. They are so far away. They have no kina and the clothes we see have been handed down by their wantoks in Wagu. Everything they have tried has failed. No buyers for their carving.

Too far over the mountain to carry things. No fuel or petrol down the April River. No medical supplies. The villagers are sick. And though the ground is fertile, they are not gardeners by tradition. They can hunt and gather gutpela kaikai from the forest, but where can they sell their produce? Kiawi asks for our opinion of the wokabaut; would that be a solution? Lucas explains it could be placed at the border between the Gahom land and the Begapuki land. There is a valley there with big trees. Lucas has suddenly come into his own. He speaks with eloquence, he speaks as a leader. But again there are difficulties. How to transport it? How to bring fuel for it? How to repair it? Transport and cost: these problems are circular like a snake biting its own tail.

But now the concentration has gone. People are talking among themselves. Shouting at children. Chasing off dogs. Lucas says we can meet again briefly in the morning. Everyone should think overnight; more questions in the morning. Then he repeats a lot of what we have already said. And we see how they need to hear things several times. And then Habe for the first time ever is standing and holding forth. Quietly the tokples words ripple out of him – he is inspired too. Firmly against big companies but keen on the wokabaut idea. Throughout much of the debate, Thomas stands close to me, his arms locked around me. I return the lock, willing awareness into his deep sad spirit.

After we've eaten, the village comes to life in the dark. Children are playing with burning sticks making shapes with the sparks and all the houses are burning with toktok. It's impossible to sleep. Men are coming in and out, talking loudly. Kiawi makes up a big new fire. The haunting flutes are being played full volume, on and on; with people picking up the tunes and humming. Toktok is continuous and there are criss-cross responses and interjections from between the houses. *Tupela*, which Nod and I are now jointly called, are mentioned again and again everywhere. There has never been a meeting like this; never been so many questions raised. Children and babies and dogs have caught the fever too, barking and crying in the dark. Even Nod starts growling, until I realize it is the large pig, scuffling directly under us. And Denis calls out in his disturbed sleep, whole agitated sentences in a sleep-language of his own.

After the toktok, for the record, Denis wrote down my introduction in Pidgin. Some young men translated it into their tokples.

English version Toksave

So. We are very happy to come back to Gahom. To see Thomas Yanwe and all our friends again. And to spend some more time with you in your beautiful village.

You remember last year we made a big wokabaut with Habe and Tom and Waga. We were so happy to see your big forest. To see the big, big trees and the many animals and the beautiful birds. Our hearts were so happy to see the big bush, because in our country there is no big forest, the big forest has all been cut down and the people are crying.

And so when we went back to our country, far, far away – right at the other side of the world – we told the story of our big wokabaut to our families, our friends, our wantoks and many people. And they were all so happy. They were all so happy to hear the story of your big forest. Because they have lost their forest and they are so sad.

They told us to come back to Papua New Guinea and tell the people of Wagu and Gahom to be careful, to take great care of your forest because if it is all cut down you will be left with nothing.......

Pidgin version Toksave

Nau, mipela I amamas tru long kambak long Gahom. Long lukim Thomas Yanwe na olgeta pren bilong mitupela gen. Na tu long sindawn wantaim yupela long dispela naispela ples bilong yupela.

Yu ken tingim long yar I go pinis, mitupela I bin mekim bikpela wokabaut wantaim Habe na Tom na Waga na mipela I bin amamas tru long lukim dispela bikpela bus bilong yupela. Long lukim ol bikpela, bikpela diwai na ol planti abus na ol arapela naispela pisin. Lewa bilong mitupela I bin pulup long amamas long lukim dispela bikpela bus ol I katim pinisim olgeta na ol manmeri I krai istap.

Olsem nau, taim mitupela I go bek long ples bilong mitupela, longwe longwe tru – istap stret long narapela sait bilong giraun, mitupela I tokim stori bilong dispela bikpela wokabaut, ol pren bilong mitupela, ol wantok na long planti man na meri. Na ol ibin amamas tru. Ol I amamas tru long harim stori bilong dispela bikpela bus bilong yupela. Long wanem ol iet I bin lusim pinis bikpela bus bilong ol na ol I wori nau.

Ol I tokim mipela long kambek long Papua New Guinea Na toksave long ol manmeri bilong Wagu na Gahom long was gut, long lukautim gut dispela bikpela bus bilong yupela long wanem sapos dispela olgeta bus I lus long katim, bai yupela I stap wantaim noting olgeta . . . .

Tokples version Toksave

Iseni nom monokudei Gahom ma ya fa si. Yen tomas nuwe fasi na ima we husi qao nuwi fasi.

Yom do tei fasi yuwei dagwen dama. Yom kiamgi wedi meii fitete ki ho, nedi tite fa bedo e, eim man Habe, ma Tom na ma Waga nom kaku. Nom mi bodo bodo enowe, fio fa na gagi tefi miya dadwen imo ma enomwe. Yuafu indo monu kuedi miya dagwen da nuweimsi nadi qao iyenoum miya dagwen indo si yuwe indo ma.

Ima uw huse yuwe indo ma mi iyenum – miya dagwen da mio buamsi. dasi nua nedi iquwa yuwe indo ma bida bodo. Bobu feni ma. Nedi titefa indo so behi metopuwa a keni ma.

Kani indo, biko swani husi. Lem meno gwedi-mte. Lem meivo kuedi miya indo behi wu sa fasi. Besi isu lem miya da e e nam. Lem nedi mumo haim Papa Niugini ma yai ma Wagu na ma Gahom nuwei sidagwen. Yom miya da mio bua ei a yom miya do ma tei e. Yom husi bafu eia tei e. Nakani, yom husi deba . . . .

From Nigel's journal. Thursday 7 March.
We sadly left Gahom this morning; wanted to stay another day but Lucas was anxious because the river was going down fast. So hard, in the rush of the toktoks and the pressure of having to move on, to be really present there. When we greeted Simeon – the Elder who had welcomed us into his house last year and who had now acquired a bright green plastic necklace – Rick had an aberration and called him 'Cinnamon'. The old man was delighted with the joke and gave us a warm hug and a bikpela smile.

This time as we left, Thomas, although sad, understood about our work and his wish of travelling to Wewak was not brought up again. Denis's story last night must have got to him. After a brief toktok recapping our main points, we were led back through the village and out along the beach to the canoe. Three women gained confidence and walked with us. One called Petra whispered, *'Tupela yu kam bek'* (please come back). We bundled our lightening load into the canoe and the young men and boys stood and waved and called from the beach until we were out of sight. We stopped at the bush camp to drop off Kiawi and Isaac and we were invited to saksak and dried fish. Kiawi's forthright and confident wife, dressed in a tattered black nylon petticoat, showed me a huge gash on her foot. We sat and ate the saksak in their humble, tumbledown, messy shack. They stay there for up to a year living rough, just three family units: hunting, fishing and collecting sago. As a parting gift they gave Habe a tame sulphur-crested cockatoo for Maria. He tied a string around its ankle and it became the figurehead for the canoe.

At the junction with the April River we had hoped to turn left and travel up to Niksek where the April Mission is based. There, Cathy Munagun told us, there is a different culture: they are gardeners. They don't cut the forest, they till the land beneath the canopy, just making small breaks for enough light to come through. But alas, the water level was precariously low and Albert said that the river is dangerous at the best of times and that he could not risk it. If the water is too shallow we would bagarap the engine. So we wound our way back down the April; down to the villagers that waited for us.

In Begapuki where there are the two, huge, bulging family houses close to the shore, we also discovered a few others tucked under the hill at the edge of the forest. Up in 'our' house, two women at their separate fires were making the inevitable saksak. Dogs were shooed out but pigs were welcome. One woman chewed up saksak, spat it out, put it into a coconut husk and offered it to an eager piglet. A little dark green and red parrot sat in a nook and a big noisy koki was perched in a gap in the wall. At the next house a tame hornbill was feeding from the window; it flies out to the forest by day but comes back at night. I was still eager to have a sighting of a bird of paradise, so a timid young man called Elijah took us up the hill. There was an unfinished Government house standing abandoned, with its roof collapsed and a flush toilet lying unconnected. We stood on the high hill and saw a spectacular vista of the April River, Mount Samsai and the Hunstein Range: the sweeping curves of the river; the densely foliated tree-coated mountains; the wide, flat forest basin that lay so vulnerable, so easily accessible to the monster chain-saws. Mount Samsai was impressively wide and dense, sitting comfortably in its own space – no wonder we got tired climbing it last year! Elijah took us down to the vale where the trees of paradise grow, egged on by a piercing cry. We sat by the long, thin, tall, pale-trunked trees. Small leaves dropping; gold-mustard-coloured balls of fruit. With so much fruit they *must* be here. We sat and sat and sat – but no kumul. Only plenty of mosquito bites. Oh well, one day I will be lucky.

From Rick's journal. Friday 8 March.
Our Begapuki toktok is in the relative cool of the morning. The

villagers bring a log for the men to sit on, under the trees at the river's edge. The river is going down fast; a wide stretch of sand is visible where on the way up there was none at all. There are only eight men and a few youths and boys; some have paddled downriver especially, but many are still in the bush. They used to live deep in the forest, but moved to the river's edge when the missionaries first came.These men are small, with wide dreamy faces. They speak in a whisper and their women, dressed in faded robes, come to look at the pictures too. Their reaction is dumbstruck silence. They have not even heard of the April/Salumei Project or of the big companies. No. They don't want to lose their forest. But, like the Bitara people, all they have to sell are canoes, parrots and saksak. It is not enough. It costs more for fuel home than they can earn at the market, so when they go down to Ambunti, they have to stay for several months. They have no school, no aid post, no support. It is a long way even to the April Mission; and now the white missionary has gone it is only partly operating. There is no mention of a wokabaut. And they don't want a lot of money. Just a little. They have lamps but no kerosene. A boat but no fuel. Torches but no batteries.

One of the elders, with rows of delicate tattoos over his cheek bones, responds to the story of the crossroads which Nod tells. He has followed the road of the mission, for they are the only people who have shown any help.

He believes in a peaceful life. He believes in Bikpela Papa above. Nod suggests that Bikpela Papa also believes in the forest, loves the forest, is part of the forest. *'Yes. Em I rait. Em I rait'* (yes, that's right). The tame hornbill flies over and perches on the tree above us. Nod remarks that it is not for nothing that he has joined the meeting. He knows his forest is threatened; and if it is cut down, where will he and the other birds live?

These men seem to be the least touched by greed; the most remote. It's as if they have only just arrived on the bank of the modern world. Just a minute ago, they stepped out of the ancient time and they are sitting by the river stunned. Keepers of the birds of paradise. Mist of innocence still in their eyes. Fragile. Gullible. One of them changed his name on a single white man's remark. As the current sweeps us away around a loop in the river, their dark figures are still standing motionless, arms raised in a long slow gesture of farewell.

At midday, we reach Kagiru. This is the graceful village we love the most; sad that we don't get to sleep here. Two rows of shaggy houses under a ribbon of coconut palms. A Men's House in the middle, with logs to sit on and a forever-smoking fire. Lots of baby *muruks* (cassowaries) scratching around, and the magnificent new canoe is almost completed – the dug-out inside is just being bound with dry palm leaves. These will be burnt to singe the wood as a seal against rain and sun. Here the women are less shy – big smiles from the high entrances of their houses, with fish baskets and cockatoos in cages, dangling from the overhanging roofs – women with coloured bangles, elaborate tattoos. Strong gypsy-like women, lovingly, tending their pikinini, feeding their muruks and sitting under the swaying palms. This is the only village where some of the men and women are still keeping their double nose holes open. They have plugged them with small pieces of bamboo; and the little old papa sitting beside me with the lightest dancing eyes has the pieces sticking out a good half-an-inch. Yes. Yes. He is proud of them. Yes. Yes. They are for the long curved antennae of the saksak bug at singsings.

Here, the people's skin is smooth and shining and the children look healthy. The young men are sleek and unbearably shy, but keen, and alert. I begin the toktok by congratulating them on their beautiful village. They must be wise people to grow coconut palms. If they feed the milk and the meat to their children, they will grow strong and fit. It has taken a long time for the people to gather, but once we begin, the attention is held. And yes the story is the same. They sell canoes – big canoes, their special talent; and parrots; and they rear baby muruks, another talent. But again the same story. Distance too far, so all the income from their goods is used for fuel to get home. These people seem the happiest and most wide awake. The young men listen with intense concentration to the dangers of their forest. And they have plenty to answer and ask. We are careful not to plant uncalled-for ideas into their minds. For they are happy. Uncomplaining.

Because the women aren't allowed in the Men's House, I take the photos and show them separately. I have to be *very* gentle, talk in a whisper; because they are only just daring to be with me in this way. I squat on the ground and use simple phrases in Pidgin. They nod and repeat my phrases, also in a whisper, amazed that this moment is happening: a white man squatting with then, talking with them, nodding with them.

Lucas is speaking out more and more now, and we hardly need to talk at all. He has Tupela's story off pat, and tells Tupela's story for them. But like us, he is tired; two shows a day on the April River is too much for us all! As we chug off, the motor cuts out and splutters and is hard to restart. It has become progressively more troublesome. This morning it cut out completely and we were left cooking in the heat, our frustration broken only by Lucas pointing out the sound of birds of paradise, and a rain bird on the forest bank close by.

A brief stop at Bitara and then homeward bound and out onto the Sepik at last. A mirror of blue, spreading waters, fringed with the translucent green of the high Sepik grass and the swamp trees, lit by the low dipping sun, with the vermilion flowers of the flame of the forest throwing fire onto the glass. And behind and beyond, the mountains of the Hunstein folding away in a deep blue haze. We speed on, splicing down the waterways; Lucas's eyes alight as he steers – eyes full of pride and heaven – 'This is my land' – the waves from the dugout skimming back all the way to the shore. Now the billowing clouds turn pink and the clouds in the glassy water turn pink too; three hornbills fly directly over the canoe, their jagged wings spread out like fingers silhouetted against the last sun. And flocks of tiny birds scatter away towards the hills, spinning and turning; bright colours caught and lost like butterflies pulled by invisible threads.

On and on the boat skids through the liquid magic, whistling past the slipping mountains – last sun over the darkening grasses splashing a sheen of wet gold over the water. Pink and crimson, gold and purple, the river has turned into a palette of oils, and the whites of Lucas's eyes are smouldering with the reflection of the burning clouds. Last shot of vivid orange and the splendour begins to fade – night rises up from the singing grass. The colours sink behind us as the water turns purple and white. And soon we are speeding on in the dark, the spray from the front of the canoe splashing silver under the last fading hues. Sepik dome of rising stars splashing light on the last white cockatoo shrieking into the trees. Lucas, a black shadow now, following the line of black reflected grass; and flying foxes, just black shadows too, flap across the blackening sky.

From Rick's journal. Sunday 10 March.
We spent Friday night in a swampland village on the Sepik shore. After further petrol drum deliberations in Ambunti, we finally reached Wagu late yesterday afternoon and had a celebratory game of 'bikpela pukpuk' in the creek with Jerome, Ringo and Keith. Then Maria gave her own toktok of the local news: yesterday morning she had discovered a real bikpela pukpuk – a real crocodile – snoozing at the bottom of the ladder that leads up to the house. And, shortly after, an extraordinary mystery had been

solved.

Two weeks ago, a man and a woman from Yambon village had gone missing. After a couple of days, search-parties had gone out, but had not found any trace of them. Eventually, the Wagu people had been accused of murdering them because of the acrimony between the two villages. Next, war drums were heard sounding over the swamp, and the Ambunti Police arrived to question the villagers. But then, suddenly, the missing couple returned to Yambon, quietly paddling their canoe. They thought they had only been gone a few hours and were stunned when they learnt that they had been missing for nearly two weeks. They had moored their canoe in an unfrequented place and entered unfamiliar territory to hunt. They had shot a possum and, walking further into the bush, had lost all sense of space and time. Eating only the one small possum, they had wandered aimlessly, drawn as if in a dream by a force over which they had no control. Eventually, they had found themselves back at the canoe and had been perplexed to hear the war drums beating in their village. That part of the forest is inhabited by a powerful Masalai who guards it against intruders. The Masalai had taken hold of the erring couple and had walked them round in circles to teach them a lesson. Denis, who translated the story, concluded: 'If you had heard that story in Wewak you would not have believed it; but now that we have been upriver we know it is certainly true.'

Nod and I would have loved a whole day off to listen to Maria's stories; I bet she's got a bilum-full as big as the one she keeps her betel nut in. But the Toktok Tour goes on, and this morning we find ourselves back in the canoe heading for the other end of the lake. Through the enveloping walls of Sepik grass, we turn off down a short channel, and there is Ygae village, built on a slope above the water – like a small version of Wagu. A big group of villagers have gathered to watch us arrive and we are led up to the Men's House, already crowding with strong-faced, bearded men and youths. It is extra hot today. But here we go: toktok number six.

The joint village Councillor for both Ygae and Wagu, who acts as an adviser in village affairs, is sitting in the corner, arm outstretched gripping a beam, an older man with heavy sagging body and watering eyes. He's clearly unsure of us. Something is different in this village. Shuffling. Suspicion. The pictures do not have the usual spellbound response. These men have already seen forest destruction: they have already been tricked and abused. This is the village that Martin Golman told us about, that has a

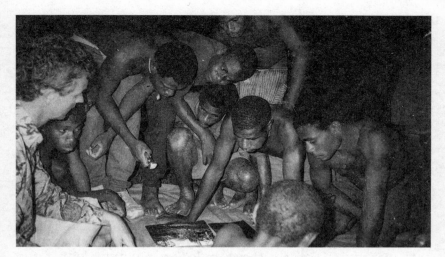

Boys of Wagu
viewing *toktok* photos.

Pikinnini Forest Company.
Denis T. Waliawi holding guitar.

wokabaut which is owned by Ambunti Council. The men work for the Council in fortnightly shifts of five. They receive only 25 kina for the two weeks: the national labourers' minimum is 45 kina per fortnight. The landowner, Wandei, and his son David, in whose forest the wokabout is cutting, only receive a pittance in royalties and are not paid by the cubic metre, which seems to be the legal requirement. Furthermore, after nearly four years of cutting eight to ten trees a week, which works out at around 2,000 trees, there is no sign of benefits to the village. No school. No aid post. On top of all this, the imperfect planks, the seconds, are *sold* back to the villagers if they want them for building; even David and Wandei have to buy back their own wood. Little wonder they are suspicious of Tupela. Are we come to cheat and exploit them too?

When we express our outrage at their reports, the angry eyes begin to open their doors. We remind them they are the papas of the bush – *they* have the power to say yes and no. And if they're not satisfied with the deal, they should go to Ambunti Council and say so. But they have already been. The Council don't care. The Government have no interest in the people of the village. We try to get facts and figures from the Councillor. How many hectares have already been cut? What is the annual quota? Why is there no replanting scheme? His dark skin is flushed now. But he has no answers. Where is the contract? Where is the long-term plan? He shakes his head. He doesn't know. He hasn't see them. He is illiterate. The young men are fiercely with us now; eyes growing by the minute. Only David is looking away, full of consternation and shame; and Wandei is wearily nodding off, craving only peace and quiet.

For the first time, women, standing close by, have dared to join the debate. Rebecca, Maria's cousin and the primary school teacher, speaks up. And another woman – peering in between the heads and limbs of the men – is coaxed and encouraged to speak too: 'Yes. We need things explained to us. We need an expert to come and give us guidance. Explanations. Only then will we be able to stand up for ourselves'.

In the nefarious midday sun we set off for the sawmill in the canoe, sliding under fallen tree trunks through the winding green-water swamp, with David, Wandei and a couple of other senior men. Petrus is at the helm. He has been strongly supportive of us; mind ticking fast; fully aware of the dangers.

'How far?' we ask.

'Yes' Lucas answers.

'Ten minutes or an hour?'

'Yes'.

'Which???'

'Yes . . . ten minutes'.

Probably an hour later we finally moor. There is a bush camp here and an older woman in a scarlet rag leans out from her shack to welcome us with a firm handshake. And Steven, a young man with cropped head and striking features, offers to take us to the mill. Only a few minutes' walk and we reach the controversial, much-discussed machine. A cleverly compact invention: small circular-saw blade on a light fold-up metal frame. Saviour of the forest? Or bringer of destruction? Here it sadly looks like the latter. A huge kwila tree, dense red hardwood, has just hit the ground. And around and beyond, great mounds of debris and sawdust have been left. No cleaning up and no replanting. And worst of all, no canopy. *All* the big trees within sight have been felled.

Steven is vocal: 'It is like a bad garden – and the forest is not growing back!' David is braving us too with his gaze now, and even Wandei is sitting up and listening. We stress the need for replanting, the need to cut one big tree and leave one so as to maintain some canopy which will protect the ground from both sun and rain. It's simple; but it needs training. Would they like that training? Yes, please. Yes, please. David is deeply affected with guilt and rage. We stress it is not his fault. And it is not too late. The rest of his forest can still be saved. And they can take the first step tomorrow, by cutting one and *leaving* one. Steven is on fire. If he can learn, if he can train, he will lead a replanting scheme .

. . . .

Back at Wagu. Hardly have time for a cup of tea before Lucas is calling:

'Tupela, Tupela!' Everyone is here – the important people of the village – waiting and ready for the final toktok.

'We just need five minutes', Nod calls down as we hurriedly try to blow up our flattened brains.

The canvas is already spread out under the stars and the swaying sago palms are casting phantasmagoric shadows over the crouching figures.

Matthew's mother is here, and his uncle Kaniofu; and Petrus representing the young men. But Solomon is still in the bush making his canoe. And the dark horse of Wagu is also missing. We have not seen him on this visit. Word has it that he is in Wewak drinking and spreading dissenting rumours about us. Is he in favour of foreign loggers? Is he being bribed to cross us? No one knows; or at least no one will say. And one other person is missing too: Matthew. We shout out for him. He's going to sleep but is persuaded to come and join us. Sleepy, sheepish, big feet clattering down the ladder from his nearby house.

Of all the villagers we have met, the Wagu people are the most confused. Half uprooted from their traditions, dislodged from their beliefs, they have been the most exposed to outside influence, and the least helped by their own social core. They have no Luluai like Kiawi anymore; their Councillor is based in Ygae. Some of them are at loggerheads with each other; some of them are at loggerheads with themselves. Nowhere is the conflict between old and new being played out with such agonizing groans. Nowhere is the pull of 'West is best' so strong. Petrus's passionate words from the first toktok are repeated with full force. Life is changing on the Sepik and they want to change too. But everything they have tried has failed. Crocodile farming, a rubber plantation and now the makaus have gone from the lake. If the big logging companies are bad then they will have a wokabaut; but not one owned by Ambunti Council. They will not stand the abuse that their poor wantoks have suffered in Ygae. They want their own wokabaut. It is the answer; they have set their hearts on it. But, we ask, how much money do they need? How many families are there in Wagu? How many children to pay school fees for? How many trees would they cut each week?

After their vociferous outburst they go silent. Blank. No response to our questions. At first we wonder if we have offended them. But Denis, his eyes like two encouraging beacons in the dark, whispers that they are pleased. No one has ever taken the trouble to ask these questions before. And so they don't know how to answer them. Even the simplest questions lead to disparity. And so we steer the debate to another point. If they had a wokabaut it would be dangerous to depend on it solely. What other crafts and skills could they draw on? Canoe-building and carvings. 'Yes, carvings.' They love their carvings and they would love to sell them. But again there is no outlet in Ambunti. There is no one to buy them. Before concentration is lost completely, the Wagu men make a final statement. Despite their spirits being pulled and torn in all kinds of different directions, their statement is unequivocal. They want us to help them get a wokabaut. They want us to teach them how to use it. They want us to help them make a good plan. Nobody else. Just us. Tupela. If we help them, they promise they will not allow the big logging companies in.

'The outcome of the toktok was deeply good', Denis affirmed later. But he also warns us: 'The Sepik people are changeable. And with all the different swamp winds blowing through Wagu, these people will be the most prone to changing.'

Before Lucas turns out the hurricane lamp I show him a poem I have written for Matthew. Does he think it could help him? Yes, he does. Yes it's a good idea. When he gets back from seeing us off, he will call Matthew and his mother to the house and read it to them. Matthew's mother is a wise woman so she must hear it too.

> Young man with big bright eyes
> I see you listening to the big men talk;
> Already your heart is beating fast
> For soon you will hold the forest in your hands.
>
> I write this song to give you strength,
> For many will try to steal it from you;
> And you will need to guard it well
> For it is worth more than money.
>
> Let your ancestors rest there in peace,
> Let the Birds of Paradise fly there forever,
> Let your hunting grounds remain safe
> And let your children enjoy it too.
>
> In my country, the forest is gone,
> The people have woken up too late.
> Please learn from our mistakes,
> Please show us another road!

❖ ❖ ❖

From Nigel's journal. Tuesday 12 March.
The Land of the Unexpected brought us a day in Ambunti that we did not want: once again no vehicle was able to pick us up at Pagwi; so, once again we were stuck in my least favourite place. Arrived yesterday from Wagu in the heat – the hottest day on record. Lucas has brought Maria and family and even she was suffering; she lifted up her shirt to expose her bright green laplap stretched tightly over her eight-month pregnant belly. Always pregnant, Maria; she must have conceived directly after the still-birth of her last baby.

We went to the Council Office to search for Julius, the Executive to the District Council, who hosted Rick on his first trip; he is in charge of the Ygae project. But he left in the morning to go to

Wewak. Then Lucas informed us that we had been summoned to a meeting with the DOIC. Walking faster than I have ever seen Lucas move, he hurried us up the hill. At his desk in his small, dilapidated office, the DOIC sits and only writes letters; he has no funds to do anything else he tells us. He sat rubbing and pulling constantly at a sore eye, an aura of hopelessness surrounding him. We all sweated profusely as we worked to keep his circular mind on track. We asked him pointed questions about the Ygae project. He wriggled uncomfortably. 'No one works together here'. I watched him carefully: his body language was not of a devious man, but of a frightened man unable to speak his mind for fear of losing his job, his livelihood. We left him at four-fifteen: seven minutes overtime.

Feeling uneasy about the uncovering of mismanagement, exploitation and corruption, we went on to a short meeting with a tall lanky American man who runs the mission. When we broached the same subject of payment and royalties in Ygae, he became very peculiar: his pen fell apart; he answered the phone; he picked up dust from the floor with a new cement-laying tool, all the while smiling a big fixed smile. Then, without warning or apology, our meeting was peremptorily brought to a close. 'You will not make yourselves popular here by asking too many questions', is the sentence that sprang out from our talk. It was said as if directed to our questions pertaining to the Council, but the meaning was double-edged. Lucas told us that he had come as a missionary and then resigned and has now become a business man. The local people had tried to get rid of him, but he made promises and was allowed to stay. Now he runs the mill, the Post Office, the Bank, a workshop for mechanical repairs to vehicles and outboard motors, and he runs the Mission plane services. He is gradually taking over the whole of the Ambunti services while the locals go *raun nating* (are unemployed). This meeting left my body feeling slimy, greasy, unclean.

Next, Lucas took us to meet Anskar, a local elder of repute. He looked like a sage, with shaggy, ageing hair and a grey beard. We found him and his wife Hendik sitting in their haus win. She was weaving a two-tone fishing basket out of Sepik grass and he was making a handle for an axe. In our talk with him we learnt that Anskar is aware of the Ygae situation. What was he doing about it? Nothing it seemed. Hendik listened intently and spoke out about her concern for the forest. I showed her the pictures. Anskar has seen the destruction in the Gogol valley with his own eyes and yet has not warned his own people. Why not? Silence. No answer.

These people see what happens and yet it appears they are powerless to take effective action. This man was fully aware, yet it seemed he would sit in his haus win and do nothing. On our way back, Rick looked hungrily at a fruit tree that drops only bitter fruit, indicative of the bitterness of the whole situation. I picked up a sweet-smelling frangipane flower and put it in a button-hole of my shirt to try to combat the putrid smell coming from my clothes.

In the sweltering, tin-roofed DPI house where we are staying, we cooked rice and lentils on the impossibly smelly kerosene stove which made the house even hotter. Served with baked beans, my stomach hoovered them up happily. On the verandah, gasping for a breath of cooling wind, Maria laughed at *longpela tupela kukim* and did not enjoy our food. Back inside the tin oven, Rick asked Lucas if he would like to write his version of our journey. He would. This is an extract from his account:

Our trip to the Big Forest

On Monday 4.3.91 we left Wagu and travelled up the Sepik River and went into April River. We slept in Bitara village a night, in the morning we have some toktoks with them and then we've travelled all the way to Gahom. From there we've seen many good things from the big forest, plenty of good things we have seen.

So, after talking with Gahom people, we've travelled down and we've spent a night in Begapuki and talked with them, and then to Kagiru village and also we've talked with them for some hours and then we've travelled all the way back to Wagu village. So the people of April River were very happy to see us and also to hear what we have spoken to them about the big forest.

We didn't go to the Niksek Mission because there was a low flood.

We've talked with the people asking questions about their livings and conditions, marketing and some other things that they do, and they cannot do. Also they've asked us plenty of questions too. One big thing is, they don't have enough earnings to support and enjoy themselves and that's why people are moving from place to place like nomads.

Because the Government did not think about those people who are living at the back of our Country or Province, this makes the people so unhappy. So what we can do is to help these people, to give them some ideas to make some things so that they should look after their forest and they themselves do the work to get liklik income to enjoy themselves to benefit their communities. That was what we have talked about.

And also we have ended up our trip in Ygae village. There we have seen many people come together to hear from us, and also we have visited their mobile Sawcamp. That was our first time to see the Sawcamp and we all were happy to see the Saw, and also we were happy to see the beautiful forest. Also we have talked with many people in Ambunti too.

So to end up my story I would like to say thank you to Richard, Nigel, Denis, Habe and myself for our big trip to April River and the big forest or the Forest of the Paradise which cannot be destroyed by any other companies.

Thank you.

Lucas Ketapi

V

On our return to Wewak we found that Raymond, the dare-devil goblin driver, was still in post – but Bruce Samban was indeed gone. His car had been stoned and he was in refuge at his unfinished house along the coast. Graham Campbell had also gone, with no message to us, no address and no phone number. All that enthusiasm, all those ideas, all his interest and support for our work, gone like a puff of smoke into the blue. However, our previous week of diplomatic manoeuvres had not been completely invalidated. Martin Golman had not been suspended and neither had the other Departmental Secretaries. They belong to the Department of East Sepik which is the local branch of the National Government. It was Bruce Samban's Provincial Government, one of nineteen, that had been ousted, along with its Ministers such as Damien Sarawabe, whom we had met, and its local government representatives such as Andrew Wamnai. Wewak itself was in strife. Violence had erupted at the news of the suspension and the misappropriation of two million kina. A special notorious police squad had been flown in and a temporary Administrator had been appointed to reconcile the books and hold the Province together. But, although the domestic news was grim, the Indonesian invasion that we had heard about had not developed into anything more than a minor fracas with the border villages. By way of fortification, we had ensconced ourselves in a holiday flat run by the Australian Baptist Church. One of two prefab units, it was situated high on the jungly hills overlooking the town and surrounded by an austere and supposedly rascal-proof barbed-wire cage. For the circumstances it was ideal. We had the luxury of a shower, a fridge and a phone. We had shade from a clump of coconut palms and we were in walking distance of a market and the Government offices at Kreer Heights. Once installed, with our putrefying river clothes clunking round in the superlative washing machine, we were well set up for the busy week and a half ahead.

'Who are you? What do you want?' The voice on the phone was frightened and belonged to Julius Sawai, the District Council Executive at Ambunti whom we had failed to meet. It was our first priority to catch him before he went back upriver and he came to see us immediately at our unit. A large, clouded man, he quickly dismissed the Ygae situation. It had all been sorted out. The villagers had only complained because we were strangers. They were just crazy. But yes, of course he would like our help. Of course the people needed to be trained to clear up and replant. But he had no funds for such things. We broached a couple of other ideas. How would he view a ferry service on the April River for the villagers to bring their produce to Ambunti? And would he welcome the establishment of some kind of training scheme: in trade-store management perhaps, or in outboard motor maintenance, so that the local people could run things themselves and not depend on the mission business? Julius listened with his heavy body pushed forward. He had been the king of Ambunti for a long time: alone upriver in crumbling, hopeless conditions; alone upriver unchallenged, unchecked and unsupported. His dark eyes warned that he was not used to interference: 'You write to me. You deal with me.' He handed us his address and left without a smile.

Our next priority was to meet with Bella Seiloni, which we did the same morning in the vacated Premier's office. He had been the Acting Secretary at our first audience with the Premier; now he had just been appointed Deputy Administrator and was still awaiting the arrival of his new boss. Rotund, with sanguine energy and an infectious laugh, Bella reassured us that the Friends of the Sepik need in no way be impeded by the Government's collapse. He had read our initial reports with delight and he would liaise between us and the new Administrator. Sustainable ideas were natural to him and his fiery eyes danced when we spoke of the bikpela bush. Concerning the April/Salumei Project, he elucidated the political channels along which the proposal would have to pass, and recommended that we discuss it further with Martin Golman and, later, with Father Momis, the Minister for Provincial

Affairs in Port Moresby. But over the Ygae situation even Bella was evasive: 'That's Ambunti Council for you.' Laugh, laugh, laugh. 'But the villagers are being treated like slaves', we retorted. More gales of laughter. Even he, it seemed, would not stand up for the rights of the village people.

A few hours after these meetings, I lay on the bare wooden floor of our new bedroom suite. My neck had cricked with a massive muscular spasm and I could hardly move. Was my body telling me something? Did we need to slow down again; was half a million hectares of virgin forest proving too heavy a load? Still, at least the seizure occurred obligingly just before the weekend, so while Nod socialized with Denis and his family (which included a pet hornbill and a cassowary), I lay with my head on *The Sojourner* by Marjorie Kinnon Rawlings from the 1956 Melbourne Book Club. Throughout my own little sojourn on the floor, our toktoks and East Sepik's formidable problems blasted through me. How to appease the monster of so-called progress? How to assist the Hunstein Range people without disrupting their fragile autonomy? How to reconcile the needs of the villagers with the needs of the bureaucratic Wewak Departments? How to satisfy Kiawi *and* the Department of Forests? By Sunday night something had begun to emerge, to slither out from underneath the mountain of paradoxes and contradictions: a local Sepik company that is non profit-making and initially funded with overseas aid. It would have a co-ordinating umbrella to service and monitor village-based logging, with a policy of carefully selected cutting and rigorous replanting. Other artefacts and forest products would also be encouraged and exported along with the sustainably produced timber. Profits would be ploughed back into the Province for other alternative rural industries and the improvement of services. A company that would employ the local unemployed and handle the timber and goods from source to final destination, thereby eliminating the middle man and minimizing the opportunity for back-handers and corrupt dealings. 'You don't look very rested.' Nod said when he got back. I wasn't. But we did have the kernel of something to work on.

Our follow-up meeting with Alois Jerewai, the Provincial Secretary, was arranged for 9 a.m. on Monday morning. I was scared, but keen to get feedback on my ideas. It was hopeless hatching grand concepts unless they met with Melanesian approval. But Mr Jerewai was just rushing off for the Port Moresby plane and so we were palmed off with his apologizing Deputy. A tall, refined man from the island Province of West New Britain, Michael Malaga ushered us onto smart white chairs in his tiny, stifling office. Taking occasional notes, he listened with rapt attention to my April/Salumei proposal. He had studied *The Barnett Report*. His own island had been decimated by clear-cut logging. His own people had been stripped of their traditional livelihood; even the collection of firewood had become a major problem. Michael Malaga spoke with restraint, but his elegant, slender hands twitched and his lucid eyes mirrored his own personal sorrow. Yes, a new approach was needed. And yes, our suggestions tallied with his own ideas. But PNG was not used to the concept of international funding; we would need to prove its plausibility through action. It was also essential that we met and spoke with the big chiefs in Port Moresby. Only with their support would sustainable strategies stand a chance. For me just to have these ideas taken seriously was a major breakthrough, and under his superbly diplomatic manner I could see that Michael Malaga was as enthusiastic as we were.

Martin Golman also listened intently to the ramifications of our local Sepik company idea. Was it truly viable or was it fanciful vaguery? Martin quickly seized on the prospective assets: would eco-timber really sell at a premium? Was international funding really a possibility? Could one really do without the middle man, who in Martin's own experience had always increased prices and reduced the profits? As I spoke I could see his mind reeling, stretching and trying to bridge the gaps and make the links that would be necessary. The next step, Martin advised, should be a written proposal and, echoing Michael Malaga, he urged that we meet the bikpela men in Port Moresby. At the commencement of our meeting, Martin had assured us that we didn't have to throw him down the mountain. He had indeed used our contribution to get to Angoram and confirm that the Malaysian malefactors had halted operations. 'If that happened in the Hunstein Range I would give up my job and go and defend the land myself', he declared. Knowing about forestry malpracice is one thing, but witnessing the devastation with his own eyes had proved to be quite another.

'*No rot – lanowna tasol*' (no entry – landowners only): the rough sign hangs from a metal barrier crossing the track. Nod and I also need to witness East Sepik's first major logging operation. Our guide, who shall remain nameless for security reasons, jumps out of the truck and pushes against the barrier. Ah good, it has been secretly unlocked for us as arranged. We drive slowly down the winding track. Smashed trunks; smashed branches. The contract for the first stage of the operation had stipulated the clearing of no more than fifteen metres either side of the road; but again and again this has not been adhered to. And 'snigging' has taken place (the cutting of trees outside the agreed limit). Surreptitious, illegal side-tracks lead off through the trees and, close to them, giant trunks are piled, their position betraying where they have come from. The loggers' camp is a makeshift shanty settlement in a three-acre clearing of mud. Drums of fuel and other waste are strewn around, and half a dozen yellow bulldozers stand idle. As we pull up we notice half a dozen Malaysian men also standing idle, leaning against the wall of their dormitory, drinking beer and looking bored and peeved. Nervous, our guide slams closed the door of the truck and, hitching up his trousers, goes to speak with them. As they converse together in unsmiling, broken English, Nod notices one of them sidle off to one of the bulldozers and bring out a large sheathed knife. But our guide returns to us safe. They had thought we were opposing loggers.

Fifteen kilometres on we reach the sea-shore. Either side of the wide mud bath, the forest hangs right over into the water. And beyond the cleared mud bank, a crude and hastily erected jetty has been built. Beyond the jetty, the unobserved sea stretches calm and readily navigable. How easy for those priceless giant hardwood logs to disappear off shore without any export procedures at all! And how easy for that snigging to continue and the suspension to be ignored without the permanent presence of the Department of Forests. Apparently, the nearby coastal villages were in favour of the project; it gave them undreamed of access to Wewak. But their triumphant new road, symbolic of a triumphant new life, has been built so shoddily, without proper drainage and without a structural base, that I doubt it will last a year. In some places erosion has already started. As we turn round to leave, a truck full of the Malaysians from the camp comes hurtling down the track and screams to a halt. They laugh loudly with dead-pan eyes and, with exaggerated movements, mime their pretended intention to swim. Our guide is visibly relieved when we reach the metal barrier and bump back onto the Wewak road.

Meanwhile, amongst Raun Isi spears and spectacular masks, Green Light Productions was in full swing. Peter Hunnam in Sydney had confirmed that WWF Australia would indeed fund the Raun Isi tour, and so we already had proof for Michael Malaga and his colleagues that overseas funding wasn't just a pipe-dream. The four chosen actors worked with exhilarating dynamism and their usual colourful inventiveness. In the early evenings we had meetings with Denis and Lucas Kou. Lucas's story still had too much of an urban touch and Denis's play was too sophisticated. Carefully, they married and adjusted their ideas; and, with Denis's fresh experience of life in the Hunstein Range, they tailored their drama to suit the forest villagers and clarified the environmental message that would be most helpful and practical for them to hear.

Following on from our earlier meeting with the Departmental Secretaries, we were keen to continue to encourage a forum for sharing views and building trust. And so on the Friday, our last day in Wewak, we held an open rehearsal and invited the Department of East Sepik to attend. Most of the Secretaries did; some had never been to the campus before. And, together with Raun Isi's neighbours and friends, the audience greatly outnumbered the studio's motley assortment of stools and broken chairs. By now the play had been christened *Pikinini Forest* and the actors performed with bewitching zest.

The scene is a village bordering on to the forest and the jocund village Councillor enters and summons his people. He has good news: a logging company has arrived to bring wealth and fortune to the village. The Operations Manager – a fattened Lucas in a pair of khaki dungarees – appears with a cosmetic smile, smarmily plying and 'greasing' the unsuspecting villagers with gifts. But one old man is suspicious. He sniffs his presents warily and throws them back. For a moment the logger's cosmetic smile slips off; he is angry. He had bribed the Councillor to smoothe the way; what is the Councillor playing at? For a moment the villagers are startled, but the logger is soon sweet-talking them again. Roads, schools, aid posts are all lavishly promised. That night the logger inebriates the villagers with beer to ensure that they will sign their land away. Only the old man stays apart, refusing to join the ribald mob. In his sleep he is visited by a masked Masalai who warns him of the impending dangers and counsels him not to forfeit his land recklessly. In the morning, much to the loggers' dismay, he will only sign away one portion of his land.

Years later, Lucas – now an unfattened youth in shorts and T-shirt – returns to his village, his education downriver completed. The youth goes hunting and is perplexed to find no game. He bumps into the village Councillor who tells him that he will have to travel far over the mountains to find wild pig and cassowary. Since the logging operation, all the wild animals have disappeared. Next, an old couple appear – with Alex as a hilarious *meri* (woman) – causing eruptions of hysterical laughter from the audience. The old couple are off to cut a tree trunk for their new house, but again they will have to wander far over the hills. The young man is mortified; his boyhood memories of the lush forest are dashed to the ground. Sadly, he enters the village empty-handed. Meanwhile, the old man who sold only part of his forest catches his brother stealing wood from his land and tries to shoo him away, but the brother won't go. Since the logging operation, he has lost all his trees; he has no wood of his own. Both are stubborn. Both are belligerent. An argument ensues. And, as is typical of an argument in PNG, no stops are spared.

During the commotion the Councillor appears. Both men turn on him; it was his fault. He is under attack from the two raging old men and, fearful of losing his life, he implores their forgiveness for his misguided actions. But, incensed beyond reason, they raise their spears and are only halted by the plaintive song of the youth: the *Pikinini Forest* song that urges the people to take good care of their land. The old man starts laughing. The old man starts hooting. The youth's pretty song is no news to him, he has already taken care of his forest. Where the loggers cut, he replanted and now his own pikinini forest is growing strong and tall. The forest for his children is alive and well. In PNG presently there is much dissension between the wisdom of the elders and the book-learned knowledge of the educated youth. But now our youth of the story venerates the old man: 'Look, this old man has had no education and yet he is the one who has saved his forest.' The play ends with a hip-swaying chorus of the youth's song, and Lucas's riveting last note would have cracked the window panes had they had any glass in them!

The audience's response was avid. Joe Mande stood and made an impassioned and impromptu plea for Raun Isi to be respected better, better supported and better utilized. And in an unprecedented surge of good will, he offered Alex a cigarette for the first time in theatre history. John Wasori of the DPI, who informed us he would have to leave in the middle, didn't; he was so engrossed he forgot all about his crucial meeting and was only sorry and tantalized that the play could not include a message from him about coffee beans. Michael Malaga shook our hands strongly and hoped that he would be able to take a performance to West New Britain. Only Martin Golman remained silent. We were afraid that we had pushed the environmental message too far. Had we lost him? Had we overdone it? In fact we hadn't: he was so moved he was almost tearful. And he was very surprised that the actors knew how loggers behave. 'This was a good play, a good message.'

When his name had been mentioned in the story he had felt quite overwhelmed. He had a few minor points to suggest, including a clear indication of how his Department could help the villagers in such a situation. The *Pikinini Forest* tour was to retrace our Toktok Tour steps, and Martin gave it his unconditional blessing.

That evening we had a final meeting with Denis. We had asked him to be the Field Co-ordinator for Friends of the Sepik; he had already accepted. 'For three years', he told us, 'I have had a deep hunger to help my people. And now at last, this will give me an opportunity to make something of this desire.' We warned him that it wouldn't be easy; that there would be many forces against us. And that soon we would be back on the other side of the world unable to give him day-to-day support. Denis had thought this through already. He was fully aware of what he was taking on, and he was keener than ever. Nod showed him the Angel Cards and explained their use. Would he like to have a go? They had helped us and maybe they would help him. Enthralled and slightly awed, he laid them out, face down, in the form of an arrow. 'What quality will help me in the Friends of the Sepik work ahead?' Denis turned over 'obedience'. A shocked surprise from us all. I thought of white oppression, colonial rule. But Denis didn't: 'The people of the villages obey and live by ancient rules, and now, split between the old and new, they are like glass, easily shattered. Even though they want to change, they must be helped still to continue to obey those laws. And I must continue to obey my hunger, my need to fulfil my desire.' Denis was keen to turn over one more card. Nod suggested he try the one at the tip of the arrow. Denis turned over 'joy'. 'Of course', he said 'I am a hunter too, I have to aim and fire. What better way than with joy?' We had talked a lot about the Masalai and the supernatural powers of his people. Now he was very tickled to be tasting white man's magic.

In Port Moresby we continued our theatre work. For our two-week project with the National Theatre, we had suggested looking in greater depth at Papua New Guinea's omnipresent dilemma: the conflict between old and new, and the struggle between rural village life and the lure of the Westernized city. We believed there was learning mileage in it for both the Melanesians and for us in the West. William presented us with a workshop outline. Inspired by his own Bougainvillian situation he had called it, 'The Dawning.'

'The Dawning' was in three parts. In the first, we would focus on the harmony and humour of the Papua New Guinea village. In the second, we would look at the alienation and disharmony of a city settlement. And in the third, we would explore the possibilities for a new way forward. The eleven participating actors were mostly from different Provinces and different regions. To encourage authenticity and naturalness, each actor worked using his or her own tokples; the rehearsals boasted an extraordinary mix of no less than seven completely different languages. But we weren't the only ones to set ourselves up with a hectic timetable, William was concurrently casting and rehearsing PNG's first television soap entitled, *Warriors in Transit.* He had co-written it and he was directing it. And so in the mornings we workshopped together and in the afternoons we parted ways, and Nod and I met the representatives of the other environmental NGOs and knocked on the doors of the national politicians. Simon Pentanu became our 'ambassador'. Even with his help the doors were difficult to locate and even more difficult to open. The higher echelons seemed to be built on quicksand, and the labyrinthine corridors seemed to be ceaselessly shifting. While Simon was trying to track down Mr Karl Stack, the Minister of Forests, an article appeared in the national daily paper. Its caption read: 'Eight important questions for the Minister of Forests.' The eight important questions were a shocking summary of the appalling recent violations, both environmental and social, that totally contravened the Forestry Department's supposedly sustainable and nationally orientated policies. The next morning, Mr Stack had gone and a new Minister, as yet unnamed, was being installed.

So instead, we met Andrew Tagamasau, the Deputy Secretary. Luckily he was a Sepik man and showed immediate interest in our Sepik adventures. He was small and dark, with a sharp energy. He reminded me of Campbell – alack where was Campbell? We had not managed to track him down either; and he had not answered my letters. Andrew Tagamasau looked out of the window when it came to the White Paper. The new proposed policies would take time; they were being worked on. With quick-fire alacrity he swung the conversation back onto us. His eyes, like shiny black beetles, scooted over the floor, up to us, across to the window and back to the floor. Many people had come to him with sustainable ideas; but as yet no one had offered a practical and financially viable plan. If our proposal contained this, he believed his Department would be interested. But he cautioned us that we should hurry: his Department was already preparing its own proposals. He would read our report with interest and pass it on to the new Minister when he had settled in.

The next meeting that Simon chased up on our behalf was with the Minister for the Environment and Conservation. 'I have an interview for you at two o'clock', Simon informed us over the phone. Tomorrow at two o'clock we sat outside the Minister's office and waited. Two-fifteen; two-thirty. Simon tapped on the Minister's door and a worried assistant assured us the Minister was expecting us; he would be returning shortly from lunch. And so we continued to wait. Two-forty-five; three o'clock. Simon tapped on the door again. Yes, it was confirmed that the Minister was definitely somewhere in the building; at that very moment they were trying to locate him. Three-fifteen; three-thirty. The Minister was nowhere to be found. The following day we learned that this Minister had gone too. And on our way to Simon's office in the central, modern Parliament building designed in the form of a mighty haus tambaran, we passed another bikpela chief who muttered that the now ex-Minister whom we had sought the day before, ought surely to be behind bars.

So we tried Paul Wanjik, Minister of Works and Member of Parliament for the Ambunti region. Simon confirmed that he would be delighted to meet us and would be interested to hear about Friends of the Sepik. Hopefully, we rattled off to the barricaded Ministry of Works a couple of miles down the road. Paul Wanjik's office had the air-conditioning on full and we sat in the antechamber shivering. His First Secretary, John Harangu, came to shake our hands and informed us with remorse that the Minister had just received bad news. His uncle in Maprik had just passed away and he had left for the afternoon flight. John Harangu was civil and earnest. Exasperated, and cold for a change, we briefed him on the purpose of our visit. He was a Sepik man as well and expressed concern for the forests of his Province. The kind of proposal we had in mind was certainly what was needed and he would draw the Minister's attention to any correspondence that we cared to send him. He was also shocked at our account of the Angoram project and sincerely seemed to have had no idea of its existence at all.

Meanwhile, back in his office, Simon was trying to trace the whereabouts of Michael Somare. Everyone had agreed that it would be excellent if we could meet the father of independent Papua New Guinea himself. He was now the Minister of Foreign Affairs and was presently involved in complex negotiations concerning an attempt to reopen the Bougainville mine. His Secretary and Assistants sent Simon on a wild-goose chase and finally he had to admit defeat.

Concerned that the not so indefatigable Tupela might well be nearing the brink, William and Puele whisked us away for an Easter weekend respite. Along an almost unpassable road, we travelled for four hours to reach Paramana, Puele's family village on the coast. We stayed with Puele's cheekily impish auntie Ena who, stretching up to pat our shoulders, said in her tokples that she wished she had brought us up. Paramana had a vast grey beach. On it, the villagers' numerous grey and mottled pigs strutted and played. At the end, mango swamps descended right into the oily water and behind it, a great wall of coconut palms brushed against the luminous evening sky. We lazed under the house and supped on fresh fish, black swamp snails and extra-sweet coconut milk. Ena asked us to sing for her and when we did she laughed with raucous abandon and taught us 'good morning' in her tokples: 'pouhe pouhe namana,' When it was time to leave she shook her head sadly. Nod whispered to Puele that he wished he had a present to give to her. But Puele assured us that *we* were the present. For the entire weekend Ena had been the envy of the village, and she would always remember Tupela with pride and joy. We returned to the fray with renewed vigour. And, at the eleventh hour, doors began to open; maybe Ena had brought us luck.

A meeting with Father Momis, the Minister for Provincial Affairs, was arranged. He was a Bougainvillian and Simon knew him personally. After an energetic workshop morning and a hectic afternoon of faxing and phoning, we sat outside his office at four o'clock on tenterhooks: trying to assemble our addled brains; trying to believe that we were really going to meet a Minister at last. At four-thirty we were ushered in, and sat in comfortable chairs in a small circle. Simon; Aphraim, the Minister's Assistant; Bernard, an economist; and Father Momis. All Bougainvillians. All polite and discreet. Father Momis is a well-known, long-term, die-hard member of PNG's political institution. He showed us courtesy, spared us unhurried time to talk, but remained partially secluded behind a protective veil of political decorum. He sat comfortably between me and Nigel, elbows on the arm rests of his chair, and his chin lightly supported by his cradled fingertips. He listened attentively to our sustainable ideas. When I strayed off the point he closed his eyes, when I veered back he opened them again. Before we went into the meetng Aphraim had whispered to Nod to emphasize our theatre connections and when he did, Father Momis's veil lifted a little. He loved culture. He loved theatre. And we discussed his sorrow that the forced introduction of the

English language had eroded much of it away. He concluded by saying that he would have preferred it if we were the Friends of Papua New Guinea, and not just the Friends of the East Sepik. We replied that it was always our policy to start small. Grand schemes so often failed, but if one threw a small pebble into the water the ripples would spread. Father Momis nodded. His parting comment was: 'I would be very happy to collaborate with you'.

On our last morning in Papua New Guinea, we had the honour of meeting Bernard Narokobi, the Attorney General. Mr Narokobi is one of the country's most renowned politicians. He has a reputation for impeccable integrity and is also well-known for his radical pro-Melanesian views. Without a trace of pomp or affectation he welcomed us into a small and unassuming room. Hardly any introduction seemed to be needed. His wide Sepik face, fringed with a full Sepik beard, showed immediate interest and our trek into his forests seemed to be enough. If only he had known, he would have invited us to his own village.

Our proposals met with easy approval. In fact, we discovered, he had begun to work on a very similar proposal of his own. He searched in his briefcase, pulled out a small exercise book and opened it at a few handwritten pages. He also had a non profit-making organization in mind; something to truly benefit the local people. To him, roads were the most immediate need; not big highways, but solid tracks. So that the *lapun* (old) men could walk without stumbling. So that the women could carry their goods to market. Mr Narokobi's gaze was deep and direct, there was an air of youthfulness about him. He is a writer, too, of both books and plays, and when he heard about our theatre work he telephoned his wife immediately to see if she could arrange to bring us some copies. He would look forward to reading our report. And we stressed how much we looked forward to receiving his comments so that we could unite his ideas with ours. His time was pressed and, apologizing for his haste, he had to rush off for a meeting on mining, though we sensed he would rather have stayed and chatted more about the forest.

A couple of nights before this meeting, I had woken up yelling 'help' at the top of my voice. My heart was pounding and it had taken a while to dare to move. My nightmare was about the rainforest:

I am involved in a replanting scheme and I am standing amongst the rows of fresh, green, newly planted trees. Suddenly I am aware of a dangerous psychic force. It swells, seizing me; and, like a huge whirlwind, it threatens to rip through and destroy the entire forest. I try to hold on, arms outstretched to protect the trees – but the vast demonic force is overwhelming and begins to hurl the trunks and branches from side to side. I know it's hopeless. I am helpless. Everything is going to be destroyed and the trees are already turning black. Horror and anguish pour through me and my yell of 'help' is a howl not only for the forest but for my own fragile survival.

The yell had also woken Nod and I related the dream to him. After all our efforts it seemed like a terrible blow of doom. But after our meeting with Bernard Narokobi, I suddenly saw it in a different light. Yes, the image was doomful all right, but I had been trying to protect the trees by myself; in the face of such a violent negative force how could I possibly succeed alone? Nod and I couldn't do it by ourselves. Like the stone thrown into the pond, the ripple had now got to spread. Fast. The cruelly buffeted people of the Hunstein Range and the pale-stemmed trees of paradise needed a wider and wider circle of support if their survival was truly going to be on the cards. A good stone for spreading those ripples would be our Friends of the Sepik Report and our Sustainable Logging Proposal. As soon as we touched down in Australia we got to work on them fast; they were completed before we left Perth. And we sent copies back to all the people we'd met. Shortly after our arrival home, a welcome ripple reached us too. It was a glowing, golden ripple carrying realistic caution but also lots of hope.

Friends of the East Sepik, PO Box 413, Wewak, ESP,
Papua New Guinea, 4 June 1991

Dearest Tupela,

Greetings and well wishes from everyone here in Wewak – we all hope you are both in the best health. It is quite a change having to write you a letter, especially after always faxing. It gives me a feeling of relaxation in the midst of business. Anyway, as you requested, the following Report is enclosed.

Pikinini Forest Campaign Report
Prepared by Denis T Waliawi

The *Pikinini Forest Campaign* is the result of a two-week long Awareness Tour which Richard Edmunds and Nigel Hughes, Directors of Green Light Productions and prime initiators of FOTS took in early 1991 with interpreter, Denis T. Waliawi. That tour involved a lot of talks, questions from both sides and presented a lot of useful information. Thus, as stated, the *Pikinini Forest Campaign* came about.

This campaign specifically involved performances of a play called *Pikinini Forest*, an environmental drama that attempts to educate local landowners in the effects of logging. It is simply an emphasis following the Toktok Tour, this time in the form of acting. Four members of the Raun Isi Theatre, a subsidiary of the Division of Culture and Tourism, were instrumental in this part.

This Report is presented in the truest sense accounting the Campaign in the best ability of presentation. By doing so we hope to receive favourable assistance to progress with future undertakings, more specifically, to support and move on from where we are now.

Wagu School   Time: 1.31 p.m. Date: 16 April 1991
In spite of the growing heat of the sun, the performance reflected determination, interest and will to achieve our aim. All ideas presented were emphasized fully with enormous energy.

Certainly a good response from the students, quietly absorbing the messages and of course a certain amount of laughters at Alex Karomo's character – but laughters and giggles were not constant which certainly gave the impression of the messages getting across. Surprisingly enough, Mr Silus, the Headmaster, was very moved by the play and expressed that certainly everything displayed in the play is practised these days. He also encouraged similar performances in future stressing that more attention be given to schools in the remote areas.

All four members performed brilliantly in spite of the soaring heat and expressed afterwards that this first performance was a stepping stone in this campaign, adding that they themselves were very emotional!

Wagu Village   Time: 5.30 p.m. Date: 16 April 1991
Similarly a powerful performance indeed and it received a good response from the villagers. Lucas this time gave it all in the song and showed increased seriousness. The presence of Andrew Wamnai, their Provincial Member, added new energy to the performers. His speech after the play reflected the same line of messages and he expressed that he had always feared such problems highlighted in the play would take place, and stressed that in spite of offers made to him he still had the interest of the people and welfare in mind.

Gahom Village Time: 5.00 p.m. – 6.05 p.m. Date: 18 April 1991
This village, it must be admitted was different from the others! Kiawi, the Luluai of the village was there right in front with the small children, with eyes glued in front, deep concentration and interest of curiosity from a very, very serious face – nodding in agreement and laughing quietly where necessary. There was never a word from him or a slight turn away from the play, he was in full concentration and it seemed very obvious that during that time his heart went out to his people and to their land.

General response from the others was also contrary to our assumptions – for we thought at the first stage, naturally, they wouldn't understand, but they in great contrast did and I personally was ashamed of my sharing of the assumption, but nevertheless, burst with joy. After the performance, Kiawi and the men were asked what they felt about the play. The following is what Kiawi expressed:

'My heart cries with tears of blood, the problems shown in the play are obvious enough – very obvious! Surely, if we are to go ahead after seeing this, then we must be *longlongs!* [stupid]
He went on to make a public announcement that they really wouldn't go for a 'mobile saw', instead they recommend Markets sought for them to sell their products, both from land and water! At 4 a.m. next morning, we all moved off quietly, getting our gear back to the canoes. We sorted out the cargo and it just worked out that a lot of space was still available. Our cartons of food from the original five had gone amazingly down to only two – a lot of eating had gone on and well-fed bodies had helped lighten the load. I was the last to leave Gahom after saying goodbye to Kiawi, the only one up to see us off. I knew he cried when we left after shaking hands – I could see his face with the streams of tears flowing peacefully onto the similarly beautiful Gahom soil under the light of the moon above.

Struggling with the canoes we got past the Sitipa junction, the engines began and we slowly moved away, disturbing the peaceful Sitipa, elegant in the reflection of the moon, leaving Gahom and the great man Kiawi once more.

Begapuki   Time: 12.09 p.m. Date: 19 April 1991

At Begapuki . . . .

Well Tupela, it seems I have come to the end. It is now 9.15 p.m. and I can smell my roasted taro being cooked for me by Rhonda my sister. I will be having it with a good cup of Lipton tea. It does sound inviting doesn't it . . . it is a mixture of the modern and the traditional delights coming together, not to destroy but to help strengthen someone who is desperate to help.

Thank you, Tupela, for giving me the opportunity to really help my people – I am not going to waste this precious item.

Lots of love and best wishes from all of us. We look forward to seeing you soon.

Your brother, Denis.

If you would like to support Friends of the Sepik, please write a courteous letter expressing your interest in the preservation of the Hunstein Range to :

The Prime Minister
Office of Prime Minister
Morauta Haus
P.O. Box 6606
Boroko
Papua New Guinea

And/or:

The Minister for Forests
P.O. Box 5055
Boroko
Papua New Guinea

FOTS itself was created through letter-writing with about a hundred letters.

Copies of the letters and reports referred to in the book are available on request from the address below.

If you would like any further information or to offer any assistance, write to:
Green Light Productions
16 Twisaday House
Colville Square
London W11 2BW